ALSO SERVING TIME

Canada's Provincial and Territorial Correctional Officers

Also Serving Time informs readers about the realities of provincial and territorial prison work in Canada. Exploring the nuances of the job, Rosemary Ricciardelli shows how officer orientations and attitudes toward prisoners are interconnected and foundational in shaping their own experiences as well as those of managerial and administrative staff and the prisoners themselves. Drawing on interviews with one hundred correctional officers with experience in a range of provincial and territorial prisons, Ricciardelli provides theoretical and applied explorations of officer orientations, interpretations, and risk propensity to show how perceptions, attitudes, and beliefs – both at the individual and structural levels – shape prison practices.

Detailing officers' experiences working with male and female adult prison populations, *Also Serving Time* unpacks how gender informs the actions and self-presentation of correctional officers. Ricciardelli confirms that tasks of daily living underpinned by pervasive risk potential shape prison work. Through the officer accounts presented, the book provides an opportunity for readers to explore how punishment and "rehabilitation," gender, and the hierarchical structure of prison management together shape officers' daily realities.

ROSEMARY RICCIARDELLI is a professor of sociology, the coordinator for the Certificate in Criminology, and a co-coordinator for the Police Studies Program at Memorial University of Newfoundland. She is an associate scientific director of the Canadian Institute for Public Safety Research and Treatment (CIPSRT), a senior research fellow with Correctional Service Canada, and a member of the Royal Society of Canada.

Also Serving Time

Canada's Provincial and Territorial
Correctional Officers

ROSEMARY RICCIARDELLI

UNIVERSITY OF TORONTO PRESS
Toronto Buffalo London

© University of Toronto Press 2019
Toronto Buffalo London
utorontopress.com
Printed in Canada

ISBN 978-1-4875-0141-9 (cloth)
ISBN 978-1-4875-2138-7 (paper)

Library and Archives Canada Cataloguing in Publication

Title: Also serving time : Canada's provincial and territorial
correctional officers / Rosemary Ricciardelli.
Names: Ricciardelli, Rose, 1979– author.
Description: Includes bibliographical references and index.
Identifiers: Canadiana 20190114452 | ISBN 9781487521387 (softcover) |
ISBN 9781487501419 (hardcover)
Subjects: LCSH: Correctional personnel – Canada. | LCSH: Correctional
personnel – Canada – Provinces. | LCSH: Correctional personnel –
Canada – Social conditions.
Classification: LCC HV9506 .R53 2019 | DDC 365/.971—dc23

Published with the assistance of the Memorial University of Newfoundland
Publication Subvention Program.

University of Toronto Press acknowledges the financial assistance to its
publishing program of the Canada Council for the Arts and the Ontario Arts
Council, an agency of the Government of Ontario.

Canada Council Conseil des Arts
for the Arts du Canada

ONTARIO ARTS COUNCIL
CONSEIL DES ARTS DE L'ONTARIO
an Ontario government agency
un organisme du gouvernement de l'Ontario

Funded by the   Financé par le
Government   gouvernement
of Canada   du Canada

Canadä

MIX
Paper from
responsible sources
FSC® C016245

For Paige Everly Ophelia C.

Contents

Preface

This project was inspired by men released from federal incarceration who described their time in remand or provincial/territorial custody as the most trying and difficult prison time they had ever served; remand in particular, they said, was loud, unnecessarily violent, and laced with stress, uncertainty, and emotional upheaval. Releasees discussed their interpretations of the inhumane conditions in which they had undergone detox (i.e., cold, immediate, and with no medical intervention), and perhaps most surprisingly, some pointed out how certain officers had tried to provide a semblance of compassion during their drug withdrawal. They remembered words of support surrounding their trial, sentencing, and visits with family, and the assistance offered by officers in navigating medical, legal, and other needs. Provincial and territorial incarceration was described as mundane and repetitive, but also as constantly in flux as prisoners came and went and atmospheres changed quickly as new prisoners arrived on units (or left). In particular, two male releasees suggested I turn my attention to the experiences of correctional officers working in these facilities and see how they "did their time."

Initially, I found it difficult to create an intellectual space in which I could be critical, reflective, and empathetic to the experiences of both prisoners and officers without displacing the concerns and voices of either. I needed to overcome this either/or dichotomy – the, perhaps assumed, us-versus-them divide between officers and prisoners – and instead focus on how officers and prisoners share a space, experiences, and realities, although at times from different standpoints. Regardless of whether it is evident or not across actions and in public spaces, I have consistently found, witnessed, and experienced that prisoners care about officers and prison staff, while officers and staff care about prisoners. Conditions of confinement are also conditions of employment – and vice versa. While this fact often goes unrecognized, it is an important and intriguing lack of distinction that inspired the research that informed this book.

ALSO SERVING TIME

Canada's Provincial and Territorial Correctional Officers

Well, you're doing time [as a correctional officer]. When you're locked up in a unit with inmates, what do you get that's more [than they get]? Milk carton comes in – the green milk trays are for inmates but the purple ones are for staff – same food, same cart, what do you got that's different? You need relief to go for a five-minute break for the toilet next door, out of the unit. You watch the same TV, you listen to the same radio, and you hang out with the same people. You do everything over and over again with the inmates locked up in there. We had bubbles, before, [where] you could go in and relax for five minutes [if] you got into it with an inmate, you know, [if] he was on stuff, you could actually go there and cool down. Let him cool off, you cool off, so you can focus on your job. You don't have that anymore.

– Anonymous male correctional officer, Atlantic Region

Introduction

Provincial and Territorial Prisons in Canada

Being locked up in jail, we get institutionalized [too].
                                                    – Anonymous correctional officer

In Canada, closed-custody penal facilities vary structurally, operationally, and in organizational style, largely as a result of differences in legislation, policy, and practice within each of the provinces or territories. And yet, some factors remain consistent across Canadian prisons, and indeed across much of the Western world. One of these factors is isolation: well into the twenty-first century, correctional facilities remain geographically and socially isolated spaces (Pratt, 2013a; Ricciardelli, 2014a). In consequence, both prison conditions and prisoner and staff needs are unnoticed in society, as citizens have "come to expect such institutions, and all the connotations and symbols they carry with them, to be hidden away out of sight" (Pratt, 2013a, p. 90). "Out of sight," however, also suggests citizens are largely unaware of and uninformed about the realities of prison living or prison work (Pratt, 2013a, 2013b; Ricciardelli, 2014a, 2014b).

Inside these socially secluded institutions are correctional officers: individuals employed to "contribute in diverse and significant ways to *Changing Lives and Protecting Canadians*" (Correctional Service Canada, 2012b; emphasis in original). Here, I cite the mandate and defined occupational role of correctional officers within the federal correctional system, which are similar to those within provincial and territorial systems – the difference being the duration of time for which a prisoner is sentenced to serve. Whereas the federal system is oriented toward the care and control of non-youth prisoners sentenced to "federal time" (two years or more), the provincial and territorial systems oversee the accommodation and management of prisoners sentenced to provincial

or territorial custody (two years less a day), those being detained or
those on remand (pretrial detention), or individuals awaiting sentencing or trial. In provinces and territories without federal closed-custody
facilities – specifically Newfoundland and Labrador, Prince Edward
Island, Nunavut, the Northwest Territories, and the Yukon – federally
sentenced prisoners may be held in one of the local facilities – a practice justified by the need to keep these prisoners closer to their loved
ones and cultural environment (Department of Justice and Public Safety,
2014a). Youth prisoners, however, are not housed in either system.
Although youth are governed under the federal Youth Criminal Justice
Act, each province and territory does have jurisdiction over youth who
come into contact with the law, and custodial practices fall under justice
and public safety, or, depending on the province or territory, the equivalent to a ministry of child, youth, and family services (i.e., Newfoundland
and Labrador youth do not fall under the Ministry of Justice) (e.g., see
Department of Justice and Public Safety, 2014b).

But What Is a "Correctional Officer"?

In Canada, the individuals we term "correctional officers" fall under the
Canadian National Occupational Classification Code (NOCC) 6462,
within "sales and service" occupations, which include occupational positions listed as "correctional service officer, prison guard, prison officer,
and correctional officer" (see Correctional Service Canada, 2013a). It
is important to highlight that the label of "guard," when applied to the
role of a correctional officer, is inappropriate and can be considered
offensive (officers are not "guarding" a person, place, or object within
their occupational role). Whereas a guard may be employed in a police
detachment lock-up, a courthouse, or in front of a building to watch
persons being held or a "thing" considered of value, correctional officers
work as peace officers. Although there is some contention around the
term "correctional officer" – often because the designation is factually
incorrect and suggests officers are employed to "correct" a person or
behaviour – it is the term used within Canadian corrections, and thus it
is how I will refer to officers in this book (the term "keeper" has not been
used for decades in Canada to refer to officers). Indeed, in the United
Kingdom and other countries, the term "prison officer" is used.
  Under the law, correctional officers are peace officers – those tasked
with maintaining the peace – and must "ensure the safe, secure and
humane custody and control of offenders" (Correctional Service Canada,
1992). Their occupational role includes "problem solving ... admitting,
supervising, and discharging offenders – along with regular inspections

and maintaining overall security" (Correctional Services Nova Scotia, 2014, p. 4). Their occupational responsibilities must supersede personal feelings or experiences that could otherwise impact their views of the people in their custody. Officers are to follow all provisions of federal law pertaining to peace officers and are also accountable for their actions under provincial law and institutional policies:

> [although] given extensive powers, peace officers are compelled to exercise such powers lawfully. They must act on reasonable grounds, without abuse of their powers; furthermore, the power to act is in some instances coupled with an obligation to act, and peace officers can be held criminally responsible for a failure to intervene in certain situations. (Correctional Service Canada, 1992)

For example, an officer can use force but will be found criminally responsible if it is used in excess (see s. 26 of the Criminal Code); can be found liable and imprisoned for up to two years for failing to suppress a riot without a reasonable justification (see s. 69 of the Criminal Code); and can be imprisoned for up to five years if found guilty of wilfully permitting a prisoner to escape from custody (see s. 147 of the Criminal Code). Thus, officers are accountable for their actions, regardless of whether they engage or fail to engage, and may be subject to discipline or legal repercussions – including criminal charges – if they fail to abide by the law. In this sense, like the prisoners in their care, they, too, are monitored, with their actions sometimes subject to careful scrutiny. Their movements on duty appear on the same monitors as those of prisoners, and they, too, must pass in and out of spaces through controlled doors (without keys or the ability to exit independently). Although it often goes unrecognized, they are also subject to the good will of prisoners, as evidenced by the fact that one or two officers working in a confined space with thirty or sixty prisoners would not, physically or otherwise, be able to stop a riot or deflate collective misconduct.

According to census data, more correctional officers work in provincial institutions than in federal institutions (Griffiths, 2010). However, the exact number of correctional officers working in provincial and territorial facilities in some capacity in Canada is nearly impossible to determine given that the role is classified differently by province. For example, some provinces may offer casual, permanent, or temporary positions; others may hire for full- or part-time positions; still others may hire for a combination of temporary, part-time, and full-time positions. It should be noted that casual employees are in rather precarious employment positions, and both part-time and casual employees do not qualify for the same benefits, sick leave, disability, or assistance as full-time employees, despite the high-risk nature of their occupation. However, given that the alternative for many individuals is unemployment, a career as a correctional officer even under these conditions is acceptable to some. Moreover, the different types of facilities that exist – including training centres, separate or joint lock-ups, holding centres, detention centres, remand centres, correctional centres, dual designation centres, jails, prisons, camps, and correctional facilities – as well as the ever increasing prison expansions – make both comparisons across facilities and standardized counts of employees working in closed-custody institutions incredibly difficult.

One misperception that I all too often face when discussing Canadian prisons is the idea that the federal and provincial systems are completely separate. The reality is that, despite the fact that Canada maintains both federal and provincial systems, correctional officers in the provincial and territorial prisons do interact with and have custody over soon-to-be federally sentenced prisoners, prisoners awaiting transfer to federal prison, and federally sentenced prisoners located in provinces without a federal prison who are compatible with the security designation of the facility. Once a person is arrested, if he or she is denied bail, because they are considered a flight risk or pose a danger to him- or herself or others, the accused is "remanded" into custody at a regional (not federal) facility (Ontario Ministry of the Attorney General, 2013). Remand custody – when the accused person is incarcerated while awaiting trial, judicial decision-making, or sentencing – is served in a non-federal correctional institution. Thus, all federal prisoners start their experiences of imprisonment under the custody of provincial or territorial correctional officers. It should be noted that, in Canada, more adults are serving time in remand than for a provincial prison sentence (Kong & Peters, 2008).

Once a person arrives in custody, he or she encounters an institutional environment in which correctional officers play a significant role. In theory, correctional officers are instrumental in the implementation of programming for prisoners, and, ideally, should aid in creating a penal environment that is conducive to prisoner "rehabilitation" (although the extent to which this can and does happen varies; see Maruna, 2012 for a discussion of the difficulties with the concept of prisoner rehabilitation). More commonly, correctional officers are prisoners' most direct line of communication with service providers, their lawyer or legal team, and the outside world more generally (Ricciardelli, 2014b; Ricciardelli & Gazzo, 2013; Robinson, Porporino, & Simourd, 1993). They are also responsible for helping prisoners receive basic necessities, from a change of clothes to toilet paper to drinkable water and medicine. They facilitate prisoners' access to phone calls, health and dental care, and they oversee meetings and personal visits. They record copious notes on prisoner behaviour and progress, monitoring them for programmatic, well-being, and security reasons. They investigate prison infractions, respond to security concerns, and may be called upon to provide first aid or life-saving transport. And, as I discuss in more detail in upcoming chapters, they may also be tasked with managing the emotional, mental, and other strains that prisoners experience, while also dealing with their own occupational stressors and those of colleagues. In short, correctional work can be and often is a mundane yet demanding and high-stress occupation.

The Occupational Context

Despite the unique and important role that correctional officers play within Canadian society, most scholarly and public attention is reserved for the persons incarcerated and for the structural, systemic, and social truths underlining the virtual and physical cage of confinement in prison. In this book, I provide a different focus. I seek to reveal some of the realities of the working lives of the men and women who *also serve time.* This view of correctional work, as a form of institutional confinement experienced by both prisoners and correctional officers, is not unique. In fact, it is an interpretation shared by the correctional officers I interviewed for this book. As one officer said of his work, "Well, you're [also] doing time." Indeed, these officers work side by side each day with the very people whom society has determined must be segregated and confined.

In recognizing the role of correctional officers, I pose questions to fulfil the purpose behind this book, which is to highlight the lived experiences of the men and women who work in provincial and territorial prisons. These officers work with prisoners during the early days of their incarceration as they try to reconcile the outcome(s) of the poor choices they have made (while, all too often, detoxing). In so doing they witness prisoners' emotional turmoil following their initial arrest and work with them in remand, pre- and post-sentencing, or while the media frenzy over their crimes and trial is peaking. Nearly every person that serves time begins in a provincial or territorial facility, including individuals deemed unfit to stand trial. All prisoners, whether intentionally or not, pose a potential risk to officers. Yet rarely if ever is any public attention awarded to the well-being or experiences of these officers.

Take, for example, twenty-four-year-old Justin Bourque, who shot and killed three members of the Royal Canadian Mounted Police (Constable

Fabrice Gévaudan, Constable Dave Ross, and Constable Douglas Larche) and injured two others (Constable Darlene Goguen and Constable Eric Dubois), before being apprehended after a more than thirty- hour manhunt. After his surrender and arrest, Bourque spent at least twelve hours being interrogated by the police before meeting for ten minutes with a court-appointed private lawyer, Mr. DesNeiges. DesNeiges stated publicly that he had never before seen such media attention nor so many armed officers in court (O'Kane, 2014). However, the media attention and concern for peace officers' safety quickly subsided once Bourque was in custody. Bourque, who blatantly opposed authority, was placed under the authority of correctional officers at the Southeast Regional Correction Centre, in Shediac, New Brunswick – peace officers who are unarmed while on duty. Many officers responsible for Bourque's custody, before he was federally sentenced to a precedent-setting three consecutive life sentences with no chance of parole for seventy-five years, also lived in Moncton and thus were affected by the city lock-down and terrorizing manhunt, as were their families (*CBC News*, 2014).

In their occupational role, these officers are also tasked with trying to reconcile their own emotions evoked by Bourque's actions, as well as by seeing any of his six siblings or his parents visit him in prison (see Blaze Carlson, 2014). After expressing hope that something positive would come from his son's actions – specifically that police be granted the power to intervene if an individual presents as possibly dangerous, and as requiring help, but has yet to commit a crime – Bourque's father explained: "We are victims. We didn't ask for this at all … Nobody has the authority to take a life" (McMahon, Friscolanti, & Patriquin, 2014). Indeed, Bourque's family, too, feel victimized.

Correctional officers must balance, if possible, the complex web of emotions that result from being in such close proximity to those who have committed criminal behaviours – the humanity of prisoners, the emotional hardships endured by the prisoners' families when visiting, and the retribution desired by the public and criminal justice systems. And yet, overall, knowledge about prisons, correctional officers, staff, and prisoners remains minimal among the majority of citizens, and is too often negatively skewed.

In the pages that follow, I expose readers to the daily realities of the correctional officers who work with adult male and female populations in Canada. I highlight some of the nuances of the job from the perspective of officers, and show how officer orientations *and* attitudes toward prisoners are interconnected and foundational in shaping the prison experiences of those in custody and those in managerial and administrative positions. Drawing on interviews with officers from a range of provincial and territorial institutions, I move beyond theoretical explorations of officer orientations, risk, and gender to show how perceptions, attitudes, and beliefs – both at the individual and structural levels – shape their work practices.

Further, data from these interviews allows for an examination of such topics as officers' motivations for entering the field, their life trajectories, future ambitions, and experiences within the prison (and beyond). The officer accounts I present provide readers with an opportunity to understand what the occupational role of a correctional officer entails, and to examine issues around rehabilitation and societal punitiveness, and how gender and the hierarchical structure of prison management and positioning shape officers' daily realities.

My two principal objectives in this book are, first, to unpack the latent and manifest essence of gender positively and negatively informing the actions and self-presentation of correctional officers – recognizing that gender is shaped by and also shapes identity, life experience, opportunity, and contextual factors. The second objective is to present some of the realities that create both male and female correctional officers' experiences when working with male and female prisoner populations in provincial and territorial prison facilities. These objectives shape my end goal of informing readers about prisons and prison work, while also showing how correctional officers interpret their occupational context – despite the pervasive and omnipresent risk that underpins the work environment for all those within these facilities.

A note of caution: my goal here is not to paint correctional officers or prisoners as either inherently "good" or "bad" people with socially "unacceptable" or "acceptable" ethical standards, morality, or values. My focus here is *not* on the mental health of correctional officers or how their employment may shape their mental and physical health and well-being (for such work see: Carleton, Afifi, Turner, Taillieu, & Duranceau, 2018; Carleton, Afifi, Turner, Taillieu, & LeBouthillier, 2018; Ricciardelli, Carleton, Groll, & Cramm, 2018; Ricciardelli & Power, in press; Ricciardelli, Carleton, Mooney, & Cramm, 2019; Ricciardelli, Power, & Medeiros, 2018; Ricciardelli, Groll, Czarnuch, Carleton, & Cramm, 2019; Ricciardelli & Spencer, 2017). Rather, my intention is to show how correctional officers are impacted by the realities of their occupational role – in many ways they, too, "do time" and are impacted by the nature of their job and the people in their custody. My hope is that in shedding light on the realities of Canadian prisons from another perspective – that of the correctional officer – I can provide a greater awareness of what is happening in our prisons and of the nature of the work correctional officers do, and sometimes are constrained from doing, because of resource, policy, and other barriers.

The empirical data presented throughout this book is drawn from a non-random sample of over one hundred in-depth interviews with correctional officers either actively or formerly employed in provincial or territorial prisons and remand centres in Canada (for more information on the method, see Appendix A). The vast and comprehensive experiences of these officers are used to provide some understanding of correctional work as caring for, controlling, and enforcing consequences on prisoners.[1] The arguments presented across the chapters flow from this positioning of their work.

Overview of Chapters

Within the context of provincial and territorial prison work experience, in this book I provide a detailed investigation into the current-day work experiences of correctional officers across much of Canada. To begin this process, in this introduction I set the stage by presenting the reader with some of the key components of provincial/territorial systems. Among other topics, I explore the processes through which provincial institutions and prisoners are "classified" and the key similarities, differences, and overlaps within and between the federal and provincial and territorial systems, as well as the diverse job requirements of correctional officers.

In chapter 1, I unpack the salient emergent themes of risk (i.e., vulnerabilities) and gender (specifically masculinities), which provide the theoretical underpinnings of the research presented in this book. To this end, I explore the role that gender plays in shaping prison work, as I reveal how processes of self-regulation are employed by officers to construct gendered strategies of risk avoidance that bear the latent function of both achieving and affirming masculinities. Then, I contextualize risk in contemporary society and explore how ideas of risk shape the prison environment, as well as the occupational responsibilities and experiences of correctional officers. In reconstructing their gendered position within the employment context of the prison, I explain how officers' navigation of experiences of vulnerability and risk are symbiotic processes and how, as a result, officers must indiscriminately select strategies for risk negation. I end the chapter with a discussion of correctional officer orientations and highlight how each is always constructed within the framework of risk and gender.

Canadian provincial, territorial, and federal governments are under increasing pressure to recruit more qualified correctional officers, who are needed in light of accelerating incarceration rates *and* the building of more and larger penal facilities. Yet, such pressures are coupled with

the struggles inherent to recruiting and retaining effective and compe-
tent correctional officers. In chapter 2, after introducing the men and
women whose stories make up the data used in this book, I examine
more closely the career of the correctional officer, seeking answers to
the question, Why corrections? Making use of participants' responses, I
present the diverse factors and experiences that motivate individuals to
make this career choice and those that have shaped the career trajectories described by interviewees.

In chapter 3, I reflect on the bulk of a correctional officer's daily role
in the field: the "99 per cent" of correctional work that is spent doing
routine, often mundane, tasks, such as ordering items, helping and providing services to prisoners, writing up reports on such activities, and
many other routine contacts that make up the work day. In this chapter,
I focus on the experiences of correctional officers working and interacting with male and female prisoner populations in order to provide
context for the chapters that follow. I examine interactions between correctional officers and prisoners and start to reflect on how correctional
work is influenced by gender dynamics and communication styles, and
I argue that prisoner–officer relations shape how prisoners serve their
time and how officers spend theirs.

It is in chapter 4 that my attention turns to the experiences of female
correctional officers. I examine their work with prisoner populations –
some male, but I then focus on my interviewees' experiences with female
populations – and the institutions that house them. Here, I provide background about the entry of female correctional officers into the field of
correctional work, and insight into how gender shapes female officers'
work experiences, including how they are viewed by prisoners and co-
workers. Topics of note include how female officers understand the
needs of those in their charge, needs that include programming, relationships, and support, with an emphasis on the too frequently reported
lack of human and material resources available to meet prisoner needs.

The focus of the next three chapters is male correctional officers and
their experiences in working largely with adult male prisoners (due to
structural limitations that often bar male correctional officers from working on units that house female prisoners or in prisons for women). In
chapter 5, I discuss the work experiences of male correctional officers,
and the strategies they use to navigate their occupational space and both
achieve and affirm their masculinities. These strategies are always gendered and shaped by power relations, and as such they further function
to help officers perform masculinities and overcome vulnerabilities –
including those thought to be inherent to their work environment. I
also consider how being viewed as "vulnerable" in the eyes of colleagues,

prisoners, and management may reduce an officer's social and professional status. In the reverse case, I present how power and privilege can be secured, even confirmed, when an officer is able to successfully negotiate his vulnerabilities at work.

In chapter 6, I draw on theories of risk to unpack some of the nuances in officer perceptions and experiences of threat. I identify some of the sources of risk that officers face, ranging from prisoner violence, to conflicts with colleagues, to institutional policies, including those likely designed with the best intentions – all threats that can impact their occupational identity, and even seep into their personal lives over time. I follow with chapter 7, where I offer a discussion of how the correctional officer occupation, for some male officers, is structured through risk-taking and, as I argue, how it thus constitutes a form of "edgework" (Lyng, 1990). In this discussion, I reveal how some officers construct their occupation as dangerous and fashion objective primary and secondary edges – the former being at the point of any encounter prone to escalation, and the latter existing within the space between criminal and civil behaviours that are occupationally sanctioned. I explore the real and potential impacts of this construction on officers' work activities.

To conclude the book, I first offer a summation of my main points and then outline my central objectives. The first objective being to lend insight into the latent and manifest essence of gender, as it works to shape how an individual chooses to act as well as self-present when serving as a correctional officer; and the second being to demonstrate some of the nuances that shape prison work in provincial and territorial facilities. Here, specifically, I speak to how experiences of prison work are similar or dissimilar for male versus female correctional officers working with male versus female prisoner populations. To this end, I seek to provide the reader with insight into how provincial and territorial prisons and prison work have changed, yet how they always remain laced with the potentiality for risk and threat and thus perpetuate feelings of vulnerabilities. Perhaps more importantly, though, I use the concluding chapter to put forth a possible vision of the future of provincial and territorial prison work, abstracted from the empirical analysis presented here. I contend that the current political climate, as it is shaped by advocacy for new penal policies and practices, alongside continuously increasing incarceration rates, may imply Canada is slowly losing the battle when it comes to keeping practices less punitive.

1

Setting the Stage

This is a provincial institution. There's not a whole lot of programs, first of all ...
it's filthy, it's gross, and it's disgusting. It's not even believable.
— Anonymous correctional officer describing work
and living conditions

In 2008–9, 23,810.2 adults on average were in provincial and territorial custody across Canada. The number increased to 25,208, on average, in 2012–13, with 11,150.7 adult prisoners being sentenced, 13,739
adult prisoners being held on remand, and 318.3 persons being held
in a temporary or other form of detention (e.g., immigration holds)
(Statistics Canada, 2014b). Reports at the time clearly stated that the
number of persons incarcerated in Canada was at an all-time high
(Brosnahan, 2013). In 2015, Statistics Canada released its latest set of
figures on incarceration rates in Canada. Although noting that rates of
provincial custody had dropped from the previous two years to a "low"
of 21,704 adults, the report also highlighted the continuation of a disturbing trend: the number of adults waiting for court dates in pretrial
detention ("remand") exceeded the number of individuals sentenced to
physical custody (Correctional Service Program, 2015; Statistics Canada,
2014a, 2014b). Such figures are released each year to provide a snapshot
of the functioning of Canada's prison systems; however, such representations, and the headings they generate – e.g., "fewer adults are being
supervised" (Correctional Service Program, 2015) – provide only cursory
insight into our prisons and their operations. They shed even less light
on the work of those tasked with ensuring the safety and security of both
the individuals within these facilities and, by extension, in the larger society. In this chapter, I review the relevant literature on prison work. As
this book draws on multiple theoretical strands, both individually and

sometimes in an integrated fashion, I then provide an overview of the
theories employed in each of the subsequent chapters.

Correctional Work

In the United Kingdom, Alison Liebling (2004, p. 484) argued that the
"largely undocumented penal project" was put in place to "eliminate
residual resistance and secure a new mode of compliance" among prisoners. In Canada, prisoner compliance is arguably advanced by "penal
populism," a concept first put forth by Sir Anthony Bottoms (1995),
reshaped by Julian Roberts and colleagues (2002), and later David Garland (2001) and John Pratt (2007), to explain how changes in penal
policy result from political actors looking to be elected. Roberts, Stalans,
Indermaur, and Hough (2002, p. 5) argued that "penal populists allow
the electoral advantage of a policy to take precedence over its penal
effectiveness." In Canada, under the former Conservative government
of Stephen Harper, a symbiotic relationship emerged between "get-
tough-on-crime" initiatives and public pressure for "crime control" that
set the foundation for mandatory minimums and a greater reliance on
the threat of incarceration (Barnett et al., 2012). For example, despite
a steady decline in Canadian crime rates over recent decades (Correctional Service Canada, 2010), the omnibus crime bill known as the Safe
Streets and Communities Act[1] legislated mandatory minimum sentences
and ineligibility for conditional release for select persons who commit
sexual crimes against children (Bill C-10, Part 2, Clauses 10–31, 35–38,
49, and 51, formerly Bill C-54), brought harsher sanctions for drug-
related offences (Bill C-10, Part 2, Clauses 32–33, 39–48, 50–51, formerly
Bill S-10), and modified the use of conditional sentencing, suspended
sentences, and probation orders (Barnett et al., 2012). The legislative
changes imposed by the Act have left many voicing their opposition,
including the Canadian Bar Association, the Canadian Civil Liberties
Association, and the John Howard Society of Canada (for more information, see Canadian Bar Association, 2011; Correctional Service Canada,
2012a; Parole Board of Canada, 2012).

In 2012, James Clancy, the president of the National Union of Public
and General Employees (NPUGE), publicly spoke in opposition to the
Act: "When people talk about Harper being tough on crime, I think Bill
C-10 demonstrates that the Harper government is dumb on crime ...
Our members who work in provincial jails are telling us that the number of inmates with mental health or addiction problems is growing dra-
matically" (*CBC News*, 2012). Clancy added that "the federal anti-crime
legislation is going to make a bad situation worse by imprisoning more

and more people ... It is an inhumane way to deal with people who need treatment, not jail time" (*CBC News*, 2012). Many have also voiced concerns about the Act exacerbating overcrowding in prisons. In Manitoba, before the legislation of the Act in 2012, calculations revealed that if the number of prisoners provincially incarcerated was to follow the documented pattern of increase, taking into account trends from seven years prior and applying such trends to the next seven years, incarceration rates would increase from 2,964 people in custody in 2012 (900 prisoners already over current capacity) to 3,964 people by 2019 (Manitoba Government and General Employees' Union, 2012). Lois Wales, former president of the Manitoba Government and General Employees' Union (MGEU), concerned that overcrowding was creating "an abnormal working environment, a hyper-vigilant working environment, and certainly an unsafe working environment," stated that:

> Whether you're a proponent for Bill C-10 or not, the reality is this new legislation will make the overcrowding problem worse. Exactly how bad it will get is hard to gauge. We simply don't know enough about it to know what affects it will have, but what's perhaps more alarming to all Manitobans is that our provincial government doesn't know how bad the situation could get. (Manitoba Government and General Employees' Union, 2012)

Overcrowding affects the safety and security of prisoners and staff, and increases levels of institutional violence and rates of infection and disease transmission. Indeed, Canada's correctional history has evolved with inquiries, amended legislation, and commissions that stagger between punitive and humanistic objectives embodied in political and practical correctional reform. Penal populism and the associated "reforms" impact men and women in custody and the correctional officers that enact conditions of confinement.

Risk, Safety, and Gender: Interpreting "Correctional Work"

My analysis of the interview data collected reveals two dominant themes in how correctional officers perceive and, in turn, shape their work: conceptualizations of *gender* (more specifically, masculinities) and *risk* (or alternatively, safety and vulnerabilities). In the pages that follow, I examine correctional work using relevant theories related to both concepts as lenses through which to develop a better understanding of the nature of this work. In this section, I focus on introducing these two concepts and the related theories upon which I draw to underpin my analysis. To conclude the chapter, I unpack previous scholarship on correctional officer orientations toward their occupational work and prisoners in order to provide insight into the various nuances of officer behaviours and attitudes found among the pages of this book.

Gender (and Prison Work)

The responsibilities tied to the correctional officer occupational role affect officers' job satisfaction as well as their professional orientation and their attitudes toward prisoners – among other lived realities (e.g., Boyd, 2011; Crawley, 2004; Jacobs & Retsky, 1980; Lambert, Hogan, & Barton, 2002; Liebling, 2008; Skolnick, 1966). The role is shaped by vulnerabilities that evolve with policy, practice, and technological change, where each is followed by the demand for officers to respond to any such change. Further, it is only in acknowledging and answering such vulnerabilities, often through a process of self-regulation, that gender is achieved, specifically those masculinities (and femininities) that are strategic for successful risk navigation. In this context, we continue to lack information about how correctional officers' occupational obligations – referred to by Liebling (2000, p. 337) as the "invisible ghosts of penality" – are tied to perceived and actual vulnerabilities (e.g., physical, emotional, legal) that shape and are shaped by masculinities (and femininities) and yet are always contextualized by the gender order. Said another way, the manner in which conceptualizations of gender are (re)constructed in accordance with the vulnerabilities inherent in culture, politics, or larger society is both inherent to, and then re-established by, officers trying to avoid risk – and such processes are always gendered. I now turn to unpacking the ways in which gender is understood, first more broadly and then in the specific context of prison work, particularly in terms of masculinities given the largely masculine and male-dominated prison environment.

Masculinities

Masculinities may be dominating (e.g., empowered) or may be dominant (e.g., common) (Messerschmidt, 2012), but they are always precarious, evolving in response to variations in social practices, attitudes, and cultural or structural changes (Connell, 2002; Connell & Wood, 2005; Zulehner & Volz, 1998). These changes are not necessarily benign, but may oppose or conflict with conventional understandings of masculinities, such that new variations or contradictory masculinities, which become dominating in status, may be produced as a result (Connell, 1992). Connell (1987, 1990, 1992) described masculinities as contested social processes that are always conceptualized in line with gender relations and operate at different levels (e.g., collective, institutional, cultural, personal) within the patriarchal structures in which they are embedded and produced. The intricate interplay that occurs between cultural ideals and institutionalized power in the constitution of hegemonic masculinity and marginalized, subordinate, or complicit masculinities also becomes ostensible: "hegemonic masculinity is not a fixed character type, always and everywhere the same. It is, rather, the masculinity that occupies the hegemonic [dominant] position in a given pattern of gender relations, a position always contestable" (Connell, 2005, p. 76). This notwithstanding, occupying a position of power is a temporal reality, meaning that it varies historically and is very much informed by contextual factors. In every context, however, one specific masculinity – hegemonic masculinity – will always prevail (Carrigan, Connell, & Lee, 1985; Connell, 1987, 1995).

It must be recognized that hegemonic masculinity is not necessarily an actualized reality or response to reality, but is just as much a symbolic entity, and, as such, becomes increasingly unachievable. Thomas (1990) and Kaufman (1994), for example, documented how non-normative masculinities may be experienced as "private dissatisfaction" or irregularities – what I argue are sites of vulnerabilities, instead of objectively viewed as a starting point for questioning the social construction of gender. This thought process and practice reinforces that hegemonic masculinity will remain unachievable, yet will always be (re)produced within the context of, and will simultaneously cultivate, patriarchal relationships and a hegemonic ideal (Messerschmidt, 2012). The idea here, as demonstrated in select studies (e.g., Vandello, Bosson, Cohen, Burnaford, & Weaver, 2008), is that any man's masculinity – his gender status – is easily threatened, and, as such, men are prone to experiencing doubts about their masculinity (i.e., there are seemingly infinite ways for men to feel less "masculine" in comparison to individuals of other gender identifications). Willer, Rogalin, Conlon, and Wojnowicz (2012) in their summation of previous research, argued that it "supports masculinity theorists' contention that men are highly responsive to their masculine status" (p. 9). If men feel their masculinity is under treat, a phenomenon that can be attributed to a "narrow definition" of what constitutes acceptable masculinity, men will be "motivated to reclaim a masculine gender identity, due to the prestige attached to it" (Willer et al., 2012). Thus, in reinforcing societal structures (e.g., the gendered order), this cycle of events ensures that men will continue to face, negotiate, and manage both perceived and real threats to their gender identity, the overcoming of which is essential if any man is to truly occupy a dominating masculinity. Of course, as Beasley (2008) argued, common or dominant types of masculinity may not always be hegemonic, such as masculinities that authenticate men's power but are culturally marginalized. Moreover, what constitutes hegemonic masculinity is dynamic, varying within and across different social, cultural, situational, occupational, and other contexts, rather than a static concept.

Vulnerabilities and Masculinities and the Gendered Prison Work Environment

For individuals, the successful negotiation of vulnerabilities within a cultural and social context begins the processes of ensuring one's dominance, by eliminating their weaknesses, if possible. It is in the embodiment or self-presentation of masculinity(ies) that hegemonic masculinity can easily become understood as molding itself into a dominating position, often in response to perceived, anticipated, or experienced vulnerabilities. Thus, those who are best able to deal with their vulnerabilities, their perceived weaknesses, are also the most able to embody hegemonic masculinity in the relevant gendered space because little can threaten their status and positioning. This position is reflective of the personally valued actualities that exist in subcultures, subgroups, and communities. If such vulnerabilities are managed and surpassed, the individual is able to attain and maintain a dominating masculine status, or, at minimum, an empowered masculine position in society, often in line with the hegemonic ideal.

Vulnerabilities in this context help to explain the transmission throughout history of hegemonic forms of Euro/American masculinities that leaned toward more calculative, rational, and regulated masculinities (Connell, 1993) – masculinities needed for the defeat of vulnerabilities in most contexts. Some men (or individuals), however, must occupy a more privileged position than others, and thus legitimate and reproduce the relations and structures underlying their dominance (Carrigan et al., 1985; Connell, 1987, 1993, 1998, 2005). As a concept, then, hegemonic masculinity is flexible, and its fluidity is a strength, not a drawback. In this sense, gender – as well as relations between and within genders – is constructed in light of its association to the vulnerabilities individuals experience. This way of understanding the effectiveness of masculinities in legitimizing a gender order in societies helps us to see that the same mechanism takes place in the correctional environment, which, as scholars have documented, is for men hyper-masculine in nature (see Messerschmidt, 1997, 1999).

This hyper-masculine male prison environment is characterized by aggressive, heterosexual, and tough self-presentations and processes of prisoner socialization (Haney, 2011; Ricciardelli, 2013; Schroeder, 2004, p. 418; Toch, 1998). In prison, dominant masculine ideals, including bravery, strength, aggression, and stoicism, are valued (Phillips, 2001; Ricciardelli, 2013), despite prisoners being disconnected from other masculine ideals like freedom, agency, autonomy, and success (Sykes, 1958). Researchers have theorized that the male correctional environment shapes the correctional officer occupation, which Farnworth (1992, p. 279) described as the "highly male stereotyped job of a correctional officer in a male prison." Thus, officer interactions are contextualized against this masculine environment laced with stereotypes that are then challenged, reproduced, and (re)negotiated. This process signifies that correctional officers must renegotiate their self-presentation in light of occupational realities that impact their well-being, identity, and agency at work. In essence, correctional officers experience in their prison work the impacts of the deprivations or "pains" tied to prison living (for a discussion of the "pains of imprisonment" as experienced by prisoners, see Sykes, 1958).

Prison environments are laced with potential risk, or sites of vulnerabilities, that must be overcome by officers. Officers then strive to create some semblance of control, while also affirming their own gender positioning through strategic behaviours such as "safekeeping" and effective self-regulation. For this reason, some officers may construct the (male or female) prisoner as a potentially "dangerous other," an individual whose needs are unmet, with each representation serving to solidify their own occupational riskiness. These officers embark on processes of self-regulation to navigate potential risk in their work environment, which include a performative masculinity (or femininity, for that matter). Responses to perceived risks are structured to optimize an empowered, rather than meek, presentation of their gendered subject position. This gendered performance affirms and achieves a gendered embodiment that demonstrates "safety" or invulnerability, and thus suppresses the potentiality of threat posed by the prisoner.

In essence, gender identity is used to reshape understandings of risk that provide new modes of defining, controlling, and neutralizing said risk – a required reality given that risk (or risk-averse) society threatens traditional understandings of gender and calls for the pursuit of a new biography of self (Ekberg, 2007; Giddens, 1994; Hannah-Moffat, 2004a, 2004b). Nevertheless, Hannah-Moffat and O'Malley (2007, p. 6; cf. Lois, 2005; Lyng & Matthews, 2007; Miller, 1991) argued that "the gender-risk nexus is capable of considerable complexity and variability" in that one's existence as an individual in contemporary society can be understood as involving constant risk negotiation and management.

Risk (and Prison Work)

In the 1990s, the concept of "risk" emerged as a dominant theme within both scholarly (Beck, 1992) and popular-science accounts of modern life (Gardner, 2009). It has been variously used to explain how diverse processes of assessing, managing, and engaging real and potential threats shape lived experiences (Beck, 1992; Giddens, 1994; Hannah-Moffat, 2004a; Hannah-Moffat & O'Malley, 2007). In general terms, risk is constituted in how people perceive their environment – perhaps in the "gut feelings" they produce, their knowledge of threat, or their diverse experiences of vulnerabilities – which then informs individual and group responses as people attempt to negate vulnerability, create safety, and sidestep potential negative consequences. In prison, identifying and understanding risk is of foremost concern for correctional staff, policymakers, and prisoners. The risk and threat inherent to prison work contextualizes the different facets of the correctional officer experiences found in this book.

The understanding of risk through which I partially frame this analysis is drawn first from the work of Beck (1992) and Giddens (1990), both of whom focus on a vision of contemporary society characterized by unfamiliar, unpredictable, but sometimes calculable, risks. In Beck's formulation of this concept, risk results from processes of globalization, diverse forms of development, and the corresponding dissolution of conventional norms, traditions, and values – realities not unlike what could motivate transgressions of the law or realities experienced in prison environments. For Beck, then, risk is in essence a human product – created by humanity – no different from our penal system, which was and is created by citizens. Implicitly, it is human intentionality, a concept central to modernization and one exacerbated by the social push toward individualization in modern times, that generates, as Beck (2002) noted, much seemingly unpredictable risk. Humans too often ignore the unpredictability of their own intentions: the risk that we generate. People then structure their behaviour to minimize "known" risk while maximizing possible benefits (Beck, 1999).

As Lash (2003) explained, however, within such processes of human action "what is intended leads to the most extraordinary unintendedness, to side-effects, to unintended consequences" (p. 51). In this sense, despite behaviours being structured to minimize known risk, the outcome (i.e., if the cost is *too high* in comparison to the benefits) of any action will always be unknown until the experience is lived and realities felt (Beck, 1999). This cost-benefit analysis inherent, whether consciously or unconsciously, to electing a course of action for any person (e.g., each person tries to maximize possible benefits when selecting behaviours to engage in, but may select to engage in riskier actions if they deem the benefit "worthy") is of fundamental value when examining correctional work.

Recognition of risk, including normative processes located in risk society, Beck (1992) argued, transforms how individuals understand the world. Individual "risk knowledges," referring to "the plurality and heterogeneity of risk thinking and the ever developing variety of risk management techniques" (Valverde, 2003, p. 9), then expose how understandings of risk differ according to the person. They are shaped by gender and other aspects of his or her lived experience and current situation that are constructed and reconstructed in the process of making decisions in response to, or in mediating, risk (Hannah-Moffat, 2004a; Valverde, 2003).

Correctional officers, then, experience risk that differs from that generally experienced by persons employed and living in free society. This risk is constituted and reconstituted across prisons, prisoners, and colleagues in light of the many diverse characteristics and contexts tied to each factor. These officers understand safety and threats to safety in light of their occupationally contextualized risk knowledges (Valverde, 2003); the heterogeneity of risk is recognized – characterized at the personal/individual level – in light of how officers identify, evaluate, and manage risk to construct safety, and this is evident whenever an individual discloses feeling vulnerable, unsafe, or worried.

The risk that correctional officers experience on duty is exceptional relative to many other occupational groups, particularly those outside of public safety, and is deeply embedded in both their assigned duties and their work environment. Correctional services is one of few occupations where the possibility of being hit by bodily fluids that have been thrown, being threatened, or being called upon to suppress a riot is very real. For example, in less than twelve months, correctional officers in Saskatchewan faced four major disturbances, including a riot at the Saskatoon Correctional Centre, and were ambushed and sprayed with mace while transporting prisoners (Saskatchewan Government Employees Union, 2016). The willingness to accept the possibility of such risks suggests there must be some perceived benefit to prison work that outweighs – in some capacity – calculated costs. For instance, the correctional officer role may inform options and acceptable venues for self-exploration, thus providing opportunities for diverse constructions of self, which in risk society is termed "individualization" (Beck, Giddens, & Nash, 1994, p. 13). Of course, for some individuals, entering the field may not have felt like an "option," nor does exiting the field seem plausible (see chapter 2).

Growing social acceptance, societal support, and even promotion of individualization has fueled demands for more opportunities, as is evident in changes in the once static structures of class, gender, and family across life courses (Beck & Beck-Gernsheim, 2002, p. xxii). But despite individualization, tradition remains an invaluable part of dealing with the unintentional outcomes – the risk – tied to processes that emerge in the tensions and contradictions inherent to living "a life of one's own" (Lash, 2001). Thus, institutions designed to mediate risk, such as the correctional system or the justice system more generally, exist to apply consequences to rule violators – any person who fails to obey laws in a way that is recognized and condoned as requiring punitive measures for social retribution or justice – (in a general sense) and to protect society from greater harm. Kelly Hannah-Moffat (2004a, 2004b) argued, over a decade ago, that an individual's knowledge of how to manage risk, and of risk itself, shapes behaviours. Individuals are then responsible for the self-management of risk, in that the choices behind the decision to act in particular ways are always shaped by identity or desired self-presentations, which are fueled by social learning and self-shaping. As I previously noted, identity is inherently rooted in gendered understandings – at conscious or subconscious levels – as gender in its many conceptualizations is a personal process *and* a reality inherent to self.

Risk-Taking (and Prison Work)

Another body of thought through which I arrive at an understanding of why some correctional officers undertake what many might see as a risky, even *too* risky, occupation is that of the allure of risk-taking for certain individuals and groups (Lyng, 1990; Miller, 1991; Simon, 2002; Lyng & Matthews, 2007). Miller (1991), for example, argued that some individuals are drawn to risk-taking, while Lyng and Matthews (2007) suggested that men may be attracted to different risk-taking behaviours in comparison to women (see chapter 7). Either way, risk-taking behaviours, whether voluntary or involuntary, are evident in diverse occupational settings, including prison work, and can be understood as risk-taking at an individual level for each officer (see Simon, 2002, 2005).

The occupation of the correctional officer, specifically those on the front line working in a unit, needs to be better understood. Officers hold positions of authority over persons thought capable of engaging in law-breaking behaviours or behaviours that could result in the violation of some person(s), place(s), or thing(s), yet officers must engage with those in their custody and do so in high-risk contexts if called upon. Prison work blurs the boundaries between "good" and "bad" and crosses the lines that serve to segregate the "criminal" from the "law-abiding citizen" in society. What makes the correctional officer's role unique is the necessary willingness to enter a space that is both physically and socially isolated, namely because of the fears the rest of society generally harbours toward those with whom the officer "voluntarily" associates. Further, within this complex site, officers must negotiate the carceral space and find ways to preserve safety, manage risk, and maintain their own personal and occupational identities within the structure of the institution.

Researchers investigating risk practices have found that males and females are both drawn to risk-taking (see Miller, 1991, for an example). Lyng and Matthews (2007) argued that men and women "may deal with risks in gender-specific ways," thus leaving gender – specifically masculinities – to be reconfigured within this new context (p. 75–6). Voluntary risk-taking, or partaking in activities deemed to be risk-taking that are rewarding and ends in themselves (see Ferrell, Milovanovic, & Lyng, 2001; Lyng, 1990), can extend to occupational practices and be embedded in gender discourses and re-conceptualizations. Ferrell and colleagues (2001) explained that edgework theorists have worked to "identify the repertoire of meanings common to particular edgework participants. More broadly, they have sought to identify the collective subcultural construction of edgework experiences, and the dynamics by which the ephemeral and the ineffable are captured within ongoing social interaction" (p. 179).

In the theory of edgework, Lyng (1990) drew attention to the dangers and powerful emotional sensations that accompany risk-taking behaviours and the need for actors to convert fear into an acceptable emotional response to risk, one that allows the actors to focus on successfully negotiating high-risk situations. The resulting sensation leaves edgeworkers feeling fully alive, while simultaneously exposing – even shaping – their future lifestyle choices in line with their efforts to maximize their sensation of "living" – what Lyng terms "the attraction of the edge" (p. 79). The objective boundary, where risk is undoubtable, constitutes the primary objective edge. The encounter of an edge that is founded on emotional sensations and personal perception – gut feelings indicating risk – rather than an objective high-risk situation, constitutes the secondary edge.

Recognizing that perhaps correctional work is not voluntary edgework for some individuals (e.g., those entering the occupation due to lack of alternatives), risk is omnipresent and correctional officers are indeed exposed to high-risk activities. Lyng (2005), among others, recognized the objective nature of risk in edgework and clarified why edgework holds an alluring quality for participants. Specifically, in a social world increasingly dominated by simulated realities and blurred boundaries, encountering the objectivity of consequential edges in edgework can be a powerful experience. Edgework, when applied to correctional officers, would suggest that some officers are not motivated to enter the field by a need to satisfy internal urges or by rewards, and instead are drawn to the occupation by their desire for certain experiences (see chapter 2 for a discussion of why correctional officers enter the field). They then negotiate the "edge," remaining as close as possible to a potential experience. Of course, how an edge is construed, interpreted, or experienced – as with all aspects of correctional work – is largely shaped by the orientations of correctional officers to their job and to those in their custody.

Correctional Officer Orientations

Liberal and/or Humanitarian Positions[2]

Correctional officers actively shape the environment in the prison and more specifically on their unit (e.g., Crewe, 2009; Liebling, 2004; Sparks, Bottoms, & Hay, 1996) – it is under their governance that behavioural conditions and formal as well as informal regulations come to be enacted. For this reason, I now turn to background information about the different occupational orientations that have been documented among correctional officers and correctional managers, to provide a lens through which the actions and orientations of officers, as mediated by gender and risk, can be interpreted. Certainly, orientations vary, but there is general agreement that officer orientation range is value based, and includes both punitive and liberal-humanitarian underpinnings. Punitive values include practices like expert policymaking, penal thinking (e.g., see Pratt, 2008a, 2008b, for more details), and strict monitoring, whereas liberal-humanitarian values include the need for more humane prison conditions in hopes that better living conditions and well-treated prisoners will positively influence "rehabilitation" outcomes.

Researchers working internationally have highlighted the different role orientations that diverse correctional officers embody, recognizing that these consistently fall somewhere on the spectrum between care and control, and from humanitarian to punitive (e.g., Allaire & Firsirotu, 1984; Crawley, 2004; Farkas, 2000; Kaufman, 1988; Klofas & Toch, 1982; Rutherford, 1994). Drawing from interviews with seventy-nine officers working in state prisons in the United States, Farkas (2000) found that officer orientations prioritized rule enforcement; negotiation with prisoners; mutual obligation toward colleagues; or human service delivery. Like those identified by Farkas, typologies provide good descriptions, and, in some instances, take into account systemic, cultural, and informal components of the prison system. Crawley (2004), for example, categorized officers into "black-and-whiters" (rule abiders), "give-and-takers" (rule benders in certain circumstances), and "care-bears" (those striving to help prisoners), while Rutherford (1994), in his typology of officer role orientations, identified the three "working credos" of punishment, humanity, and efficiency. Rutherford's (1994) primary credo involved officer orientations that were geared toward problem-free, efficient, and effective management, a persuasion he deemed to be consistently spread across most orientations (e.g., it was evident in both harmony and security orientations). More recently, Crewe and Liebling (2012)[3] developed a typology of correctional manager orientations that ranged from the "Alienated" to "Managerialist" to "Dualists" to "Idealists." This typology,[4] constructed as part of Crewe and Liebling's quest to ascertain "an identifiable 'liberal' and/or 'humanitarian' position in contemporary practice" (p. 2), draws on the work of Valerie Braithwaite (1998b), who contextualized the values of security and harmony through a study of citizens' political values. She found both harmony and security present, though largely conflicting, as value orientations that corresponded with the voting, personal, and social behaviours of individuals (see Crewe & Liebling, 2012, for more information). Suggesting that an understanding of the "other" accompanies each value orientation, where harmony values suggest an orientation toward "others" (e.g., harmonious living, consensus) and security values one toward "self-protection" (e.g., individuality, protection, safety), Braithwaite (1994) found that some individuals took on both orientations – harmony and security – and, in doing so, actively strove to rationalize a balance between the two. She called these individuals "dualists" to differentiate from those with a weaker commitment to either orientation, who she referred to as "moral relativists" (Braithwaite, 1994, 1998a).[5]

Crewe and Liebling (2012) extended Braithwaite's dualist concept to include individuals with distinctive "approaches to the task of governing … They are linked to personal and biographical characteristics, as well as formative experiences during careers. Underlying them are distinctive visions of the moral status of offenders, and different conceptions of the means and ends of prison work" (p. 4). In applying the concepts to prison managers, they argued that officers who take a harmony-oriented approach use a consensual and social-justice professional style with prisoners, while those with a security-oriented approach "prioritise internal order" and use strict and aggressive styles to manage prisoners (p. 4). The foundational components of Crewe and Liebling's (2012) typology thus rest upon the idea that both punitive and liberal-humanitarian values coexist among penal professionals. The orientations of correctional officers, whether liberal-humanitarian or neo-liberal, are then embedded in their on-the-job behaviours and are inherent to their interactions with the prisoners in their custody.

Officer Orientations and Occupational Practice

The liberal-humanitarian or neo-liberal orientations of correctional offi-cers shape their work behaviours and interactions with those in their custody, determining in essence if a relationship can develop between officers and prisoners. The typology from Crewe and Liebling (2012), in looking at the influence of liberal-humanitarian values on the penal orientation of senior prison managers in the United Kingdom, pro-vides a range of descriptions of diverse orientations that help to explain how officer orientations play out among prisoners. In 2016, I adapted Crewe and Liebling's (2012) typology for correctional officers, first, to determine how prisoners' perceptions of correctional officers' orienta-tions (liberal-humanitarian or neo-liberal) shape their interpretations of officers' behaviours and interactions with prisoners, and second, to distinguish between prisoners' interpretations of these orientations (Ric-ciardelli, 2016a). A few challenges emerged in the process. For example, it was not possible, given the parameters of the study and the correc-tional officer occupation, to discern those officers who were considered "entrepreneurs" (i.e., if officers were thought to be "innovative" in their approach) – to do justice to Crewe and Liebling's (2012) typology – so I omitted that element of the typology. Another challenge was that offi-cers, given their professional responsibilities, cannot practise a harmony or security orientation in isolation, as their occupational responsibilities prevent them from expressing either exclusively, which needed to be recognized in the adapted typology. Finally, to ensure all experiences and perceptions of prisoners were exhaustively represented, I created an additional "punisher" orientation, based on Rutherford's (1994) "pun-ishment credo," an orientation that involves extensive moral condemna-tion, loathing, and dislike of prisoners. Thus, I determined officers to be perceived as dualists with either a stronger harmony or security orienta-tion – rather than exclusively harmony or security oriented – or moral relativists, or punishers. These typologies, including the types of dualists, along with the level of harmony or security persuasion in their orienta-tion, can be seen in table 1.1.

Table 1.1. Typologies of prisoner interpretations of correctional officer orientations

Category	Sub-category: Description
Secure dualist: security oriented	**Operators:** Strong and experienced managers, who are highly skilled in operational terms, with forceful personalities (often found in poorly performing prisons, where they are tasked with challenging and difficult staff cultures).
	Managerial-Entrepreneurs: Those of a younger generation, who either tend to simplify the management task or are energetic, confident, and even effective "ideas men," focused on smoothly appeasing senior staff. Some are "technicists," particularly focused on and adept at the technical details of the job. They can also be "risk-takers" (e.g., impulsive) and sometimes overly optimistic. Managerial-entrepreneurs are driven by "performance" and committed to due process and decency.
Harmonious dualist: harmony oriented	**Moral dualists:** Highly competent, intelligent, and operationally astute, they seek to balance their value priorities and their management means. Their focus is on performance more broadly, and they grasp the wider purpose of performance targets (e.g., these are not simply to impress senior staff, but also to aid in assisting prisoners). They have a clear moral direction that is not "one-sided," such that they are sensitive to the dynamics of power and the plight of the individual prisoner. They see order and targets as being for other things; thus, institutional security and prisoner-officer relationships become mutually reinforcing rather than being in conflict.
	Idealists: Less pragmatic than their colleagues – of any orientation – they are thinker-speakers or value intellectuals. Some are even uncomfortable exercising or wielding power, as well as with their own position of authority, where they can impose punishment or consequences.
Moral relativists	**Moral relativists:** They are ambivalent dualists, without a strong harmony or security persuasion. The moral relativist is approaching retirement and/or has lost interest in the job. Some constitute a more toxic "traditional-resistant" subgroup, who are indifferent or disparaging toward prisoners. Others are disillusioned, and more liberal in their orientation. They feel alienated and are leaving the profession because they feel out of sympathy with the current organizational culture.
Punisher	**Punishers:** They are inspired by their own disregard and intolerance for prisoners, rather than by security. Marked by a general hatred and/or

(*Continued*)

Table 1.1. (Continued)

Category	Sub-category: Description
	loathing for prisoners, they are perhaps newer to the field or can be more experienced. Nonetheless, set apart from others by their intolerance for prisoners and their needs, they have a disregard for the humanity of those in their custody, and their displays of revulsion, animosity, impatience, and detestation toward prisoners can lead to challenges with their colleagues. The end goal of the punisher is to simply punish prisoners for their lived experiences and any pains they may have inflicted on others. Indeed, they may themselves seek vengeance or be persuaded by such desires.

Adapted from Ricciardelli, 2016a. Originally adapted from Crewe & Liebling, 2012, p. 4.

[a] Crewe and Liebling's (2012) categories of Managerialists and Entrepreneurs are collapsed into Managerial-Entrepreneur.

[b] Crews and Liebling's (2012) the Alienated is renamed as the "Moral Relativist."

Overall, correctional officer orientations, as perceived by prisoners, are operationalized into the subgroups of harmonious dualist, including the subcategories of moral dualist and idealist; security dualist, including operator and managerial-entrepreneur subgroups; moral relativist; and punisher orientations. The reality here is that correctional officers are often viewed, including by prisoners, as a heterogeneous group – some being "decent" and others "bad" people – and either harmonious or secure in their orientation. However, the orientations of harmony and security, unlike the punisher position, are complementary where security potentially breeds harmony and harmony breeds security. Moreover, a select few officers hold the punisher position, which breeds neither harmony nor security. Prisoners described the majority of correctional officers as dualists – with either a slightly more harmony or security persuasion. The orientation of correctional officers shapes their work experiences as well as the experiences of the persons in their custody, and this needs to be recognized as the nuances of prison work are explored across the chapters in this book. Orientations change over time, are malleable with experience, and represent a need to balance competing, even contradictory, responsibilities. They are also impacted by threats and experiences of workplace violence, harassment, years of experience, overcrowding, and other factors (Dignam & Fagan, 1996; Garcia, 2008; Hayes, 1985; Lahm, 2009a; Savicki, Cooley, & Gjesvold, 2003; Sorensen, Cunningham, Vigen, & Woods, 2011).

Conclusions

Across each interview I conducted, a select number of salient themes, including gender and risk, underlay the officer's explanations of his or her occupational experiences. I interpret these themes as foundational to correctional officers' orientations to their work – the facility, prisoners, and their occupational obligations and responsibilities. The theoretical interpretation of gender, specifically masculinities, and risk, or vulnerabilities, together shape the analyses both directly and inadvertently throughout this book. Gender and risk shape the officer-prisoner relationship (or lack of relationship), the variations in reasons why officers enter (or leave) the field of correctional work, and officers' experiences and positioning when working with male or female prisoners, to name a few examples. Scholars, internationally, support the reasoning that officer-prisoner relationships influence the degree of order in prisons and can help to secure officer legitimacy (see Crewe, 2009; Liebling, 2004; Liebling, Crewe, & Hulley, 2011; Philips, 2012) – realities that can assist with risk navigation and gender-identity construction. Although occupational security and satisfaction, role conflict, and responsibilities, among other factors, have been linked to officers supporting different correctional philosophies (see Crawley, 2004; Cullen, Lutze, Link, & Wolfe, 1989; Haney, 2011; Haney, Banks, & Zimbardo, 1973; Jacobs & Retsky, 1980; Jurik, 1985; Jurik, Halemba, Musheno, & Boyle, 1987; Liebling, 2008; Skolnick, 1966; Sykes, 1958; Whitehead & Lindquist, 1989), officers and their occupational role have been found to be influenced by the realities – like perceived, experienced, or anticipated risk – shaping the prison context.

The inherently vulnerable position of the correctional officer, the level of which will vary with how much it is either recognized or made explicit across facilities, must be acknowledged when thinking of officers' occupational orientations (see Lanthier, 2003). The ways that organizational factors, including work conditions, environments, and tenure of employment – with longer tenure tied to less favourable attitudes (Jacobs & Kraft, 1978; Jurik, 1985; Lariviere & Robinson, 1996) – affect officers' attitudes toward prisoners are also recognized by past scholars and in this book. Thus, prison work, for correctional officers, is deeply structured by gender and risk, which exist in a rather symbiotic relationship, where gendered experiences or desired performances shape perceptions of, as well as anticipated and experienced, risk, and risk, in turn, underpins vulnerabilities, thereby shaping gender.

2

Pathways: Who Are Correctional Officers and How Did They Get There?

How would you react? You got a nut case on the cell camera, and the next thing you know he's naked covering himself with faeces, challenging you with a shank. So what are you gonna do? ... You don't see that at the call centre, Sobeys, or Tim Horton's.

– Anonymous correctional officer describing another unique aspect of the prison work environment

For most of us, knowledge of prison and its inhabitants comes from television and movies, where correctional officers are frequently portrayed as tough, detached individuals who do little more than move prisoners to and from cells or tell visiting loved ones their time is up. Citizens, perhaps due to the rather hidden nature of prison work, tend to know little about the real people who occupy the role of correctional officer and the work in which these people are engaged. In this chapter, I move beyond stereotypes and media depictions to begin the process of introducing the reader to the men and women who perform this work and their motives and ambitions. I seek to provide insights into the career trajectory of correctional officers. By highlighting themes and patterns of career decision-making, my hope is to facilitate a deeper understanding of the realities that shape the decisions of individuals who become correctional officers.

Who Were the Men and Women Sharing Their Stories?

Although over 150 men and women were interviewed for the larger project, this book is based on the first 100 of these interviews (see Appendix A). These 100 men and women had experiences working with adult male and/or female prisoners serving time in provincial or territorial custody.

A total of 51 per cent of the sample worked in a correctional centre (with remanded prisoners), and 49 per cent worked in prisons housing sentenced prisoners only. In this section, I provide a basic overview of who these individuals were in terms of demographic factors.

Sixty per cent of those interviewed were male and 40 per cent were female. The male officers' ages ranged from 23 to 61, with the average age being 34 (two men did not report their age). The female officers were 20 to 58 years old when interviewed, with an average age of 36. Fewer male than female officers were between the ages of 20 and 24, which may be due to the recent push to hire more female officers or simply due to the nature of the sample. A second trend observed was that female correctional officers tended to be clustered at one end or the other of the age spectrum, with a majority either recently hired or nearing retirement. Given that researchers have noted retention issues among female correctional officers, such a pattern in age distribution is perhaps not surprising (see Camp, 1994; Griffin, 2005; Lambert, Hogan, & Barton, 2004; Samak, 2003). Retention issues may also be behind hiring strategies designed to recruit more women into the occupation, and this may further explain the higher number of younger female officers in the sample.

In relation to marital status, only one female officer was divorced and had remarried. The others were married ($n = 12$), single and never married ($n = 17$), common law ($n = 7$), separated ($n = 2$), or divorced ($n = 2$). Sixteen of the 40 women – 40 per cent – had experienced a change in their marital status during their time working as a correctional officer. Twenty-seven of the men also reported changes in their marital status since first entering the occupation. Further, 6 of the male interviewees were divorced and had remarried (some more than once), 22 were married, and 21 were single and had never before married. Ten male officers lived in a common-law relationship, and one was divorced and may not remarry.

Officers were also asked if they were parents. Of the women, 23 reported having children and some discussed their experiences of being pregnant on the job. These officers described electing to work in the "bubble" or control, or in any area of the prison where they would have little or no contact with prisoners as the pregnancy progressed. Here, a "just in case" attitude was prevalent. Both male and female officers agreed that pregnant females inside the prison should avoid taking unnecessary risks. Among the male officers, 34 had children. Unexpectedly, multiple men reported having lost a child, their son or daughter dying in either his or her teen years or as a young adult.

When asked about religiosity, 56 men reported their religious (or lack of religious) affiliation. Of these men, 30 self-identified as Catholic, although only 13 were practising; 12 identified as Christian, yet only 6 were practising; and 14 men did not identify as having any religious affiliation. Among the women, 22 identified as Catholic, but only 12 were practising; 10 reported their religious affiliation as Christian (5 practising); and the other 8 did not identify with any religion.

I must note that every interviewee self-identified as white (n = 100), although one male identified as both white and Indigenous. Thus, the correctional officer population was rather homogenous, revealing an intriguing set of research questions to be considered in future inquiries, including the following: Are correctional officers working in all Canadian provincial and territorial prisons across the country overwhelmingly white? If so, what are the implications of a lack of racial or ethnic heterogeneity among correctional officers? How is this particularly problematic given the overrepresentation of Indigenous prisoners in custody? Moreover, in what prisons or prison system (or where) is there more diversity? I also acknowledge the possibility, however, that this finding might be a limitation of the research (e.g., the provinces from which the sample was drawn) and that other studies may draw different samples.

Officers were also asked about their level of educational attainment. Of the men, 3 had not continued their education after high school (these officers were 44, 59, and 60 years of age and were not recent hires). The majority, however (n = 46), had a college diploma, predominantly in "correctional officer training," however, some were in policing or criminal justice. In addition, 18 had some university education, and 15 had a degree. Three men had yet to finish their degree, and 2 of these men were continuing to work toward completing the courses they required to graduate. Most degrees were in the disciplines of psychology, criminology, and geography, although others were in marine engineering, teaching, and history. Of the men with university degrees, 5 also had a college diploma. Conversely, all of the women interviewed had more than a high school diploma. The majority had a college diploma (n = 31), often in youth care for custodial or high-need/high-risk youth or "correctional officer training," while 10 held a university degree – criminology, sociology, political science, psychology, and teaching were named as majors. Three women had started their degree but had yet to finish, one had a post-graduate degree, and 3 with completed degrees and 2 with incomplete degrees also had a college diploma. In short, it appears that individuals interviewed from the more recent generation of correctional officers, particularly female correctional officers, had higher credentials. This finding is consistent with trends of increasing credentialism observed across other occupations (see Turcotte, 2013 for trends in educational attainment among Canadian women more generally).

Of the sample, 54 of the men and all of the women were working as correctional officers when interviewed, although I am aware of at least three people who have since left their occupational position (one is now in policing, another moved to work in federal corrections, and the third is in school full time). At the time of their interview, these officers' experience in corrections ranged from six months to over twenty-five years. Some had left the field at retirement, others due to a work-related injury, while some had moved on to a different career or life path. Many had work experience from different occupations prior to entering corrections, such as fisheries, oil, security and policing, trades and construction, service/retail, and some had been in community corrections, youth intervention, or open-custody (e.g., community corrections) positions. Some men and women had worked in the federal correctional system, although not as officers, prior to moving into the provincial or territorial correctional systems.

Focusing on interviewees' experiences when employed in provincial or territorial corrections, female officers reported having worked with different prisoner populations. Specifically, of the 40 female officers interviewed, 26 had worked with adult female prisoners, 35 with adult male prisoners, and 33 had worked with male and female youth. Male interviewees, however, had less experience working with adult female prisoners ($n = 11$) and female youths ($n = 24$) in their custody. Instead, 56 reported having worked with adult males and 27 had worked with male youth.

The officers interviewed generally had experience working in facilities designated as maximum or medium security. However, in provincial custody, maximum security institutions – particularly correctional centres with a remand population – can diversify their "security" level by providing prisoners on certain units with more incentives, goods, opportunities, and freedoms (e.g., a coffee maker, more out-of-cell time, movie nights). Higher security correlates to a specific structural design in the prison, which then shapes the experiences of those working in the institution. Of the men interviewed, 27 had worked in medium security facilities, and 44 in maximum security. Of the women, 11 had experience in maximum security facilities, and 31 in medium security.

Role Entry[1]

Aside from questions about their background and education, interviewees were also asked why they first entered the field of prison work. Analysis of the interview data revealed that interviewees generally fell into one of three groups: 1) those who viewed their current occupation as the first step toward securing an alternative correctional position (e.g., in parole, probation, or federal corrections); 2) those interested in a career in policing, either at the provincial, federal, or municipal/city level; or 3) those who viewed their current occupation as terminal, such that they intended to retire from corrections, sought promotion in their current job, or felt barred from career advancement. In this section, I explore the process of "role entry" using a thematic approach. The themes emerged through an iterative process of analyzing the data and comparing the results to similar themes found within the research literature.

Role Entry: But Why Corrections?

Motivation can be intrinsic (e.g., doing something because it is inherently interesting or satisfying) or extrinsic (e.g., doing something because of the reward, as in money, praise, or recognition) (Deci & Ryan, 1985; Wood, Wood, Wood, & Desmarais, 2002). Britton (1995), like Shaffer (1999),[2] noted that most officers – men and women – in her interviews related their decision to enter the field of corrections to extrinsic, not intrinsic, elements of the occupation. Her findings differed from Jurik and Halemba's (1984) study of women correctional officers, in which some did credit intrinsic reasons for their movement into the field. Nonetheless, not a single male correctional officer indicated to Britton that there were intrinsic reasons behind his occupational choice.

Jurik (1985) found that officers with intrinsic motivations for entering the field of corrections (e.g., being attracted to the profession because of their interest in human service work) held significantly more positive views of prisoners than those who had extrinsic motivations (e.g., being interested in the field because of job security, salary, benefits, and promotional opportunities). Intrinsic motivations have also been linked to increased job satisfaction (Hepburn & Knepper, 1993; Jurik et al., 1987; Jurik & Winn, 1987; Mottaz, 1987). Most recently, Schlosser and colleagues (2010) sought to identify why people pursue careers as correctional officers and to determine if their reasons differed from those identified in studies of police recruits.[3] They hypothesized that correctional and police officers would not significantly differ in the reasons for their career choice. In surveying 256 candidates for correctional officer positions in the northeastern United States, they revealed the top five reasons people choose a career in corrections: job security, salary, opportunities for advancement, early retirement with good pay, and the opportunity to keep the community safe (Schlosser et al., 2010).

A statistical comparison with the sample of police officer candidates surveyed by Foley, Guarneri, and Kelly (2008) indicates that correctional officer candidates, in comparison to police cadets, are more likely to report a lack of available job alternatives and less likely to report the excitement of the work as reasons for entering the field. Notwithstanding some similarities across the two professions, including wages, peace officer status, and paramilitary structure (Schlosser et al., 2010), correctional and police officer candidates were dissimilar in their motivations for seeking careers in law enforcement. Reasons cited included differences in occupational duties, as well as the value that police and correctional officers assign to their duties. For example, police recruits in Foley et al.'s (2008) study attributed more value to the opportunity to help people than the correctional officer candidates attributed to helping prisoners. Schlosser et al. (2010) suggested that not all correctional officer candidates see helping prisoners as an important part of their job, or part of their job at all, and hence, for some, the desire to be of service is less important as a reason for choosing the career.

Overall, since the 1980s researchers have suggested that rather than seeking employment as correctional officers, men and women have largely "drifted" into this line of work (Crouch, 1980; Pollock, 1986; Zimmer, 1986, 1987). These findings held true in the 1990s as well (Britton, 1995), and were also reflected in my current study, in which few of the officers interviewed reported planning their entry into the field. Instead, many drifted into the occupation as a result of both external (the socio-economic environment) and internal (personal lived experiences and self-expectations) motivations in their community and social environment. These factors together shaped interviewees' knowledge of available career possibilities and, in combination with their need for stable, well-paying employment, tended to drive occupational entry in more rural communities (or even urban centres) where fewer viable employment options were believed to exist.

In this regard, my findings mirror those of Britton (1995), who similarly observed that the rationale underlying such "drift" is that prison work is one of the few occupations that pays well, but has historically required only a relatively low level of formal education and experience (also see Bensimon, 2005). It should be noted that, more recently, many governments have increased their academic and physical expectations, if not the direct criteria, for new correctional officer recruits. As a result, the number of correctional officers with a post-secondary education employed by Correctional Service Canada or Ontario correctional services (and perhaps in other provincial and territorial correctional services) increased from 41 per cent in 1991 to 75 per cent in 2006 (Ontario Ministry of Community Safety and Correctional Services, 2013; Correctional Service Canada, 2013a). The current interview process itself requires the government to invest more time and resources into candidate selection in order to optimize the quality of officers hired – yet turnover rates remain remarkably high. Nonetheless, among my interviewees, working as an officer remained an attractive employment choice, particularly for those living in rural areas with fewer alternative options available or who had invested years in the job and, in consequence, had developed a specific skill set that they viewed as having limited additional applicability.

Role Entry: Occupational Drift and Viable Career Paths

Each of the officers I interviewed described her or his pathway into prison work; their comments frequently exemplified an experience of "drifting" into the occupation. One officer began by revealing, "I needed a job. It was never a goal of mine as a kid to say, 'Oh I want to be a guard!' " When asked what his original employment goals were, he replied:

> Nothing really, [if] I'm being honest. I'm not the most ambitious person in the world. I've never had a goal, [never thought] "this is what I want to do." As you know, I didn't go far in education. I graduated from high school and started working for the government. I graduated in June of 1972. I got a call from one of my high school teachers who said, "The government is … looking for people. We're looking for someone. And I gave them your name, and they will be contacting you." That's how I started working [here].

Many had similar experiences. For example, when finishing school or in periods without stable work, some had been referred to the occupation by family or friends. As one officer explained, "I was supposed to move back down North, down home when I made a good friend here and she said, 'Do you need a job?' So, I just started to work here." Another noted,

> I applied to go to that college in [province] and there weren't any jobs at the time. I was just looking through the paper and I saw an ad at a college for policing and corrections. I had a friend's dad who works at [a specific] penitentiary. I kind of just went with it [laughs], a last-minute decision.

A lack of employment opportunities in smaller communities and/or rural areas was repeatedly cited as a reason for entering prison work. This was particularly the case in those communities where previous "mass employers," such as factories or mills, had either relocated or gone out of business. Several correctional officers, for example, had previously been employed by such businesses, and when they shut down or left town, these individuals were forced to look for alternate employment in the area that would allow them to avoid uprooting their families.

Still other officers were unsuccessful in their quest for long-term employment that provided enough income for a family to live comfortably. Many people were "stuck" in seasonal or temporary positions: "I was fishing for two months and I was doing EI [employment insurance] for ten months a year living pay to [pay]. I fucking hated it." Even officers with advanced educational credentials, such as a university degree, and experience in different fields of work described feeling restricted by available occupational opportunities. In contrast, correctional work in Canada, it was thought, could provide employees with financial stability, including those working in casual or part-time positions, as they are able to earn a full-time salary because of available overtime hours.

Although for some officers, entry into prison work was about a lack of alternate choices, this was not the case for all. Some felt they did have choices, but, upon reflecting on the benefits of prison work relative to their current positions, saw more economic and other opportunities in correctional work. Of these benefits, job stability was cited by several respondents. Steve, an experienced teacher, attributed his transition to a career as a correctional officer to inadequate employment opportunities in teaching. He explained:

> I was teaching for a few years and doing supply work ... But I ended up getting out of that just because I wasn't getting any full-time [positions]. My degree, it covers kindergarten to [grade] 12, so I could teach anything ... It was frustrating after a while doing supply work. I was very popular. I had all kinds of work. I was just going around, never having a class [of my own]. So I actually heard about this job ... Two weeks later [an adult prison facility] called me back and offered [me a position] so I went there.

Like Steve, who had aspired to be a teacher but was unable to acquire long-term employment in this role, others had also become attracted to the potentially stable nature of full-time employment in prison work. Steve's story was echoed by others. "It was just a better career move, money-wise," one officer explained. Another simply stated, "I wanted something with pay every week, [to] live a stable life."

The need for income and stable employment was particularly motivating for those individuals who were starting out in the workforce or who had young families. One officer recalled being a few credits shy of finishing his degree when he took a job as a correctional officer. Although he had not previously considered a career in corrections, when the opportunity presented itself he was a newly married young father in his last

year of university, and he opted to take the job, putting his degree on
hold to earn additional income for his family. Others explained that correctional work provides a "better [opportunity] for me to spend time
with my family." The importance of time and proximity were particularly
evident in the words of interviewees who described the location of the
prison as a central factor underpinning their occupational entry. One of
the officers stated he would have considered joining the military if his
facility had not been built "thirty minutes away from here." The location of this new facility provided him with another option, a decision
that worked out well: "I like my job. In general, it's either really stressful
or not stressful. It goes from one extreme to [the] other, but I like it."
Further, an institution's location can serve to expose people to the possibility of prison work as an occupational choice. People become aware
of and familiar with the institution, and, perhaps as a result of exposure
to those who already work within the walls, gain some insight into what
the various roles entail, thereby increasing the likelihood that they will
consider corrections as a career choice.

The pull of family caused others to leave well-paying employment
and occupational opportunities in other provinces in order to return
"home." Several participants spoke of leaving "good jobs" and of being
unable to find well-paying employment after their move, despite years of
experience in specific occupations across different provinces. One interviewee had formerly been a police officer for six years in another province. After making the decision to return to his home province, he was
unable to find another policing position, and so returned to correctional
work, an area in which he had worked before leaving.

Tuition costs and the availability of courses are also factors in occupational decision-making. Whereas some police organizations, as an
example, now largely try to hire university graduates, many correctional
facilities welcome certificate- and diploma-holding graduates from
shorter (and therefore less expensive) programs. "Honestly, it was a
cheap tuition course," one officer explained, "a one-year course. I had
a buddy that was going through it too; we went through together. Half-
decent living and that was it. It was an easy way out." The combination
of comparable affordability, shorter duration, and ease of access – many
courses are offered in community colleges or other local settings – helps
to make a prison career a more feasible option for many who might otherwise struggle to enter a vocational field.

The ability to fulfil one's potential through career selection and development was typically raised in interviews in which individuals discussed
how they entered the occupation through their educational pursuits.
While in some cases, this pursuit was for pragmatic purposes – to earn a

certificate or complete a course as a requirement for advancement – in others, individuals simply sought to satisfy some internal need, usually related to curiosity. Common to all respondents who entered a career in corrections through education was an earlier desire to figure out which opportunities existed and how these opportunities aligned with their own interests. An officer who began his career by taking a college course on policing and corrections noted that as soon as he realized he was not well suited for policing, he really "got into corrections." Another described his entry, saying, "I took a course [because] I wasn't sure of what I really wanted to do." Having since entered the field, this officer's instinct that the job was a good fit for his personality and skills was confirmed; as he stated in his interview, "I enjoy it."

As noted, other interviewees reported being driven toward entering the field because of an interest in the people who are incarcerated – that is, a curiosity about the thoughts, behaviours, and motives of the people imprisoned. These officers did not enter educational programs with a specific vocational goal, but instead underwent a process of self-realization through learning that led them to a career in prison work. One officer expressed his initial interest in the following terms:

> I took psychology to understand human behaviour ... and I had a lot of friends from policing. I'm like, "Ah, I might as well try something different." None of my friends, at the time, were doing corrections, and I'm like, "Ah, I like human behaviour. I like seeing how society is changing. When people get caught, where do they go?" Nobody really has an answer. When you're [motioned as if to say, "in society"] you have no idea what happens behind these walls.

This officer was not alone in his interest in the people in prison. Another officer similarly observed that he was not initially motivated by a career goal, but instead by an intellectual curiosity that grew into a desire to work in the field: "I took school for it [corrections] when I was younger ... It was always an interest as far as the psychology of it. The minds of these people [prisoners] and even the people that work with them." The opportunities to observe human behaviour in these conditions had kept the officer interested in his work, which he felt was "exciting."

Role Entry: Correctional Work as a Helping Profession

For many people, helping others is seen as an opportunity to provide service to their community and to grow as an individual (Deci & Ryan, 1985; Wood et al., 2002). While it is the case that some seek these experiences

through volunteer efforts, others gravitate to a career in "helping professions" – as is the case with correctional officers. Despite stereotypical
media depictions of correctional workers as harsh, brutal, and/or devoid
of feelings, previous researchers (e.g., Jurik, 1985) have shown that some
officers are motivated to enter the field because they see it as an opportunity to work in a human-centred public service role. Interviews conducted for this project revealed similar motives among some officers.

In line with the idea of a "helping" or "human service" orientation to
prison work (e.g., Foley et al., 2008; Schlosser et al., 2010), some interviewees expressed an interest in helping others – whether that be the
prisoners in their care or "the general society" – and saw the correctional
officer role as an opportunity to fulfil that interest. Emblematic of this
view, one officer explained that his motive for entering the field came
from watching his brother get bullied. This experience made him want
to help others, particularly those who reacted to being bullied by bullying others. In his view, many prisoners could be like his brother, so
he decided, "I want to go in, [because] I know I'll do great in the field,
because I'll be taking care of guys like that." In this sense, these officers
understood that one person's negative experiences could and sometimes did lead to the continuation of a cycle of negative experiences for
others – those who hurt others, in essence, often are hurting.

Still others are proud that their employment provides what they see
as a valuable "service to the public." For example, one officer spoke
of "being on the right side of the law," explaining that, for him, "it's a
privilege to work as a peace officer or as a correctional officer, because
people look at you as – you're not better than anyone else, but you're
doing something positive." Like other officers interviewed, he saw his
work as "benefiting society and doing something that is positive." He
then added:

> I got a thirteen-year-old son, [and] he's proud of his dad as a correctional
> officer because I'm doing something that is benefiting society. His mom
> told me that, you know, "Well Johny thinks it's cool that you work at the
> jail." I never heard that before and it kind of made me feel, you know, I
> had goosebumps. It made me feel good that, hey, I'm doing something that
> even my thirteen-year-old son thinks is cool. And he tells his friends, "Dad's
> a correctional officer," so that's a motivation too. To do something that
> people would be proud of you [for]. Not everyone gets that chance. So, I
> feel good about the job that I'm doing and I do it to the best of my ability.

His words reveal his pride in his job, a pride reinforced by the positive
feedback received from his son.

Despite financial incentives, employment stability, the ability to help others, and the fact that some interviewees "like their job," interviewees' feelings about their choice of career were not uniformly positive. Pressures resulting from overcrowding on units, and the challenges associated with such problems as the confinement of higher numbers of prisoners with mental illness, meant that, for many officers, the relative high rates of pay received were no longer as attractive when they factored in increasing occupational challenges and responsibilities. Retrospectively – often when reflecting on who they had become or what they had seen or experienced – some opined, as one officer stated, that the pay just "isn't worth it." For example, as Kevin explained,

> Let's put it this way: I would never let my kids apply for a job there. I would never let them go. I would say, "No, you just don't do that." The way of life here, it's just ... people being threatened all the time, and assaulted. I have been assaulted many times over the years and stuff like that, people have been bit and tested for AIDS, tested for Hepatitis A and B, and things are just crazy.

A similar attitude emerged among many participants who felt the negative outcomes tied to prison work outweighed the positive. Kevin was just one of a subgroup of officers who spoke of "dreading" or "hating" the idea of their children entering the field of corrections.

Stepping Stone: Role Entry with an Exit Plan

Some officers spoke about their entry into correctional work as a "stepping stone" toward a career in another area of criminal justice. Among the officers contemplating, or actively oriented toward, a career in other realms of criminal justice, some described feeling they were less likely to be accepted into that field or successful in the recruitment testing without first attaining practical work experience in justice. To that end, they tried prison work as a means of actualizing their long-term career goals.

Federal Corrections, Parole, or Probation

Some interviewees entered provincial or territorial prison work because they sought practical experience that would make them more attractive as potential hires for federal corrections, federal parole, or provincial/territorial probation jobs. Among the expected benefits of such jobs cited by interviewees were better working conditions (the location of the office or institution they wanted to work within), higher salaries, and/or improved benefits. For example, one officer wanted to work for Correctional Service Canada because "it's the cushy federal job, a federal government job. Ideally, I'd like to do parole." In addition to this perceived "cushiness," "it's more of a Monday-to-Friday job." Another correctional worker stated unequivocally, "I actually never wanted to be a correctional officer." However, she observed that jobs were "slim" in her area, so she applied to work in corrections. When she received a call for an interview, she explained, the woman on the phone "talked to me about it and I ended up taking it," concluding, "that's how I landed here."

Workers within provincial or territorial institutions also see correctional work within the federal system as potentially less stressful. Reasons for this view include the fact that officers in the federal system can apply to work in minimum security facilities, which were frequently likened to "camp" by interviewees in comparison to higher security or provincial institutions. The camp analogy is deemed applicable because in minimum security settings, correctional officers no longer interact with prisoners considered actively capable of extensive violence or misconduct, as prisoners must demonstrate "good behaviour" or have a chronic health condition necessitating constant medical attention to be (re)classified to, and thus transferred to, minimum. Officers also noted that because federal prisoners are already sentenced – unlike prisoners in remand custody, who are not yet sentenced or convicted, and, indeed, have even at times been brought straight off the streets – they have already been through the challenges of drug or alcohol withdraw and detox. Moreover, the prisoners have already come to terms with the fact that they are "going away" (i.e., they are sentenced to a minimum of two years in custody) and have become knowledgeable about how to "do time." This point is apparent in an excerpt from an interview with Jake, a more seasoned provincial officer:

> My main goal is eventually [to] be [in] federal corrections ... We are getting paid nineteen bucks and forty-seven cents right now and they do the same at federal, except we gotta deal with them [prisoners] when they're on withdrawals [and] when they just did the crime. In federal they're sentenced, [and] most of the time [the prisoners are] mostly calm by that time. We deal with them when they're fucking badass and stuff like that.

In short, correctional officers view federal minimum security settings, and the prisoners housed there, as providing officers with, as several stated, an "easier go." Officers value this, particularly as they start considering or nearing the end of their career, when they may be less inclined

to want to deal with chronic violence, chaos, and some of the other conditions they face in higher security institutions. As Jake also stated of
his desired career trajectory: "I would like to start in maximum [at the
federal level], go right for the hard core right away, and then eventually
go, in ten years, to [names the minimum security prison] and finish my
last ten years there."

Policing

Many interviewees had also entered the field as a stepping stone toward
a career in law enforcement, while others entered as a "fallback." Correctional officers who viewed their employment as a gateway to a position in policing tended to self-identify either as open to the prospective
career change or as actively working toward becoming a police officer.
For example, one officer offered the following about himself and his
current and future employment: "I just wanted to do law enforcement ...
Yeah, I did [want to be a police officer]. I still somewhat do." When
asked, another officer revealed that "down the road, it's definitely ... I'm
not going to lie. It's [being a police officer] definitely one of my ... I
would like to [go] down that road." Others were actively in the process
of applying for policing jobs. One officer reported "going through the
process with the RCMP," and another similarly stated, "I'm in the process
right now." Another officer admitted that his "dream job" was to work on
a "SWAT [team] with the RCMP." As these comments show, some officers
were and remained oriented toward a career in policing. Given that a
number of other officers referred to former colleagues who had left correctional work for policing (and that some of the officers I interviewed
are now police officers), corrections clearly is viewed as a stepping stone
to such a career goal.

And yet, not all individuals who entered corrections with the intention of moving into policing remained committed to that pathway. Some
interviewees realized, once they were on the job, that they liked working
in corrections and saw it as a permanent career choice. For instance,
one interviewee explained that at the start of his correctional career
he decided to defer his acceptance into the Royal Canadian Mounted
Police training program at Depot for a year. He reported that, when he
took the position in corrections for that year, he thought he would end
up in policing:

> Really, it was about just wanting to do a job. I was completely ignorant to
> anything that was going on. I had no idea what it was like and then I got
> in there and the first day, I remember looking around and I was like, "This

is a government building?" And I was like, "I'm never going to be able to work here." And [yet] after two or three shifts with the staff that I worked with, I was home.

Although this officer felt at "home" working in prisons, for other interviewees the choice of corrections over policing could be more accurately described as bittersweet. Correctional work, for these respondents, had remained a fallback employment opportunity: they wanted to be police officers, but were ineligible for reasons beyond their control (e.g., past injury, uncorrectable poor vision):

> The reason why I couldn't get into [the] RCMP was 'cause of my vision. I've tried so many times to get corrective surgery and if I could get in now, I'd do it [join the RCMP] in a heartbeat ... [but] I was never a candidate for the corrective lens part of it ... Then a friend of mine took a corrections course. And it was along the same lines as what I wanted to do for policing. And I read up on it, and researched it all, and that was something that I was interested in. I love my job.

As this officer's words show, ineligibility for policing and less stringent entry requirements for correctional work together fuelled some interviewees' decision to first enter corrections, which was, for some, "the next best thing." Others lost interest in policing after working in prisons, citing reasons that included the need to relocate every four years in some police services, having to deal with victims of crime, and a preference to leave work at work. As one male correctional officer reported,

> The difference with us and a police officer is that you're a cop 24-7. I'm a guard for twelve hours, and I go home [and] I'm not a guard anymore. That's the way I gotta do it. That's the only way I can handle it.

And in the words of another male officer:

> I don't think that mentally I would be able to handle looking at somebody and telling them I found their daughter in the woods. So I looked at corrections as a way to be [in] the best of both worlds. I can still make a difference but I'm making a more controlled choice ... For my safety, mentally. And as well ... [there's] better time for me to spend time with my family.

The officers quoted above recognized their capacities and were turned off from the policing occupation because they thought it would interfere with their daily lives.

Role Exit

As can be seen in the preceding section, several officers had planned career trajectories that included leaving correctional services for other employment opportunities within the criminal justice system. These were not the only individuals to speak of role exit. Other officers were happily anticipating and planning for their retirement, while still others spoke of quitting the criminal justice field altogether. Such results are not entirely surprising. A wealth of research in Canada (Correctional Service Canada, 2001) and elsewhere (Camp, 1994; Kiekbus, Price, & Theis, 2003; Lambert & Hogan, 2009; Lambert, Hogan, & Tucker, 2009; Slate & Vogel, 1997; Stohr, Self, & Lovrich, 1992) reveals that officer turnover is frequently high within prison and correctional facilities. For example, at the federal level in Canada, where statistics are more readily available, Correctional Service Canada estimated in 2001 – even before overcrowding was so grave an issue – that nearly 13 per cent of federal correctional officers exit the field within the first thirty months of their employment (Correctional Service Canada, 2001; Management and Training Corporation Institute, 2011; also see McShane, Williams, Schichor, & McClain, 1991, for predicted turnover rates in the United States). Such numbers are not uncommon in Canada, and are potentially higher in provincial and territorial institutions where officers are known to take more sick days or stress- or health-related personal leave due to occupational strain (see, for example, Bensimon, 2005; Doucette, 2014; Forum on Corrections Research, 2014).

Researchers looking at the dynamics driving high turnover within this occupational group have uncovered a number of significant factors, including general job dissatisfaction (Lambert, 2006; Lambert et al., 2009; Lambert & Paoline, 2010), lack of promotional opportunities (Jurik & Winn, 1987), and stressors within the work environment (for more information, including studies looking at work environment and turnover that have generally produced mixed, even contradictory, results, see Cullen, Clark, & Wozniak, 1985; Grossi & Berg, 1991; Jurik & Halemba, 1984; Lambert, 2006; Lambert & Hogan, 2009; Lambert & Paoline, 2010; Lambert, Hogan, Altheimer, & Wareham, 2010; Slate & Vogel, 1997). Specifically, Byrd, Cochran, Silverman, and Blount (2000) found that job dissatisfaction, in comparison to other correlates such as work environment variables, was the strongest predictor of a correctional officer leaving the occupation.

My findings are consistent with this research, with the officers interviewed for this study citing similar reasons for leaving or wanting to leave their current employment role. A man who had been a full-time correctional officer in a provincial facility for over twenty years – what he called a "life sentence" – explained that he left correctional work after a traumatic experience (a young prisoner died in his arms). As a result of this experience, he felt unable to continue working in an environment in which tragic events are not uncommon. Other officers continued working in prisons, but acknowledged being under tremendous occupational strain and expressed genuine unhappiness and dissatisfaction at work (see Ricciardelli & Power, in press; Ricciardelli, Power, & Simas-Medeiros, 2018). In fact, in all the prisons I visited, morale was never high.

I would also note that officers cited other reasons for wanting to leave their current employment role. Among these were pay, job security, lifestyle factors, and the desire for new challenges. It was apparent that many did not necessarily intend to stay employed as correctional officers, and were either open to resigning at some point or were counting down the days to retirement. Some spoke of wanting to teach at the local community college, or simply to do something different, although they were not quite sure what that would entail. One officer had given himself a deadline (to which he ultimately adhered): "It was a decision ... one way or another I was going to get out of that jail. I'd even put a deadline like May the 1st of [year]. I was not going to work there one more day longer."

Conclusions

The themes that did emerge as motivations in my analysis aligned with natural socio-ecological systems: individual, family and community, and societal. Many interviewees had drifted into correctional work, a drift resulting from the location of the prison, the comparatively low cost of the courses required for accreditation, the stable income with benefits, or a lack of alternative career options (see also Britton, 1995). This combination of affordability and ease of access to required educational programming – courses being offered in community colleges and sometimes locally – made a career in corrections a feasible option. For others, corrections was a stepping stone to a primary occupational goal, which often came under the rubric of social justice, community safety, or criminology. Some had abandoned previous career paths, often due to a lack of stable opportunities for employment in corrections. It must be recognized, however, that few interviewees ever stated that the specific vocational identity they were trying to actualize was that of a correctional officer. These diverse movements into the field were all laced with processes of obtaining self- (and societal) awareness and the learned ability to direct their career choices based on this self-realization.

Many interviewees had also sought out a career in corrections as a way to garner meaning from their personal experiences (e.g., observing a social injustice) or through the influence from their friends and family (e.g., having a friend who worked in this field). Others, often victims of difficult economic times, struggled to find jobs and turned to corrections as a reasonable alternative – a move that, as we saw, was perhaps indicative of career compromise. The importance of these occupational positions, however, as well as the high rate of turnover in correctional institutions, makes it essential for government to recruit high-quality staff who will perform effectively. In this sense, by understanding why some men and women enter this field, training and recruitment processes can be aimed at informing potential candidates about their occupational responsibilities and demands. Providing accurate information about the correctional officer role and aligning expectations and occupational realities is essential. If correctional officers enter the job, after training, with accurate expectations, officer retention is more likely to be optimized in ways that will also benefit the persons in custody.

Such knowledge is of value to government, as it can be used to increase the effectiveness and efficiency of recruitment strategies, interview processes, and training. For example, finding that a subset of my sample had originally aspired to be police officers, but did not pursue this job due to physical limitations (e.g., serious injury) or the realization that the position was in some way undesirable for them, suggests that aiming recruitment efforts at individuals with specific interests in corrections may not be necessary. Instead, it may be worthwhile for governments to also consider recruiting from police foundations or police training programs. Overall, it is only with greater insight into the motivations of persons entering the field of corrections that administrators can refine their recruitment process, assist with pre-employment screening (Schlosser et al., 2010), and perhaps help foster positive prison environments that together can help in the hiring of effective employees and thereby sustain long-term retention.

3

"99 Per Cent Boredom, 1 Per Cent Sheer Terror"

My role [is] basically everything. You gotta be a guard. You gotta be psychologist. You gotta be a nurse, because they come to you with all kinds of problems. You got a headache, or they go through withdrawals or they lost a relative, death in the family, so you gotta deal with them. Basically, being a psychologist and you gotta be a friend, and you gotta be an enemy. A multitasker, basically.

– Anonymous female correctional officer describing how she sees her occupational role

Much of the later chapters of this book are focused on risk and reactions to risk as central themes in how correctional officers – specifically male correctional officers – view their occupational life, respond to its challenges, and relate aspects of their work to others. However, such a representation is unidimensional. While it would be unlikely, perhaps impossible, for one author to be able to accurately represent all aspects of any particular occupation within the confines of a book, I do not wish to provide the reader with the impression that the bulk of the work that provincial and territorial correctional officers in Canada do is fraught with constant turmoil and danger – no matter how overcrowded the prisons, whatever the conditions of confinement, or the gender of the custodial population or officers. Indeed, much of prison work is rather dull and repetitive, even ordinary; just imagine if your daily life was to occur within a series of encaged spaces (and with people who were involuntarily confined). Specifically, it has been suggested that prison work is much like war: "99 per cent boredom, 1 per cent sheer terror."[1] Thus, my focus in this chapter is on some of those aspects of correctional officers' work that constitute part of the other 99 per cent of their work life. A significant part of that 99 per cent is spent working with prisoners, relating to prisoners, ordering prisoners, speaking with prisoners, helping prisoners, and providing prisoners with access to services and other things that make up a day. With this in mind, I turn my focus in this chapter to the experiences of correctional officers working and interacting with male and female prisoner populations. In the first section, I examine the nature of the interactions that correctional officers described between themselves and their prisoners. What I reveal is the extent to which correctional work is influenced by gender dynamics, experience, and individual beliefs and communication styles – themes that I return to in the following chapters. In the present chapter, I argue that the nature of these relations speaks to how prisoners will serve their time and how officers, who are confined along with their custodial population, will spend theirs.

Correctional Officers and Prisoners: Attitudes and Interactions

Correctional officers play a fundamental role in shaping the prison environment (e.g., Crewe, 2009; Liebling, 2004; Sparks et al., 1996), as it is under their governance, and in direct contact with prisoners, that the behavioural conditions and formal regulations of the prison environment come to be developed. Officers' attitudes, and thus behaviours, are further impacted by the violence, harassment, and assaults that threaten their occupational health, and by other diverse job-related stresses that they experience to various degrees while on duty (e.g., job dissatisfaction, high burnout rates) (Dignam & Fagan, 1996; Ditchfield & Harries, 1996; Garcia, 2008; Hayes, 1985; Lahm, 2009a, 2009b; Lambert et al., 2009; Lambert, Altheimer, & Hogan, 2010; Sorensen et al., 2011). Organizational factors (e.g., working conditions, policies) can also impact officers' attitudes toward prisoners (e.g., Jurik, 1985; Lariviere & Robinson, 1996). As such, officers are thought to have much influence on the day-to-day lives of prisoners (Guenther & Guenther, 1974; Jackson & Ammen, 1996; Simourd, 1997). Researchers have therefore paid close attention to officers' attitudes toward and interactions with prisoners. Since the 1970s, correctional officers have been found overwhelmingly to hold negative attitudes toward prisoners, describing prisoners as sneaky, untrustworthy and not dependable (Chang & Zastrow, 1976), incorrigible (Farmer, 1977; Plecas & Maxim, 1991; Poole & Regoli, 1980), and at fault for their current predicament (Nacci & Kane, 1984). Moreover, officers have been found to hold less favourable views of prisoners in comparison to other correctional staff (Antonio, Young, & Wingeard, 2009; Lariviere & Robinson, 1996; Young & Antonio, 2009). The relationship between working conditions, work experiences, and personal well-being can impact both occupational and personal stresses for officers (e.g., Samak, 2003; Seidman & Williams, 1999). Officers are, then, clearly impacted by the work environment, and this environment in turn shapes their interactions with prisoners while on duty; thus, prisoners must indeed experience some repercussions from the potentially adversarial conditions in which officers conduct their work. Furthermore, we must remember that correctional officers in Canada have been documented victims of violence, or threats of violence, on-the-job stress, and other unpleasant circumstances resulting from their employment (e.g., Boyd, 2011; Seidman & Williams, 1999), yet they continue to exert a profound influence on the lives of prisoners as they govern and structure prisoners' penal experience (Guenther & Guenther, 1974; Jackson & Ammen, 1996; Simourd, 1997). This fact supports the importance of continued investigations into correctional officers' perceptions of prisoners (e.g., see Lariviere, 2002, on this work in a Canadian context).

Researchers have also noted that officer attitudes are more negative toward prisoners who are mentally ill or thought to be incarcerated for sex-related offences (Kropp, Cox, Roesch, & Eaves, 1989; Lavoie, Connolly, & Roesch, 2006; Weekes, Pelletier, & Beaudette, 1995; Ricciardelli & Moir, 2013; Ricciardelli & Spencer, 2014, 2017; Scrivens & Ricciardelli, 2019; Spencer & Ricciardelli, 2017). Yet, other officers do have more positive views of prisoners, including of sex offenders (Cullen et al., 1989; Toch & Klofas, 1982), and such attitudes and associated interactions are influenced by organizational factors such as occupational responsibilities (Jacobs & Kraft, 1978), work conditions (Jurik, 1985), and the prison environment (Lariviere & Robinson, 1996), as well as the length of time one is employed in the profession (more time is correlated to less favourable attitudes) (Jurik & Winn, 1987). Factors such as occupational security, satisfaction, and role conflict have also been linked to officers supporting different correctional philosophies (see Cullen et al., 1989; Jurik, 1985; Jurik et al., 1987; Whitehead & Lindquist, 1989).

For decades, such factors as prisoners' gender, race, and education have not been found to impact officer attitudes – instead, it was the tendency of officers to blame prisoners for their situation (e.g., they committed the crime, thus they are responsible and must deal with the consequences) that shaped officers' negative attitudes (e.g., Jackson & Ammen, 1996; Jurik, 1985; Lariviere & Robinson, 1996).[2] To examine this further, researchers have conducted studies – though there are relatively few thus far – from the perspective of prisoners in the United States (Collins, Iannacchione, Hudson, Stohr, & Hemmens, 2013), England (Crewe, 2006), and Canada (Ricciardelli, 2016). Crewe (2006), for example, investigated the male prisoners' relations with and attitudes toward female correctional officers in a medium security training prison for men in England. He found that although female officers were viewed "the same" as the males – e.g., when all officers were "evaluated on the basis of their practices rather than discourses in which gender characteristics are presumed" (p. 396) – the officer's role and identity took primacy over their gender. Yet, in terms of "sexualization and sexual desire, cynicism about professional motives, masculine validation through female contact, and chivalry" (p. 396), gender was privileged over professional identity and practice. In Collins et al.'s (2013) survey study conducted in a state jail in the United States, they found that, for both prisoners and staff, race was not significantly correlated with a rehabilitative goal orientation, while gender and education for prisoners only influenced a non-retributive goal orientation.

Boyd and Grant (2005), in their prison study, did not find any differences in the ratings of male and female correctional staff in terms of their use of communication, empathy, and discipline and control. Females, however, were rated as more professional than males. Notably, their findings only pertain to adult male units – not units housing females – where the prison culture itself may hamper the expression of empathy and communication. Finally, Kjelsberg, Skoglund, and Rustad (2007), in their study that included prisoners and employees in four Norwegian prisons, found that prison employees working in female-only facilities held more positive attitudes in comparison to prison employees working in male-only facilities. Thus, differences exist according to the gender of the prisoners in custody, although the nuances of these differences may vary across units, facilities, provinces, and countries.[3]

More recently, researchers found that negative views are attributable in some cases to penal policies that undermine officers' authority (e.g., instructions from those higher in command outlining what officers can or cannot provide for prisoners) in ways that can escalate negative or even volatile interactions with prisoners (e.g., an officer may not be able to fulfil a request due only to administrative command rather than best practice) (e.g., Crichton & Ricciardelli, 2016; Lariviere, 2002; Merecz-Kot & Cębrzyńska, 2008). Merecz-Kot and Cębrzyńska (2008) specifically noted that approximately one-third of their sample of correctional officers had experienced repeated aggressive acts from their co-workers and/or superiors. This is not surprising given that correctional officers, as civil servants, hold one of the lowest status position in the prison hierarchy – they are just above the prisoner, and as a result, they must comply with orders and protocol or their occupational position will be compromised, even terminated (Lanthier, 2003). Moreover, any aggression between colleagues has a ripple effect on officer-prisoner and prisoner-officer interactions, and, in consequence, can create or even escalate negative interactions with prisoners (e.g., an officer may not fulfil a request if it is an administrative command rather than a best practice), thereby encouraging a hostile work environment.

Overall, researchers studying imprisonment have demonstrated how the organizational and operational nature of prisons – for example, the rigidity of the institution and the active and stringent management of each prisoner's time and space – influence the type of relationships that develop between prisoners and prison staff (e.g., therapeutic, punitive, comforting, or disciplinarian) (e.g., Kruttschnitt & Gartner, 2005; Pollack, 2009; Ricciardelli & Perry, 2016; Ricciardelli, Perry, & Carleton, 2017). Institutional structures also shape the relationships that prisoners construct, and then use, with other prisoners and staff. For example, some scholars argue that prisoners' social relations can be interpreted as a practice of resistance against the restrictive prison environment (Bosworth & Carrabine, 2001). Yet others, like Rebecca Trammell (2009), argue that experiences of alienation and isolation in prison encourage the development of intimate and rather deep friendships among female prisoners. Researchers looking at staff-prisoner relationships have also tried to understand how these relationships may, arguably, perform a rehabilitative function for prisoners. Given that researchers have found female prisoners to be more oriented toward "rehabilitative" or "treatment" goals in comparison to male prisoners (e.g., Jurik & Musheno, 1986; Zupan, 1986), there is the potential that female prisoners will be more open to interacting with correctional officers in order to facilitate this process.

Interactions – Female Officers and Their Prisoners

When the female officers interviewed spoke about aspects of the "other 99 per cent of their work," those working within female prison facilities or units emphasized what they saw as the importance of interacting with the prisoners. Often, perhaps a result of training or common occupational jargon, this process of relationship building was described as necessitating being "firm but fair" with prisoners. When asked to provide examples or describe what "firm but fair" was in practice, officers explained that it involved being patient and communicative, as well as being open to assisting prisoners without prejudice and creating a means for positive and supportive officer-prisoner relationships to develop. "You gotta be firm but fair and communicate with them," one officer explained. "We have to communicate with people, and I think that's 98 per cent of the game here, [it] is just communicating consistently." She then provided a scenario in which she had interacted with a new prisoner who was expected to give medical staff some problems:

I was supposed to come first thing this morning with you [the interviewer/ author], but we were having a doctor's clinic, and one of the nurses come to me and says, "We expect to have trouble from this one woman offender, she's newly admitted, she won't be happy that she's not receiving some of her medication while she's here, so we want to have two staff instead of one" ... So when I'm taking this woman offender down, I've dealt with her before, she could go off any second, but I felt the need to take her [a]side before we even went into the clinic, and [I] said, "Listen, you're probably gonna hear some things you're not going to like, and as a result I want you to behave well. I expect you to be respectful, if there's any negative behaviour we're going to have to end it and you'll have to go back to the unit." And I think that's fair, she knows my expectations so there's no question afterwards. I think ... taking those few seconds here and there is only fair to the prisoners and to the staff [to let them know] what your expectations are about how things should go. If we're told to tuck in our shirts, I have to tuck in my shirt and I hate tucking in my shirt, well you have to tuck in your shirt. We have to communicate with people.

The officer's solution was to speak to the prisoner beforehand, explain what was to happen and why, and then communicate a clear set of expectations around the prisoner's behaviour. As her words reveal, fairness and consistency seem to be valuable aspects of the officer-prisoner relationship.

As I describe in more detail in chapter 4, much of the communication between female officers and prisoners is centred on officers responding to the various needs of their charges. Some interviewees worked within institutions that actively treated relationship building between staff and prisoners as a critical step in meeting prisoner needs, particularly those needs centred on desistance, and in this way the culture of the facility supported and encouraged open communication. A staff member from one of those institutions said of herself and her co-workers, "We try, like we're really trying. I know my peers, especially on my shift, we really try to form a good relationship with our prisoners and try to get them through their woes and their trials and tribulations and stuff." Exemplifying her commitment to relationship building, she then added, "I hope that we're doing fine."

Among female officers across various institutions interviewed for this study, there was an entrenched belief that female officers are more receptive to prisoner needs than their male counterparts, including being more aware of, and responsive to their physical well-being and emotional states. Why the female officers considered themselves to be more sympathetic, even empathetic, was never clearly articulated, although some suggested that male officers are more likely to act like "authority figures" and "tell jokes" rather than to "listen" or "talk" to the prisoners. As such, their conclusion was that males are less likely to care for prisoners in the same ways that females were believed to care for them. Some female correctional officers attributed this to their ability "as women" to be more empathetic as well:

> I find being a female, you can relate more. I find I'm more able to put myself in their [the prisoners] situation than a male officer would even bother. And I think that's the biggest thing, being able to relate to them better.

However, how correctional officers actually manage to empathize with the prisoners in their custody was rarely explained in any detail, beyond "that could have been me," nor backed by empirical evidence or externally verified. It is likely, instead, that traditional understandings of female socialization prevail as a dominant discourse, shaping their self-perceptions as well as their perceptions of other female officers. To exemplify, an officer described how, in the profession, "we have a little bit more of a sympathetic ear, a little bit more of a softer [approach]" – an interpretation that supports gendered readings of traditional notions of feminine traits. Indeed, it was believed that female correctional officers often feel more tolerant of prisoners' antics and moods in comparison to male officers, and are more responsive to prisoner needs – particularly when working on female units. As one female officer put it,

> I don't think that the males are as tolerant of it as we are. No, I really don't think they are. Again, it depends on who the female [prisoner] is ... [but] it might be just that pat on the back that she needs today. Regardless of who it's coming from, she's having a bad day ... I tend to think females will be more receptive to it.

These qualities of understanding, patience, acceptance, and sympathy, to name a few, are perceived by officers as not only cultivating a higher possibility for female officers to foster relationships with female prisoners – relationships that encourage understanding rather than assertion of control – but also to create an environment that allows, even encourages, the officer to garner insight into the circumstances that have shaped each prisoner's trajectory toward criminal behaviour. Such findings are consistent with Crawley's (2013) work with correctional officers in the United Kingdom. She found, through her interviews, that officers not only described prisons as "domestic spheres" but also as "emotional arenas" (p. xii). Prison work, then, was a form of emotional labour, requiring staff to bear a performative attitude and employ a range of strategies of emotional labour.

To be clear: it was not simply the case that female interviewees saw themselves as more empathetic or sympathetic than their male colleagues; rather, during their interviews, these interviewees' words revealed that their practices, actions, and views embodied a degree of empathy or sympathy for their prisoners. One officer, for example, expressed tremendous empathy for a female prisoner with whom she had "bonded" after discussing the details of the woman's case. "I see her side of the story and it's very concrete," the officer said. "You're like, 'Woah!' But this could have happened to any of us, if we were in her shoes." As a result of understanding this woman's story, and being able to see herself in her position, she believed they had developed a relationship built on "mutual respect." Another officer demonstrated sympathy through her revealing insights into the intergenerational nature of criminality and how familial and social forces shaped the futures of many of her charges. Of the women in her prison, she said, "they've never had a chance since birth; they were born into it":

> I've dealt with a lot of females and my heart went out to a couple of them because they didn't have a chance. And they had no family, no friends, no support. I've been in an institution where we had ... males and females, and I've had like a mom, dad, sister, kid, grandmother, all in the jail at one point where they were all getting visits together. So no one had a chance.

Another officer recounted a prisoner telling her that "my younger kid's in juvi ... I can't support 'em cause I'm here in the unit." Many officers described the difficulties voiced by incarcerated women as distressing because they were away from their children and therefore not able to provide for them. These officers also felt sympathy, even understanding, for the women in custody who were believed to "end up in trouble with the law because they are very old school." An officer explained that, for women accustomed to traditional patriarchal families, if their husbands abandoned them, some became destitute and felt like the only option was to turn to the streets (see Stein, Leslie, & Nyamathi, 2002; Williams, 1998; Yeater, Austin, Green, & Smith, 2010, for a brief introduction to some of the trials and tribulations faced by homeless women). Another officer explained, "that's the only life they know ... We've got all different walks of life, and it's different for each one of them." Similarly, a female officer in another institution pointed to structural forces that leave impoverished women with few choices:

I've had them [female prisoners] say to me, "Welfare will give me this much
money to live off of and by the time I pay rent and phone and get a few
things to eat, the only thing I can afford to live off of is bread and water. So
of course I'm going to go on the street and prostitute myself. Of course, I'm
going to get involved with drugs and try to sell them. And then I get hooked
on doing them so that's why I end up coming back into a place like this."

The officer continued to explain that the cycle of drug use and imprisonment follow too many women of lower socio-economic status upon
release because they lack financial and social supports. This reality is
intensified by the fact that, when some women enter prison, their "families turn their backs on them and they're lost." Once released from
prison after six or seven months, "they're all sober and rehabilitated and
then they're thrown back out and then they have nowhere to go."

These excerpts not only show the social and personal positions of many
incarcerated women, but also the degree to which some female officers
are aware of the women in their charge. Said another way, by being suf-
ficiently open to engaging with the women in their custody, the female
officers interviewed had been able to learn much about these women,
including many details of their life histories. One officer, for example,
explained that it was because of the relationships she had developed
with the female prisoners that she learned about their need for clothing
post-release; as a result, she had brought clothing to the prison rather
than donating it directly to a shelter, as she had initially planned. This
knowledge reveals a marked difference from the less intimate knowledge that correctional officers generally have of male prisoners. Hearing
women's stories, overall, invoked sympathy, and, in some cases, empathy,
among officers. Particularly compelling in this regard were the stories of
women who wanted to change but did not know how:

I found that there's a select few that my heart kinda went out to ... [They
were] wanting to change and not knowing how ... The females see what
they're doing and have the want to change. And it might take a hundred
times in, it could be a very long process, but they seem to have the motivation and they want to actually take the steps. Even if they're just going
through the process for that time they still want to at least go through it.

This officer was not alone in her thinking: many of the officers interviewed felt that prison does help some female prisoners because it can
function as a stepping stone whereby each time "in" removes them from
otherwise very destructive life situations (e.g., abusive relationships).[4]
Moreover, if they are fortunate enough to be placed on a female unit

with staff who genuinely care, these prisoners may develop some sort of support network to help them meet their needs in prison – an arguable benefit for women who may have lacked (or even those who did not a support network in the community.

Officers also explained that some women with careers that allowed them to successfully contribute to society, and who have strong family relationships and support networks, suffer greatly when incarcerated. Their view was that, for these women, prison either negatively impacts or altogether ends their ability to reintegrate into their previous life. These women may qualify for more opportunities post-incarceration, yet they are marked by the label of "offender," which all too often negatively impacts their career and access to social supports in the community:

> A lot of women had good careers and they made bad choices so they ended up being in here, but they got the label of offender. Now they're in the system and they can't get out. I'm not defending them. You can see the cycle 'cause I know myself, I have seen women come in and they've been in here for an impaired charge. Well I have a friend that's coming in with an impaired charge so I think, "Wow, she comes into a place like this and she's going to be labelled as an offender, but she's my friend." Then you have your ones that keep coming in, the prostitutes and the drug addicts, and the ones that keep doing fraud and whatever. And everyone just gets put in this one big label: "Offender."

Officers also described the struggles of prisoners they saw as "stuck in the system" without resources, who would very likely cycle through the prison system again and again. An officer who made a point of saying she was not "defending" prisoners in her custody also spoke sympathetically of those who "keep coming in" because "they are now labelled 'Offenders,' " which she saw as preventing individuals from moving on from criminality (such findings have also been supported by LeBel, 2012; Link, Cullen, Frank, & Wozniak, 1987; Link & Phelan, 2001; Link, Struening, Rahav, Phelan, & Nuttbrock, 1997, 2013; Moran, 2012; Winnick & Bodkin, 2008a, 2008b).

For many female officers, the accruement of the "offender" or "ex-prisoner" label was viewed as unjust in those cases where they believed female prisoners had been sentenced for "ridiculous reasons." These women had either been convicted of a crime that did not "fit" the severity of their sentence, or were being punished for something they were forced into doing for financial or other motives. In such instances, correctional officers stated, the women should not be held accountable to such a degree that they are imprisoned, as they unduly suffer for actions

that were not motivated by an innate criminality or other perceived
moral defect. That said, officers also acknowledged they were not in a
position to impose judgement. An example of a "ridiculous" reason was
provided by one officer:

> I have a woman offender on my unit now. She's here for assault with a
> weapon. And what it was is, they were at the bar, both drunk. The girl started
> mouthing at her, she replied and eventually the other girl shoved her and
> so she went to throw her drink in her face and the cup went flying. Assault
> with a weapon. That's ridiculous to me. She serves till February, first-time of-
> fence. Twenty years old. It's a bar fight ... What happened to the days when
> two people had an issue, they dealt with it, and then they moved on or they
> stayed away from each other. But now it's like the tiniest little thing [results
> in a charge of] assault.

Here, the officer does not condone the behaviour of the "perpetrator."
Instead, she explains that the prison sentence, from her perspective,
does not abide by the principles of sentencing in that it is too severe relative to the offence committed. The accidental slip of the cup from the
"perpetrator's" hand is articulated by this officer as being unworthy of
incurring an assault charge and closed-custody incarceration.

Despite their expressions of empathy or sympathy, officers clearly
stated that it was not permitted for such feelings to impact their professionalism or how they engaged with prisoners when on duty. As was
explained to the interviewer, "You have to check yourself at the door ... As
a professional you're, not forced, but encouraged to take a self-inventory
and know who you are as a person." Thus, whereas in some cases they
might have felt sympathetic toward one prisoner, or, conversely, unsym-
pathetic toward another, they recognized a need to put aside biases and
not permit their personal feelings to influence their ability to perform
their job in a neutral and professional manner – despite any bonds or
understandings that might develop between staff and specific prisoners.

Barriers to Communication and Relationship Building
between Female Correctional Officers and Prisoners

While it is the case that many, if not most, of the female correctional
officers valued communication and relationship building as tools of
their craft, analyses of the interview data reveal two major barriers to
the effective use of such tools. The first is officer attitudes. It was not
wholly the case that all officers were empathetic or sympathetic to all
prisoners. Like other humans, officers have personal beliefs and biases

that structure how they view the world and the people within it, a fact that several acknowledged when they spoke of having to put aside their biases to be "professional." That said, some officers tended to frown on those prisoners within the system who appeared to be wasting resources or not seriously committed to desisting from crime or "rehabilitating." Such attitudes are evident in the words of one officer who described why she did not believe that all prisoners who attend programming actually benefit from it:

> We offer programs but, from my experience, they'll put on the show: "Oh, I wanna go to AA and I wanna go to GED." But they go to GED to look at the male teacher and they go to AA to gossip with one another. The occasional few are serious about it but you see so many repeat offenders with the adults that you get a little discouraged after a while ... [It's] not the way we're set up.

For the correctional officers who attribute program attendance to prisoners wanting to "gossip" or "look at the male teacher" – instead of an interest in the actual programs and associated possibility for personal growth – it is disheartening. Further, this example works to reinforce the importance of the prisoner's desire to change if any program is to be effective.

The second significant barrier to relationship building is resource limitations, both material and human. Inadequate material resources include gaps in offered or available programming and in treatment options:

> We are not a drug rehabilitation centre. We're not here to get you clean, you know what I mean? ... But a lot of them, that's what they expect. Like, you shouldn't expect that. You broke the law or whatever. But rehabilitation on the women's side really [is] working with the women, they go to things like church and AA and stuff like that, but really there are not enough resources for them to get the proper help a lot of them really need, [and] it's unfortunate. But ... we've got to do what we've got to do and when you're working with all these people that have all these mental disorders ... it makes it harder ... Being incarcerated is a consequence of their actions, [and] I don't consider it rehabilitation. If you want to go to rehabilitation go to rehab because you're a drug addict, because you're a kleptomaniac, whatever, but jail [is jail].

Like the female officer quoted here, many correctional officers specifically speak about the inadequacies of Alcoholics Anonymous (AA) and detox and addiction programs, and agree that Narcotics Anonymous (NA) is an absent but needed program in facilities. These were predominant emerging themes across interviews:

> Especially with the females, drug rehab is huge ... I work the remand unit, [and] we spend so much time dealing with withdrawals that the majority of our days we either have a new person coming in on withdrawal, [or] we have somebody that managed to smuggle something in that's now withdrawing ... So we were told, like, "Go and see what's out there, go see what we can have for programs." But when we run up ideas about drug rehabilitation programs [management says] "No, no, no, we're not a treatment centre, we're an institution." We had a really hard time finding stuff that we could actually use in here. Like, even our AA program, it's not actually AA. It's, like, an introductory meeting every week. So the ones that go week after week after week, they're not getting the full benefit of being in AA. They're going to introductory meetings, week after week. They're still not getting the benefit of it. But if we could actually run some sort of drug rehabilitation program in here, I think it would make a massive, massive difference.

As these excerpts demonstrate, access to detox and addiction programming is either limited or non-existent. The idea most often put forth is that if female prisoners, once released, are to actually survive in the community, they must acquire some necessary skills, like learning to cope and how to remove themselves from unhealthy situations. Programming is inherent to treatment plans and is encouraged for prisoners, albeit the quality and availability of programming and associated resources varies across regions.

This lack of programming is compounded by a lack of human resources in the form of trained persons available to effectively run programs and provide guidance and treatment for prisoners. In many institutions, when asked about who was running select programs, the response was either community volunteers, correctional officers, or other staff. Access to any sort of psychological services appeared to be minimal, or, most often, non-existent:

> Our worst thing is to not have somebody for the fallback. Right now, I've been working since January with the females [female prisoners]. I was the first one, my partner and I were the first ones to get the females from [name of other prison that previously housed female prisoners in the province], so we were the first ones to have full contact. We set them up on the unit and said, "Here's your home for the time you are sentenced" ... They kind of took it seriously but kind of didn't take it seriously ... For example, [they have no] social workers or a full-time nurse or full-time doctor, psychologist,

psychiatrist – that makes it very hard for us. And they [management] just say, "Talk to them calmly, keep your distance, [and] if they get agitated put them in their room." But they getting agitated and [me] putting them in their room [will not work]. I've seen those prisoners come out of their room too, so that part worries me the most, [that we do] not have the structure here for them to have a fallback and a place for them to go and be treated just for that ... Every unit should have a nurse, a psychologist, a psychiatrist, a doctor, a social worker. They should have all of that.

Another officer working in the female unit at a predominantly male prison spoke at length about the problems that the lack of trained support creates for officers – problems that can increase officers' occupational risk. She explained that not having a

social worker or full-time nurse or full-time doctor, psychologist, psychiatrist, that makes it very hard for us. We have to take all that, especially if they have a fall[ing] out with their dad or boyfriend, and they have such a disorder that you're shaking your head because you don't know how to treat [it] ... They should have something for them to fall back on so that we can just focus on punishment [and] what needs to be done, [so we can] be correctional officers ... But it's never going to be like that, I understand that, from funding, from lack of interest, to whatever it may be. That part scares me, that maybe one day we will have a fall[ing] out with prisoners that are mentally ill and they [will] cause a riot. Not only do they hurt themselves, but they hurt us. Knock on wood, in the last five years we've had threats of riots but never had any – not compared to the damage at [name of another prison removed] that they've had. But yeah, that scares me a lot.

As evidenced by these officers' words, the lack of trained personnel available within institutions creates extra demands on the time and energies of female correctional officers, leaving them unable to respond to the emotional or other needs of the prisoners. "If I have one woman that's upset and crying," one officer explained, "I can't spend hours sitting down talking with her because I have to make sure my partner's safe, I have to make sure the rest of the unit is safe. I can try, but I can't set aside hours to help them." This same officer then referenced the additional pressures that come from a mixed population, which includes not only those with active mental illnesses, but also individuals with lower cognitive functioning:

We get people here with mental illness and they're just mixed in with everybody else. We try to keep them separated as much as we can, but at the same time we can't give them any special treatment, and sometimes they just don't understand; they don't have the comprehension level to understand rules. And so they're getting secured, [but] it's a comprehension thing. We don't have the time or the programs to deal with people like that and to me that would help a lot, especially drug-use programs. I mean, I've got a whole unit over there, [and I can only] think of one person who is not in for a drug-related charge.

This officer is hardly alone in feeling the stresses and challenges tied to having special-needs or high-needs women in custody. Further, even if treatment options are available, it is possible that a prisoner might qualify for cognitive behavioural therapy or another type of intervention because of the particular testing employed and yet still not be able to benefit from treatment for a variety of reasons. Stories like this shed light on some of the barriers officers face in building effective relationships within their facilities, relationships that assist their charges in having their needs met, but that, importantly, also increase the safety and security of those housed within a unit. They also demonstrate the general failure of the penal system to meet the needs of the prisoners in custody and to recognize correctional work as a caring profession involving emotion labour (Crawley, 2004, 2013), as well as to provide adequate resources for the officers who do this work. As an outcome of such shortfalls, prisoner-officer relationships can be strained as safety concerns among officers (as well as other staff and prisoners) are left unaddressed.

Interactions – Male Officers and Prisoners

Like their female colleagues, several of the male officers interviewed spoke of a perceived need to interact with, understand, and provide services to the prisoners in their charge. These correctional officers believed it was part of their role to "try and treat inmates like human beings" because, as they variously explained, it was only by "listening to inmates," by being "willing to talk to prisoners," and by "trying to help people who need it" that they could do their job – which is to provide services and support to prisoners – effectively. Some officers even linked their occupational role specifically to "rehabilitation" and the belief that they could and should help prisoners to move away from addictions, criminality, and/or other antisocial behaviours. For example, an officer stated emphatically, "I try to help people … That's how I view my job, to try to help people. I'd like to think that my job is more about rehabilitation." Other officers in this group were also more likely to see their relationship-building activities as a productive part of helping individuals in need and/or fostering a better work environment. They also thought that their work benefited society to the extent that they were able to help change prisoners' views.

One officer spoke at length about his willingness not only to change prisoners' attitudes, beliefs, and behaviours, but also those of his fellow officers. He was of the belief that if prisoners were shown kindness and understanding, some of their real or perceived antisocial attitudes and behaviours would diminish, a result that might reduce future criminality. He explained:

> I find the more contact we have with the inmates, the more interaction we have, the more they realize we are human beings, the more we realize they're human beings. We all have our faults and some of us are damaged on both sides ... Some of the most amazing people I ever met are inmates ... I had an argument – not an argument, a discussion – with somebody on the staff. It's just, "These guys should get nothing" and "The food's too good for these guys" and blah blah blah. I said, "Think of who we're dealing with," and I challenged them and asked them to look at it from their [the prisoners'] point of view. Some of these people were socially conditioned to hate "the man" and hate society and [told] law enforcement are crooked and they're idiots, and [so] they're predisposed when they go out into society, and it's our job to prove them wrong. When you go to jail, or before, when you're arrested by the police, we represent society and what it's supposed to be. We guard that. And for us to act and fulfil their perception of us, to confirm their suspicions by not giving them [what they are entitled to] or [by] treating them like garbage or treating them bad, before they even deserve it ... reinforcing all those things that they were taught ... [But because I treat them well] you can see them looking at me and you can see the wheels start to spin. And they start to think a different way. And what I like to do is go out and disprove that, get rid of the misconceptions, and a lot of inmates respond to me positively because [of] simple things.

Male officers with similar value orientations toward their work – that is, those who saw building relationships with prisoners as a necessary component of their daily occupational life – generally held more positive views about prisoners compared with those who saw their work solely as the monitoring or movement of prisoners. For example, they expressed views that suggested they did not uniformly see prisoners as being "bad people at heart," but rather as men who had made "mistakes" or were "unlucky." One male officer explained that, through working in the prisoner admissions section of his facility, "I learned about prisoners, and there's always three huge things. They didn't have any education. They were on drugs or they didn't know their dads and they hated their dads. They were beat by their dads." Prisoners with addictions were at times viewed sympathetically, and the inability of some to stay clean once they left prison was not simply attributed to moral failings or character weakness, but rather to deficits within the current penal system, a system that fails to provide support for newly released prisoners. One officer opined that it would be useful to have mandatory treatment after release: "Like, have a jail – this is a crazy, crazy thought, but – have a jail and then have a rehab centre where it's mandatory for them to stay in the rehab centre, because a lot of guys in here need it." Lacking positive supports in the form of addiction counselling or pro-social family and friend circles, many of those released will, he suggested, "get back out into that scene, and they've been sober for sometimes two months, sometimes almost two years, and then they get back out and they overdose."

Some prisoners were described by officers as "ignorant." At first glance, such a comment would appear to be highly negative. However, unpacking the context within which such characterizations were made reveals that the term was employed in a rather sympathetic manner, to describe, for example, some individuals' failure to know what is in their own best interests because they lack alternate visions of what their life could look like. Referring to the bragging that can take place on the unit, one officer observed that

> some of the things that guys have said to me ... they live in a completely different world. They've literally looked at me and said, "Well you should work for me on the outside. You wouldn't believe how much money you can make and all the girls," and this and that, and I'm like, "You're in jail right now and you're telling *me*. How much money did you make?" "Oh man I make, like, five grand a week." And I said, like, "Yeah, but you've been in jail the last two years of your life. You're out for like two weeks at a time." But they have no idea. Completely ignorant, it's complete ignorance.

To be clear: not all of the male officers interviewed were sympathetic to, or particularly interested in communicating with and/or developing relationships with, those in their custody. The informal norms governing male prisoner culture mandate that prisoners do not engage with staff (see Sykes, 1958; Ricciardelli, 2014a, 2014b). Underlying such attitudes are two interrelated dynamics: perceptions of prisoners as inherently distrustful and potentially dangerous, which I see as being coupled with a desire on the part of these male officers to maintain an outward, uber-masculine bearing or posture. In short, these officers did not see relationship building as a central, or particularly necessary or useful, part of their work, which was instead cast as maintaining the peace in a hostile environment through the active monitoring of their charges and the quelling of potential problems.

The main rationale provided by some select officers who opposed or failed to build positive relationships with prisoners, as their female colleagues were more likely to do, was repeatedly expressed as a profound lack of trust, and, in some cases, active dislike or disdain. Some stated their belief that officers who actively engage with prisoners, counselling them or trying to provide rehabilitative or other services (termed by one officer as "saving" prisoners), are vulnerable to being taken advantage of by "predatory inmates." To this end, I was warned: "You still got to be careful because you can't really trust any of them because they are criminals." Speaking of the prisoners in his facility, another officer openly said, "I believe everybody's trying to get something from me. They're lying, they're manipulating me." A prison supervisor, however, observed that, when it came to trust issues, there were noticeable similarities among correctional officers and prisoners: "Every prisoner [and] guard has trust issues ... Guards and inmates, a lot of the times they're very similar people personality-wise." As this supervisor's words reveal, working in prison or living in prison – both ways to experience prison – shapes both correctional workers and those in custody.

I would also note that male officers' adverse views were sometimes shared in comments linking prisoners – either as individuals or as a generic group – to certain negative qualities. Aside from being cast as "liars," prisoners were at times described by some officers as "unintelligent"; they were also linked, unintentionally or otherwise, to more primitive, irrational creatures: "These guys with their lower-level intelligence, they react with their base instincts rather than taking a second to think before they react." Another officer saw prisoners as malcontents: "They're constantly demanding stuff and they're never happy." These views were particularly evident when male officers spoke about repeat offenders, who many deem to be social burdens, unable to survive and achieve success as *men* in free society. The "revolving door" of prison living was considered their chosen lifestyle: "They made the same choices, murderers and rapists, they did it many, many, many times and you *can't* change from that." Some officers even suggested prisoners "deserve" to be incarcerated because they have agency and are without "remorse" or a desire to change, and thus do not belong in the community: "They laugh, they get arrested, they're in jail," or, "there are some inmates that I do not want on the street." In expressing such negative perceptions, these male officers affirm their perceived moral and social superiority over prisoners, which they can also assert in encounters with prisoners. Further, such beliefs also allow them to bolster their presentation of the "dangers" shaping their occupational role, thus enhancing their self-image as men who negotiate a dangerous terrain (this is discussed in more detail in chapter 7).

Investigating and Responding to Trouble

That a select few officers would downplay the importance of relation-ship building and communication skills within the prison setting is wor-risome when we consider the extent to which they are called upon to investigate and respond to potential problems on their units or within the larger prison setting. Without the ability to de-escalate emotions or convince recalcitrant individuals to act in accordance with their orders, officers have few alternative routes by which to gain compliance, and these largely centre on the assertion of power and, at times, the use of some type of force or restraint. An officer described a typical scenario in which lack of prisoner compliance can increase stresses, not only among officers, but also more generally across the unit itself: "We'd had to secure the entire unit because too many guys were getting punched out. Too many things happened too quickly. We'd shut her [the unit] down for a couple days." The response from officers was twofold: "to try to figure out who the ring leader was" and to "make some moves" among the prisoners – by placing them in new cells – in an attempt to change the dynamic within the unit. There were also instances, as one officer explained – "a lot of times, at least four or five" – during which prisoners staged sit-ins and "refused to go to their cells." Not only were such events "stressful," but given the high ratio of prisoners to officers as a result of institutional overcrowding – described variously as "20 against 5," "60 to 3," or even as "we had all four units with 25 on each, and we had 30 men at the gym. It was crazy. You couldn't move; everything just sucked. It was just a pressure cooker" – resorting to physical methods of extraction could precipitate an escalation of the situation. Thus, in an attempt to prevent possible violence, the officers tried to "go over and talk to them, [to] get them into the cells." In such situations, hyper-masculine postur-ing or physical threats would have been not only wholly inadequate, but potentially dangerous.

In addition to episodes of interpersonal violence, officers are also called upon to respond to prisoner deaths by suicide.[5] While officers should be trained to respond professionally to these and related medi-cal emergencies, they can be, and often are, a source of trauma for the officer – or, in other cases, they present the responding officer with a situation that results in feelings of moral ambiguity. An example of the latter was provided by a recently retired officer who assisted in trying to resuscitate an offender who was "in for sexually molesting his eight-year-old nephew." As the officer explained, the prisoner was on a suicide watch and had been placed in a "baby doll," a special gown that the man should not have been able to tear or set on fire:

> It's a fire retardant suit, like a dress, a gown. And this thing had a hole to put your one arm through it and another hole to put your other arm through and then a hole to put your head through. You weren't supposed to be able to tear it and it wasn't able to light on fire ... [He wore it] because he was on a high suicide watch. He couldn't use it to hang himself because he couldn't rip it. And he couldn't use it to start a fire because it wouldn't burn, plus he wouldn't have matches anyways. (If he had a T-shirt in there he could rip it all off and use it to hang himself.) So anyways, this guy was very creative, and in their segregation cells, [they had] stools that were actually mounted into the floor, and he took the arm hole on the one side and put it over that, put his head through the other arm hole, and forced his way down to the ground and then just started rolling like an alligator, to asphyxiate himself. And he was successful.

Although in theory, the prisoner should not have been able to experience death by suicide while wearing the baby doll, the officer reported that the man was likely already dead when he found him in his cell, as he was "blue." The officer explained that he "was the second on the scene" right after the on-duty captain, who was already attempting CPR. As the officer said of the situation, "you're doing your job, trying your best to resuscitate this guy to the best of your abilities, but in your mind you're thinking this creep just sexually molested an eight-year-old child and here I am trying to save his life." In the end, though, he explained: "your humanity takes over and says 'I don't give a shit about him, but you do the job that you're paid to do.'" Of note in this officer's words is the observation that his "humanity" was based not on a positive desire to save the prisoner or see him as a person outside of his conviction, but instead to do his job while always remembering the violations that prisoner had caused with his crime.

Getting Things/Moving People

As prisoners in provincial and territorial facilities are not at liberty to access even basic necessities on their own, correctional staff are tasked with providing assistance in a range of areas, from handing out food trays, to passing out mail, to responding to requests for basic provisions (such as toilet paper, toothpaste, and commissary items). As such, much of an officer's time can be spent responding to requests or "getting things" for prisoners. As with nearly everything in a correctional facility, there are rules and regulations governing how, when, where, and under what circumstances prisoners can receive certain items. These rules, and the need for staff to abide by them or face possible discipline, can be a source of conflict. Officers spoke of facing constant requests from some prisoners who refused to accept no for an answer. "When you can't have something, you can't have something," an officer explained. "I don't care how much you bug me or annoy me, you're still not going to get it. But then if you bug me or annoy me I'm going to lock you in for twenty-four hours because I've told you 'No,' so kind of leave me alone ... I'll tell you the reasons why you can't have it. And if you can't have it and I don't know the reasons why, I will find out for you."

In a similar context, officers also supervise the distribution of food to ensure that prisoners receive their food allotments. This rather mundane task can become a source of conflict for prisoners and staff if prisoners try to secure extra food rations. Not surprisingly, some will test the officers by trying to take more than they are permitted. An officer explained: "Like, for muffins in the morning, it says, each inmate is allowed to take one muffin." He then provided an example of a typical exchange over "muffin counting":

Alright, they come in, "Can I have two?"
    "No."
    "Well, what the fuck?"
    "No. It's one per each. The kitchen counts the meals, so one each. You take two, buddy, it means someone won't have any."
    "Well, it's not my problem."
    "Well, it's mine. So, I'm telling you."
    Then the next day, "No" [laughs]. Stupid, right?

He concluded by sharing the following: "There's not a whole lot of jobs that you're gonna come in and get a guy in a bad mood that'll call you a goof, piece of shit, cocksucker, for twelve hours straight."

Prisoner transport is another, often relatively routine, officer responsibility that may occasionally become problematic. Prisoners requiring medical treatment, as an example, must be ferried to and from appointments by two officers. One officer related a story involving the transport of a prisoner for dialysis treatment at a local hospital. Although the transport itself was without incident, while there the officer encountered a male nurse whom he recognized as a former youth prisoner from his time working in a youth custody facility. He described the former prisoner as "a kid that got charged under the Young Offenders Act for murder. I remember he got two years and he murdered two kids." Now released, he was working as a nurse on a ward of the hospital.

> I knew it was him. But now he's a nurse, and I couldn't say [anything], and I knew exactly who he was, because I saw the name, but I couldn't say anything and there's that part of you that's like, 'God, I just want to tell everybody who works with him, everybody here that ...' But who am I to make that determination that he's a risk to anybody ... to try to ruin this guy's life for something he did two lifetimes ago? It was a precarious situation.

This officer was trying to reconcile who a person was versus who they are – in many ways asking the age-old question: When is a person no longer the person who first committed the crime?

Also Serving Time

As can be seen from the title of this book, and throughout the proceeding chapters, one of the themes that emerged from the interviews was the notion that officers, both male and female, also "serve time" – and, in many respects, serve their time (on the job) alongside the prisoners they are tasked with supervising, being as much influenced by the environment as are the prisoners. This message was brought home in an interview with a female officer who spoke about how much her views of prisoners had changed over time. When she first started, she said, "I was surprised, because when you're just somebody that has never worked with the offenders, you just have this view from TV and stuff, like they're all scary looking. I was amazed at how normal they were." This realization was her "biggest shock ... Just normal people that made bad choices, that is how I view them." She conceded that "sometimes they can be a little looney," which she attributed to the fact that they are "cooped up for most of the day," but she admitted that "I'd be a little looney too." Reflecting on this, she added, "By the end of the shift, *I'm* sometimes a little loony." Not only did the prison environment have a similar effect on this officer as on the prisoners under her supervision, but she observed that the prisoners themselves had an influence on her. "You start talking like them," she noted, because she spent "more time with the offenders than I do with my family." As a result, officers "[pick] up on the lingo and their little sayings and you'll catch yourself and be, like, 'Oh my God, what am I saying?' " A male officer at another facility made a similar observation: before beginning prison work he never swore, but after spending five years in an environment in which the word "fuck" is a part of regular vocabulary, he said, "of course, you're gonna use that."

Other officers similarly described their experiences of "doing time" and the effect it had on them. For example, a retired officer who had begun work in a large jail in the 1980s described that facility as follows:

> You have to imagine there's an area ... maybe 25 [feet] long by 10 feet wide. And you're at a desk in the middle and on one side there's a door, a solid door that's locked and it has a cut-out with a grill. And that's where the inmates can come and talk to you. So there's a door on your right-hand side and a door on your left-hand side. And behind each of those doors there are thirty criminals.

These thirty criminals, the officer continued, were intimidating, not because they were serious offenders, but because of the architecture of the space. As he explained, every twelve-hour shift at that facility "consumes your life ... and you've gotta go back in the next day." He reported that working at this institution made him feel as though he, too, was serving "a twenty-year sentence at the jail. I used to say to people, 'I just did a twenty-year sentence.' " In his words, being on duty felt "like being in prison yourself." What was most concerning for him, and something that was echoed by other officers, was that "I felt more comfortable inside a range with thirty guys who have committed various crimes, like I said, from murder down to impaired driving. But I felt more comfortable on a range, where there are ten cells with them, than I did at the shopping mall. It had become my territory as well." It was for this reason, among others, that he knew it was time to retire and leave prison work.

Conclusions

For male and female correctional officers working with prisoners of any gender, much of prison work entails a mundane routine, with small doses of, arguably, rather unhealthy excitement – perhaps even terror. Officers occupy a position of status vis-à-vis prisoners that is further influenced by gender dynamics, which, to some extent, inform communication styles as well as formal and informal prison structures. Many female officers interviewed felt they were communicative and had personable and assistive relationships with the female prisoners under their care, although this was not a universal norm – officers do have diverse personalities. However, the level of communication and relationship building among these officers was much higher in comparison to male or female officers working on all-male units. Interviews showed that more personable communication between female officers and prisoners provides officers with insight into the plight of the female prisoners in their custody *and* into the women's overall positioning.

Officers put forth that over time, prison is either detrimental to, or, in some cases, can help, prisoners who have become "lost" in the community. Many officers believed that individuals can be helped if they are able to acquire support networks, overcome addictions, and learn valued skills when incarcerated. Some officers felt that more is needed after prison, like mandatory "rehabilitation" programs. Many suggested that available programs are rather ineffective in design or scope, and that needed programs such as NA, and human resources like counsellors and psychiatrists, are either too limited in supply or non-existent. As a result, these responsibilities fall on the correctional officers themselves, who lack the training, skills, and even the time when on duty.

4

The Female Correctional Officer

You can't act like a baby. You're not going to get any respect if you start crying, especially on a male unit ... You do not want to cry or show them any sort of insecurity. But sometimes you have a shitty day and sometimes you do cry.
– Anonymous female officer discussing gendered norms in prison work

In 1986, speaking of corrections, and in particular the role of the correctional officer, Zimmer posed a provocative question: "Can women really do the job?" Her question reflects the uncomfortable reality that women in correctional work have historically faced gender-based discrimination, largely generated from the belief that women are inherently incapable of engaging in this form of "man's work" (see Jurik & Halemba, 1984; Jurik et al., 1987; McMahon, 1999; Pollock, 1986; Zimmer, 1986, 1987). Recognizing that gender dynamics shape correctional officers' occupational experiences, I turn my focus in this chapter to the experiences of female correctional officers working with some male, but mostly female, prisoner populations. I first provide background about women's entry into the field of correctional work and then examine how gender shapes their working experiences, including how they are perceived by prisoners and their male (and female) co-workers. Further, I highlight how gender structures the nature of correctional work, specifically how it shapes available responses to the challenges correctional officers face within the prison environment.

Previous Work on Female Officers

Women have been eligible to work as correctional officers since the 1970s, although they were discriminated against by select colleagues and management as well as subject to harassment (see Britton, 1995; Jacobs & Kraft, 1978; Jurik & Halemba, 1984; Jurik et al., 1987; McMahon, 1999; Pollock, 1986; Zimmer, 1986, 1987). In 1984, when Jurik and Halemba asked male and female correctional officers about the source of the problems they faced on duty, they found that both male (52 per cent) and female (56 per cent) officers answered that their supervisors were the source. Differences, however, were found in the gender of officers who attributed their work difficulties to prisoners – 36 per cent of males versus 3 per cent of females – and to colleagues – 12 per cent of males versus 41 per cent of females. Nonetheless, the authors did not find support for gender differences in correctional officer job satisfaction. Later, Britton (1997), recognizing the conflicting interpretations of the role of gender in correctional work, sought to disambiguate what she called "the empirical paradox" (p. 86). She argued that, based on data from the Federal Bureau of Prisons' *Prison Social Climate Survey*, female officer job satisfaction is a complex concept and its indicators are not clearly or directly related (see Gilman, 1991; Saylor, 1989, 1991; Saylor & Wright, 1992). The majority of female officers, she found, were largely satisfied with their occupation, despite past qualitative data suggesting otherwise (Britton, 1997).

Gender differences, however, do influence the job stress that correctional officers report, with female correctional officers reporting more job stress than their male counterparts (Cullen, Link, Wolfe, & Frank, 1985; Jurik & Halemba, 1984; Jurik & Winn, 1987; Van Voorhis, Cullen, Link, & Wolfe, 1991; Wright & Saylor, 1991, 1992; Zupan, 1986). Perhaps these experiences are tied to the dated notion that "the job requirements of prison guards seem to be in direct contrast to the traditional norms for women's behaviour," and, although "expectations for women have changed ... to be sure, [it is] not so much that women's ability to perform jobs traditionally held by men goes unquestioned, especially if the job entails the exercise of power and authority" (Zimmer, 1987, p. 415). Zimmer may have written on the subject in the late 1980s, yet her writing is still gaining some traction today among those who believe women should either not be correctional officers or should only work on female units. A small percentage of the men that I interviewed, less than 10 per cent (and more commonly men working in higher-security or remand facilities), did not believe female officers *should* be working with male prisoners, often claiming that women are "smaller," "less strong," or "too caring" and "emotional."

Nonetheless, beyond studies of workplace stress and harassment, few scholars have explored in depth the work of female correctional officers. Some of these studies are by those international researchers looking at correctional officer competence as mediated by gender within prisons (Bowersox, 1981; Boyd & Grant, 2005; Britton, 2003; Farnworth, 1992), the gendered "organizational logic" of prisons, where one gender is privileged over another, or the experiences of women working in different prisons (Britton, 1997, 1999). In her seminal work, Zimmer (1987) interviewed seventy female officers, other correctional staff, and men incarcerated in New York and Rhode Island. She found that the on-duty actions of female officers challenged the assumed rigidity of the correctional officer role, and that female officers did their job in innovative ways, specifically when they faced barriers to success, using "predetermined appropriate definitions of work behavior" (p. 417) – which reshaped their occupational role. Her findings differ from Jurik's (1985), who found that male and female officers did not have substantial differences in their on-duty behaviours (or attitudes toward prisoners). The overwhelming majority of men and women I interviewed valued working with female officers and singled out some of their specific skill sets (e.g., the ability to "talk down" a situation; verbal skills). Female interviewees, specifically those working in higher-security men's facilities, however, described a period at the start of their career in which they needed to prove their abilities, and they felt that this was not experienced in the same way by the new male recruits. Nonetheless, researchers have long shown that male prisoners do respond well to female correctional officers, generally adhere to their directions, and that some even behave better with female officers (i.e., are less vulgar and refrain from hurting or threatening the females) in comparison to males (e.g., Zimmer, 1987).

The Workplace of Female Correctional Officers

In Canada, female officers can work in both male and female units, which have significant operational and organizational differences. Formal structures regulated by legislation, policy, or prison administration shape the gendered nuances of the correctional officer occupation. Such policies range from how many men versus women can be housed in a single cell, to the material possessions men and women are allowed to have in prison, which all complicate the officer's role. Regarding the latter, to exemplify, only female prisoners are allowed unique personal items such as diverse cosmetics (e.g., lipstick, mascara).[1] On the other hand, men are given generic hygiene and grooming provisions (e.g., mini-deodorant, toothpaste, three-inch-long toothbrush). Thus, women are more prone to disagreement with each other over personal items, which adds another element of possible conflict between prisoners that an officer must navigate and try to reconcile.

More trying, however, are the limitations on how officers can interact with prisoners of the opposite sex. For example, an officer cannot perform a strip search or place their hands – even to stop a rule-violating behaviour – on any "private area" of a prisoner of another sex (or, often, gender). Informed prisoners can use these gender boundaries to their advantage, if desired. A female officer, for example, explained that when trying to take contraband away from a male prisoner, she was cautious to always keep her hands above his waist. The prisoner, recognizing this formal boundary and the female officer's need to respect it, elected to drop the contraband into his underwear to ensure she could not confiscate it. The challenge here was, first, that her hands were metaphorically tied; she could not take control of the situation. Second, she had to acquire the assistance of a male officer to help locate the contraband through a cell and person search; at this point, however, the contraband is often already in circulation or consumed. For safety, it is optimal to have a male officer take over the incident, yet to maintain status and authority the female officer would prefer to finish dealing with the situation on her own. A second example described by multiple officers was of a female prisoner who would remove her clothing, fully aware that male officers, particularly those on the Emergency Response Team, could neither enter her cell nor extract her from her from it if she was naked when engaging in misconduct in her cell. This former prisoner was notorious in her unit for using the prison rules to her advantage. Such examples reveal different strategies by which prisoners have tried to exert power over officers and add a degree of havoc to the operation and harmonious functioning of the prison. Taken together, then, the gender of the correctional officers and the prisoners do indeed shape the experiences of officers when on duty. Perhaps because there are fewer women in prison in comparison to men, there are also fewer women's prisons or units. As such, female prisoners tend not to be segregated by security classification and instead are housed together (see Trevethan, 2000). Moreover, in prisons with only one unit available to house female prisoners, there is no protective custody possible for women with specific needs, and the only way to offer protection to a female prisoner targeted for victimization is to move her to a segregation cell.

Perhaps it is for these reasons that the female correctional officers interviewed felt they had a greater role to play and more responsibilities when working with incarcerated women. Because male correctional officers are often barred from such units, and feel they are more restricted in terms of their ability to have any contact with female prisoners (see chapter 3), female officers must assume greater responsibility. In one institution, after male prisoners were transferred to another institution

and the unit was re-designated for women, female prisoners were introduced, which meant that female correctional officers were now responsible for the care and control of the adult prisoners in custody. As one
female officer explained,

> [there is] a change in the dynamic right now because of the women offend-
> ers coming in, because there's no males working over there typically. They
> say "they're not allowed to," which I don't agree with. That's bullshit, be-
> cause for years females [correctional officers] have had to work with youth
> males and adult males.

As evidenced in this officer's words, while adopting a larger responsibility over one segment of the prisoner population can place an unfair
workload on female officers, it also provides some women with more
employment opportunities. For example, these female officers could
assume more of the positions on the Emergency Response Team or fill
supervisory/managerial roles that they believe might otherwise have
been assigned to men.

Unlike their male counterparts, who do not work regularly with the
opposite gender, female officers can and do work with male prisoner
populations. When working with male prisoners, some female officers
felt, in the words of one officer, that preference is given to male officers
when "picking a person for a job." Although it was not a universal theme
among interviewees, the existence of an "old boys club" was reported by
some. For example, as one female officer explained:

> Males ... always had an easier time being accepted. The casual [labour]
> males would come in, and if they played hockey with one of the guys, well,
> all of the sudden they're getting other duties thrown at them and it's kind
> of like, "Okay, I've been here for how many years, when exactly do I start
> getting those opportunities?" That has changed a bit with the women
> offenders.

As shown in the above excerpt, female interviewees felt they were denied
career opportunities before the female prisoners were transferred into
the facility. However, the inequitable division of labour and career
opportunities are two of several areas in which female officers described
double standards in their treatment. Some women also noted that
management at their institutions seemed inordinately concerned about
female prisoners making allegations against male staff, yet lacked similar concerns about allegations being made toward female officers by
male prisoners. These concerns were, again, tied to the issue of who was

responsible for supervising which (gendered) segment of the prisoner population. While the division of labour provides increased opportunities for female correctional officers, it also reveals an attitudinal fault line in terms of which employees managers direct their concern toward. It is in this context that a female officer expressed some anger over the disparate valuing of employees. Referring to how women are viewed in this light, she said, in an imaginary dialogue with her bosses:

"Well, you weren't so fucking concerned about allegations against them [from male prisoners against female officers], now were you?" Allegations by them against us, but the males [correctional officers] can't work with the female women offenders because they're supposed to be so much worse for making allegations. Thanks. We always just sat with that threat [when working in men's facilities] … But like I say, it does come with the down side of them saying that the male correctional officers shouldn't be working with them but they never worried about us [working with the males].

Despite management's concerns over the potential for accusations of inappropriate conduct by male officers, when working in male facilities female correctional officers were likely to be accused by their male colleagues of "flirting" with prisoners. That such allegations would arise is not unusual, as researchers have similarly documented incidents in which casual conversation between male prisoners and female officers was misconstrued by others as sexual in nature (e.g., Pollock, 1986; Zimmer, 1986). Ironically, female officers in my sample felt they were expected to listen to prisoners and be sympathetic, but that doing so was interpreted as "flirting" by other staff.

Remarks or accusations about flirting from male (and female) colleagues were upsetting for many women since they served as a reminder that they are subject to double standards in terms of how their conduct is viewed. A female officer explained:

Years ago, when we had the male adults, I've lost it at times when I've heard comments like, "and she flirts with the clients." I absolutely lost it … I had that comment thrown at me once and I just looked at them and said, "I can have the exact same conversation as you would have in the exact same tone. You would be a good guy developing rapport with the clients, I would be inappropriate and a flirt." So I have very little use for that.

As in this officer's experience, female staff expressed some apprehension about how their actions toward male prisoners were being interpreted by their colleagues. In 1995, Britton wrote that "the implication here is that inmates will inevitably attempt to solicit female officers sexually, and that women will find it difficult to resist due to 'natural' heterosexual attraction" (p. 127). Consistent with these findings from decades ago, I, too, found some evidence that the (rather incomprehensible) belief that incarcerated men are, in some way, too desirable or manipulative for female officers to resist remains. This thought process may inform the accusations of flirting directed at female officers from select colleagues and management.

Interviewees also spoke about being catcalled and subjected to inappropriate sexual comments, which they felt were ignored by some supervisors and management. Female officers working on male units felt that attention was often focused more on their behaviours than those of the prisoners, particularly regarding any unwanted sexual advances. In this context, simply being female at times appeared to equate to having to deal with unwarranted and unwanted sexual interest and comments. Perhaps this challenge is, to some degree, tied to Britton's (1995) findings that "male officers and supervisors worry that female correctional officers will be willing or unwilling victims of seduction by male inmates, or that they will let their sexuality be used against them in more subtle ways" (p. 139). The onus is then placed on the female correctional officer rather male prisoners.[2] In this sense, we can see that concerns are gendered, directed at female prisoners or officers rather than at the actions and comments of male officers or prisoners.

Working as Women with Women

As in larger society, in prison no one is immune to knowledge learned through discourse (see Foucault, 1981; Foucault & Sheridan, 1972). It has long been recognized that women in prison are subjected to stereotyping, prejudice, and discrimination – all realities that will impact, no matter how unintentionally, perceptions and attitudes toward female prisoners (Fox, 1984; Freedman, 1981; Sargent, 1984; Schram, 1997). In the United States, the Office of Justice Programs (1999) noted that female prisoners are stereotyped as overly emotional, passive, and childlike (Fox, 1984; Freedman, 1981; Sargent, 1984; Schram, 1997) – although not exclusively – which has led to tighter controls being imposed by prison management and limited understandings of what constitutes appropriate roles for women (e.g., emphasis on parenting over work). Reacting to this report, Schram, Koons-Witt, and Morash (2004) explained that "in this vein, there is a related history of paternalism towards women, and paternalism has often been the basis for limiting women's behaviors and activities 'for their own good,' that is, in order to take care of them" (p. 26). Such views create challenges for supervising female prisoners because these negative stereotypes need to be mitigated or differentiated from truths if the actual (as opposed to assumed) needs of the female prisoners are to be met. Moreover, how women express their needs, in light of such negative stereotypes, can be misconstrued as unnecessary or exaggerated. Clearly, such beliefs can influence how institutions and the people within them treat female prisoners.

Correctional officers recognize that although all prisoners are removed from their families, children, friends, employment – indeed, everything they value and care about – some female prisoners also have histories of intimate-partner violence and abuse.[3] The gendered realities of patriarchy also play a role in shaping both the incarceration of women and the conditions of confinement they face. In response, officers have understood that many incarcerated women will be in rather precarious emotional states – exacerbating the countervailing negative stereotypes tied to women more generally (Jurik, 1988) – in comparison to men (despite the similarities in their situations and losses). In 1984, Pollock, studying correctional officers' perceptions of female prisoners' emotionality, found that not only were they viewed as being "prone to irrational emotion[al] outbursts" and as having a "shorter fuse than men," but that officers also felt they had to "watch what they said to female inmates and be more sensitive to how women might react to them" (p. 84) in comparison to male prisoners. Female prisoners are thus more likely to be viewed rather homogenously in terms of their emotional state, while male prisoners tend to be viewed more as individuals – with some being more emotional, aggressive, or weak than others. The fact that the emotional well-being of female prisoners is viewed rather uniformly (e.g., that they are emotional, even "bitchy" and "moody," and that this intensifies with the menstrual cycle) evinces the prevailing stereotypical nature through which female prisoners are read. They are viewed through a very traditional gender lens (see Wolf, 1991).

Perhaps unsurprisingly, in my interviews with female officers, some female prisoners were sometimes described as catty and competitive. This competitiveness, which is inherent to traditional, even hegemonic, understandings of masculinities, is viewed through a different lens when ascribed to women. Whereas men are perceived as inherently competitive, such that "the best man shall win" (of course not exclusively), and this competitive nature is viewed positively, even idolized, in the male prison environment, being competitive is viewed as a potential trigger for altercations among female prisoners. It is, instead, conceptualized problematically and tangled with negative connotations: "We had minimum, medium, max parole violators, federals, all jammed into one [unit]. So [there was] always bullying going on."

In interviews, officers who worked with female prisoners discussed female displays of dominance as a type of "competitiveness" in which women take turns "bragging" about their crime or about previous stints in prison to show toughness. To illustrate, one officer mimicked what she frequently heard in the unit:

> "Oh, my crime's bigger than your crime. I'm in here for murdering some-body and you're in here for stealing a tube of lipstick, so you do what I say or I'm going to beat you up." And I tend to say it to a lot of people. Just think about it, you throw twenty-four females in one room, they're sharing one phone, one TV, and one hairdryer, and one shower – let me know how you'd make out. Really [you hear a prisoner telling another that it is] "my turn on the phone, will [you] fucking get off!" ... There is no "*can* you get off?"

This officer explained that the "competitiveness, almost bragging" that goes on constitutes a version of verbal victimization or bullying – a nega-tive act representative of relationships of power and control within the prison social structure. Although this, too, is common in men's prisons, where the status hierarchies are known to structure prisoner conduct (see Irwin, 2005; Irwin & Cressey, 1962; Ricciardelli, 2014a, 2014b; Sykes, 1958; Trammell, 2009, 2012), the actions of women, interpreted accord-ing to their position on a similar sort of hierarchy, are often construed negatively. The social hierarchy among men, for example, tends to be tied to their masculinities and criminality, and is then normalized. Among female prisoners, however, women who strive to be in positions of dominance are viewed as "power-hungry bitches," while those in more subordinate positions are thought to have identifiable needs or be "suffering" in light of their conditions of confinement and associated deprivations:

> Now that we have women [in the prison], who are bitchier – we have a group of fucked up women who are living here, they have mental issues, they have drug issues, [and] they're separated from their families. They are separated from jobs and all that. Then you take a group of power-hungry, bitchy women and put them in the same group with them trying to tell them what to do. It's fantastic [sarcasm].

Identifying and responding to such threats is the job of the officer, as is keeping peace among prisoners and preventing predation. This task is made more difficult, however, by the diverse nature of the women who enter prison, and the unique challenges they face. In other words, they have complex physical, mental, and emotional needs that can render them highly vulnerable.

Moreover, in speaking about female prisoners, female officers tended to agree with the perception that these prisoners are more "needy" than their male counterparts, as one officer stated, and that working with female prisoners requires different approaches and skill sets than those applied to males. Some of this apparent emotionality was explained by female officers as being a result of biological factors – in particular, women's monthly hormone cycles.[4] The fact that women menstruate was reason enough for correctional officers to refer to female units as more stressful workplaces (see Koff & Rierdan, 1995; Parlee, 1982; Wolf, 1991 for discussions of the social taboo of menstruation). One officer stated, "when a lot of groups of females hang out they tend to get [on] the same cycle. And I've had twenty-four females … [menstruating at] the same time, and … they're very emotional." Rather than adopting a dismissive attitude, this officer emphasized that "they're just needy. Being a female, I know how moody we can get [laughs]." Notably, the notion that overseeing an entire unit of women – in some cases, upwards of thirty-two women confined in a communal space – sharing the same cycle is challenging was put forth by a number of interviewees. This is a space where both correctional officers and prisoners lack direct access to medications, food, and other material or human resources (e.g., a nurse) that might help make the unit more comfortable and manageable for prisoners as well as officers (Office on Women's Health, 2014). For some officers this was only being exacerbated by "females [being] very emotional; [they] lead with their emotions constantly" – not surprising, given that emotions are central to interactions.

Prisons are organized by informal and formal norms that shape what constitutes acceptable emotional language and expression – which varies between male and female prison environments (see Irwin, 2005; Irwin & Cressey, 1962; Ricciardelli, 2014a, 2014b; Sykes, 1958; Trammell, 2009, 2012). Emotionality is considered a trait unique to female prisoners, one that plays a predominant role in structuring their prison environment; this is a far cry from correctional officers' experiences working on men's units, where men tend to suppress emotions.[5] The "prisoner code" – meaning the informal norms governing prisoner conduct, documented most notably in men's prisons – ensures that men adopt an emotionally and physically tough posture in order to avoid being seen as a weak person who can then be subject to predation (Irwin & Cressey, 1962; Ricciardelli, 2014a; Sykes, 1958). According to this code, any expression of emotions or personal revelations to staff violates the norms of acceptable prison behaviour. It is necessary to not only avoid being labelled as weak, but perhaps more importantly, in terms of one's own safety and security, to refrain from talking to staff so as to avoid being seen as a "snitch" or "rat" (Ricciardelli, 2014a, 2014b; Sykes, 1958).

Recognition of the gendered nature of such dynamics, and their impact on how male and female prisoners interact with prison staff, is reflected in an interview with a female officer who had worked in both male and female units:

> Adult females have a lot more needs compared to the men. Men, I find, don't need – they probably need it, but they don't ask. Like, "I'm alone; I need someone to talk to." They need someone to vent to. Most men are angry, they go in their cell. I think that's what's considered normal, [otherwise] they look weak. But [working with the women] I enjoy actually. A lot of people think I'm crazy, but I enjoy working with the women, 'cause I find a lot of it is in your approach with them. If I seem approachable, they can come to me with things, you're more likely to find out if there's things on the unit. Stuff like that. So I enjoyed the women, because you sit down and a lot [of] people think they're losers and that, [but] they're really not. You hear so much more about their life. With a male offender everything's all trapped in.

Beyond revealing some of the nuances of the "prisoner code" in men's prisons, this officer speaks to the view that some correctional officers hold of female prisoners. As Crawley (2004) wrote about correctional officers, the informal "feeling rules" in prisons dictate what constitutes appropriate versus inappropriate emotions and what feelings can or cannot be expressed – norms to which prisoners, just like prison staff, must adhere. Crawley attributes such norms to the fact that female prisoners are more likely to open up to staff about being lonely.

Another officer spoke of this gender dynamic and its impact on officers' ability to openly communicate with prisoners by comparing how males and females respond to questions about their well-being. Females, she stated, are more likely to respond honestly to questions or concerns about their physical, mental, or emotional state. Conversely, if a male prisoner is asked if there is anything wrong, "he would say, 'no' ... because they [males] just shut you off." Moreover, aside from the ability to positively interact with female prisoners, the lack of the male "prisoner code" operating in female units provides the officers who work with women certain advantages over their colleagues in male units. Female officers described being able to more quickly recognize when a female prisoner is not doing well, perhaps due to a difficulty coping or a physical illness. This ability to discern how prisoners are doing by their self-presentation and mannerisms is a product of being freer to build casual relationships with female prisoners, and thus being more aware of what is going on in their day-to-day life. One of the officers explained this as follows:

> Yeah, with the women, you know more about them. When I unlock a cell in the morning, I can tell she's having a bad day today, because you can just tell when their day changes, when their attitude changes. And you can go to her [and ask], "Is there anything I can do?"

As this excerpt shows, it appears that prisoners who express their emotions and disclose their life experiences provide more opportunities for correctional officers to offer support, act as a sounding board, provide comfort, and, in some situations, try to rectify a situation before it escalates.

According to Crawley (2004), emotions, or how a person feels "inside," are articulated through language, as "the language of emotions is a means by which human beings communicate and convey meaning(s)" (p. 413). Because humans communicate with a purpose, as argued by Vygotsky (1987), Crawley puts forth that emotional language serves the functions of structure and expression – they are performed according to norms and expressed so as to relate to others. While some officers clearly enjoy the opportunity to engage in what has been termed "emotional labour" (Hochschild, 1983, 1998), others experience the act of receiving emotional confidences as a source of role strain and occupational stress. This is perhaps not surprising, given the emotional investment required to spend hours in what is, in essence, a counselling capacity, without any formal training or institutional guidance and support. For example, one officer who enjoyed working in the female units explained that

> although I didn't mind working with females – I did good working with females – it was just, I was more stressed out. You were constantly on edge, and constantly dealing with the emotional factor and constantly dealing with ... a different level of emotions ... because guys tend to hide their emotions and females tend [not] to.

This officer, like others working in female units, spoke of being physically and mentally drained as a result of listening to the histories of the women in her custody. Many of the female officers similarly reported feeling an almost inescapable sense of obligation to listen to prisoners' stories, which often involved horrific experiences, in many instances sympathizing with female prisoners but feeling otherwise unable to help. These listening experiences, in turn, were seen as taking a personal toll on many officers, which often manifested in a form of "burnout," vicarious trauma, or compassion fatigue (Figley, 1995; Pearlman & MacIan, 1995; Pearlman & Saakvitne, 1995; Saakvitne & Pearlman, 1996; Stamm, 1995).

Other officers referenced the emotional demands that come as a result of having to supervise prisoners with low cognitive functioning, whose inability to fully understand and process their environment and its rules places enormous time demands on officers who must find ways to gain their compliance. Yet, they have neither the time nor personal resources to provide for all these prisoners. Moreover, any prisoner who begins to monopolize an officer's time may also create animosity among the other prisoners on the unit. One officer described her experiences with female prisoners with low cognitive functioning:

> The inmates I find the most stressful ... [are] when you have somebody with a mental illness on the unit because, one, they annoy the rest of the unit because they get special attention, and then, at the same time, we've had women here who are almost sixty but have the mental ability of a five-/six-year-old. I've literally played hide and seek with them while they're in their cell. They'll duck down and I'll be like, "Where'd you go?" And the other inmates are like, "Come on," but it's like having a five-year-old on the unit. Yes, she may be old enough to be my grandmother but at the same time [it's her] cognitive ability. And she's here because she would assault group home staff when they told her no, and that was one of the rules [i.e., to not say "no"] when she came, whenever these people come in.

This officer then explained that one source of strain comes from the fact that some prisoners are triggered by the word "no." As another officer explained,

> Usually we get an email saying, "Don't use the word 'no' with them. Try explaining it because the word 'no' is a trigger." You know how hard it is to direct somebody without using the word "no"? And you'll catch yourself, and you're like, "Please don't do that" ... I find those the most stressful because you're trying to handle a unit full of people at this level [motions with her hand] and then one at this level [motions again] and try to split your time between the two. And they're usually very needy because they don't understand why they're here and you're just, like, ready to pull your hair out ... [It makes me feel] just worn out. It sucks the life out of you by the

end of the day. Those days when I have somebody like that here I'm ready for bed by the time I leave here. I find it physically and emotionally draining, those kinds of days ...

Indeed, officer stress levels fluctuate with the needs of the different women on the unit; these prisoners also affect other prisoners, who may in turn get irritated by the extra attention some prisoners require or receive. Perhaps out of a combination of the aforementioned reasons, the male and female correctional officers I interviewed largely preferred to work with male prisoners. As one officer explained: "everybody will ask me, 'Well, who would you rather work with?' I say, 'I would take one hundred guys over five females' ... I've worked with them [females] a lot, and I've dealt with them a lot. And I respect females a lot and they respect me, but a lot of females tend to become very catty." Such views are consistent with Pollock (1986), who found that a majority of the male and female officers she interviewed (66 and 72 per cent, respectively) preferred to work with male over female prisoners. Britton (1999) also found that officers in state prisons preferred to work with incarcerated men because (among other factors) female prisoners were "seen as emotional and irrational" (p. 455).

Working as Women with Men

Several of the women interviewed for this study either worked in male units at the time or had previous experience working in prisons for men. It is interesting to note that women working in male units cited issues similar to those experienced by officers working in female units – although often they were contextualized differently. For example, overcrowding (frequently emphasized as more pronounced on male units) and interpersonal conflicts, like prisoners bullying and preying on other prisoners, were described as a common source of problems:

> [When] a unit is overpopulated, and you have different behaviours ... and you have guys who can't adapt to the outside and that's why they're in here. And they tend to bring their outside life in here. If an inmate outside tends to be a bully or a drug dealer or whichever assault or nature of charges, they tend to bring it in here. And the bullying continues ... That's my stress.

Just like their colleagues working in the women's units, female officers working successfully with male prisoners often reported being able to resolve issues relatively quickly because they had built up a reputation for being fair and respectful. One officer explained that "dealing with

inmates is fine with me; I'm a very personable person." She then noted
that part of her strategy for "dealing with inmates" is to "have huge respect
[for them] … because I know that they give it back to me." The marked
difference in the relationships that correctional officers described having with female versus male prisoners is that they referred to establish-
ing connections with and passing time "listening" to the women in their
custody. With the male prisoners, however, officers talked about being
respected and having a good rapport, rather than having a "connection"
or "relationship." One officer explained that the optimal tactic for interacting with male prisoners was for "you [to] come in and … build a
rapport with them. I have [a] great rapport with some of them." Thus,
according to the officers interviewed, it is not about cultivating interpersonal relationships – "listening" and providing support – with the male
prisoners; instead, it is about being fair, consistent, and respectful. The
fact that male prisoners are not to engage openly with staff, according to
the "prisoner code," means that interaction between male prisoners and
correctional officers is minimized, a reality that reduces the emotional
labour tied to correctional work.

Hans Toch, in 1981, not only supported that penal regulations often
bar friendship-oriented relationships between officers and prisoners
(see Toch, 1978, 1981, 1992), but also that female officers are more able
to violate such rules than males. Perhaps this is because female officers
will not experience the same disapproval from colleagues and management, given the fact that they already lack the approval of male officers
and others, a phenomenon that begins when they first enter the occupation. Female officers are also, for the same reason, more "free" to create
such relationships compared with their male colleagues. But these
relationships with male prisoners will always pale in comparison to the
emotional affinitiesdeveloped through, or expected from, working with
female prisoners.

For instance, a female interviewee, after realizing she would never get
along with all the male prisoners on the unit, said, "some of them I have
some negative rapports with. It's just human nature. Some personalities
are going to clash with other personalities." Comments about conflicting personalities were readily described by interviewees in reference to
both male and female prisoners, although female officers did tend to be
more sympathetic to female prisoners in comparison to male prisoners.
Even females who were considered exceptionally "difficult" (e.g., some
had reduced officers to tears by the end of a shift because of the pure
frustration and torment they would cause) were just that – "difficult" –
while male prisoners would at times be described as "bad to the bone,"
"undeserving of freedom," and "evil."

Many female officers felt that their gender could sometimes play a role in suppressing incidents before they escalated: "sometimes when a situation arises and a female shows up, a lot of inmates will ease up. 'Ok, I'm done, I'm done. I'm done!' " This view was echoed by male officers, like one who said of female officers working within male facilities: "a female is a lot better to have in a situation than a male, if you have the right female ... A lot of times you want to have a woman [with you] 'cause a lot of them [male prisoners] have respect for their moms." And, in some situations in which male prisoners have attacked female officers, other male prisoners have stepped in to protect the officer: "I've had male staff and male inmates haul male inmates off me." Another officer reported incidents in which male prisoners shouted, " 'Get clear of her! Get clear of her!' before dragging male prisoners away from the officer." In many institutions, although this is becoming less common, female officers had a degree of security in light of the old-school mentality that "no real man ever lays a hand on a lady."

Respect for, and/or protectiveness toward, female officers is not, or arguably is no longer, universal in male units. Interviewees in select provinces (but not all provinces) reported instances of female correctional officers being victimized by male prisoners – something completely unheard of in prior decades. In one particular prison, female officers had been physically assaulted on both the male and female units. Nonetheless, females working in male prisons or units acknowledged that, as women, they faced certain challenges because of their physical demeanour (i.e., size) or because of gender stereotypes, which resulted in them being perceived "as weak." In consequence, some male prisoners would, as one officer stated, "tend to test you a lot more than they would a bigger dude." Another explained that she "struggled" in the beginning working with adult male prisoners. She first found the experience to be "very intimidating" because "these guys are old enough to be my dad." She was forced to "fake" a degree of confidence that she now has internalized; she considers it second nature to her self-identity:

> I'm a different person here than I am outside of here. Mind you, working here has changed how I am outside of here as well. I'm more confident, more outspoken, more willing to voice my opinion, and I swear a lot more, but that's about it ... Being an authority figure changes you.

As her words evidence, this officer's increased confidence is a positive outcome of her occupational experiences, which is noteworthy given that most discussions of correctional work are focused on negative experiences and outcomes.

Female officers also, as previously noted, face unwanted sexual comments and behaviours. For example, one spoke of being "catcalled" and "hit on by inmates." Another said that by the end of the day, when working in male units, "you just feel like a piece of meat ... you feel gross about yourself." To minimize the potential for such reactions, some female officers with experience working in correctional facilities explained that they typically dress and present themselves as "gender neutral" – that is, they consciously avoided wearing anything overtly feminine or too fitted with their uniform, or any item of clothing or make-up that might otherwise draw attention to their gender. A female officer with decades of experience provided an example of the advice she would give to new females working in male facilities:

> You need to be wearing a shirt underneath your shirt. You can see right in through your thing [uniform shirt]. And you should be tying your hair back. And you don't need to be wearing bright pink lipstick ... There's a time and place for that. And it brings attention to you more than anything. When you get catcalled, when you get hit on by inmates, you're opening a window for yourself. So why do that? Then that puts your partner in the situation of telling them, "Ok ... you gotta be not talking to her that way."

Again, here we see how female officers are, in some capacity, made responsible for the actions of others, the idea being that if "she" is catcalled, for example, "she" must have done something or worn something that caused it. This variant of victim blaming, evidenced in this officer's words, places all responsibility for the men's behaviour on the women. Speaking of herself, she continued:

> I find that you should come to work [looking] professional and neutral. I don't go out of my way to look good to come in here ... [Being female,] my hair's never down. It's always back in a ponytail. I've had inmates who have been, like, "Oh why don't you wear your hair down?" And I'm like, "Because I'm in a correctional facility." So I make sure that my clothes are not tight. Or, like, I try to not, I try to be, I guess, as less feminine as possible while I'm working. Because when people, all my staff members, see me outside I'm totally different. I paint my nails. I wear heels. I wear dresses. People are like, "What!?!"

Female officers are also careful about how they interact with male prisoners. Whereas male officers are able to use humour to communicate with male prisoners, females who similarly "joke" with prisoners may find themselves accused, as I previously noted, of being flirty or otherwise inappropriate. An officer said, "there's a fine line there, because if the female officers tell jokes with the adult males, they're flirting, which I was accused of once." This same officer was told by a manager during an evaluation, "You're a little too friendly with them." When she pressed for an explanation, she was told she was "borderline a little flirty." She found this double standard troubling: "Me telling jokes and treating [prisoners] as a human being is not me flirting because I'm a woman, it's me treating them as a human being."

Male officers also observed that female officers in male units are treated differently, and, in some cases, are subjected to unwanted sexual attention. For instance, an officer noted that "it's easier for me to be a male in a male institution. As female[s], they're surrounded by social prejudice here." Some officers felt that this prejudice was rooted in male prisoners' efforts to be found attractive by the female officers: "They've got guys – 'Oh, hey honey' – trying to hit on them." While this officer was of the opinion that all of the female officers he worked with remained highly professional, he also thought their presence in male facilities could create challenges that were unfairly experienced by female staff, from prisoner behaviours to the reactions of male colleagues and, occasionally, supervisors. The consequence was, as echoed by some male interviewees, an added layer of possible conflict and challenge when working with a female officer, particularly someone who was described as "very feminine," "attractive," or "hot" in their self-presentation on a male unit. Interviewees described it as simply one more possible source of concern, additional work, or tension on a unit, another "thing to deal [with]," because any prisoner who makes any comment or gesture should be disciplined.

Nevertheless, most female officers preferred to work with male prisoners. In large part, such preferences are attributable to the perception that women are both catty, as previously noted, and also "mean," thus creating interpersonal conflict among female prisoners that can be rather difficult to resolve. A female officer with such a view explained that when men fight, the particular issue in question is then squashed, but "when females have a fight, they're enemies for life. There's no forgiveness." This, according to her, makes working with females more difficult than males. The same officer reported that, given the space constraints on female units, and in prisons more generally, whenever there was a problem between two females, "we couldn't separate them." In prisons that had multiple male units and only one unit for females, any female prisoner who wanted space from the unit did not have that option. A female prisoner could not be moved to another unit, or even to segregation, because such units were occupied exclusively by male prisoners. Perhaps the fact that male prisoners tend to hide their emotions, which meant that this officer spent less time managing emotional outbursts and conflicts in her male unit, and thus was no longer "constantly on edge," contributed to her preference for working with male prisoners.

Programming: Unequal Access between Male and Female Units

Programming is not consistently offered in provincial and territorial prisons; it varies with the institution, prisoners' gender, and security classifications, and it may be coordinated by volunteers or professionals, but is often the responsibility of correctional staff. Female officers reliably reported that female prisoners have more programming options and services available in comparison to males:

> I think there's a huge double standard that exists with male and female prisoners. Females have more expectations, [they] expect more, want more, [and have] fought for more from years and years of [fighting for] equality rights. But it's gone so far that I believe ... females do have more rights than males now. The equality isn't [there]. I think that they should both have it [the access to the programs]. I think that it's important that a child has both their parents in their lives. Maybe females are more apt to be a member of the family and be more emotionally connected, but if a father wants to have a part in their child's life [then they should have help to] have some [part]. That's my opinion, but I think that if there is a program that can be used for both genders then it should be used and [it should] be accessible.

This officer went on to suggest that female prisoners appear to have "more rights than males," and not just more opportunities for programming, but more accessible opportunities. Officers specifically argued that male and female prisoners deserve equal access to programming and services that encourage active parenting and support family unification after prison; such programs should not be exclusively offered to women, as is the case in some institutions. Officers who had worked with male and female prisoners in the same facility explained that "the female adults, they have a lot more than the male adults ever had," despite the fact that many believed male and female prisoners have similar needs:

> The adult females, I think they're quite like the males that we had here. They're just as needy, and they all have the same backgrounds as the men, just the female version obviously. I think that we're going to do better with the female population, adult population, than we did with the males because when the males came here, from my understanding ... [they] didn't

have the support. They had AA or church – [a] few churches came in to talk to them, a few support groups – but nothing concrete. Now that we're supposed to become the only female institution [in the province,] I think that the programs are a lot more solid and they have the time – we have the time to rehabilitate them [the females] *compared* to the men ... [It's so much more] compared to the stuff that we had to work with [when we had] the men.

Another officer offered the following:

We didn't have a whole lot of programming here for the adult males. All we had at that time was your AA and church services and stuff. Because we weren't set up for them. But now, with the females, we have a lot more stuff. You have your education programs, your mentoring programs, and stuff like that. We were so overhoused if you will. We just didn't have the capabilities or the space to offer them the same services we're offering the females.

The latter excerpt supports the view that female prisoners are provided more programming than males because there are fewer of them, and, correspondingly, there is a higher staff-to-prisoner ratio in comparison to adult male units. However, despite female prisoners having more programming, officers still reported that females were not getting enough programming. Specifically, they, like the male prisoners, might be able to "get their GED in here, read, go to AA, but they don't have anything really in the way of Narcotics Anonymous."

Conclusions

Despite emergent themes highlighting a focus on more negative characterizations of female prisoners, female officers appeared to be more sympathetic to the plight of female versus male prisoners. However, they consistently did recognize the stresses and challenges that lace the prison experience for all those incarcerated (e.g., losing employment, being removed from children and family). Interviewees reported that opportunities for bullying are equally common in female and male prisoner units, but that they are tied to different factors in each. For the female prisoners, the rules that allow them additional material possessions in comparison to those provided for men – like make-up and so on – are also potential sources of conflict. It should be noted that the rules surrounding items culturally read as indicative of femininity vary by province and by institution. Elizabeth Fry Societies and Stella's Circle are strong supporters of women who are incarcerated, and are proponents of empowering women, including through helping them maintain their femininity, when in prison. On the other hand, among incarcerated men, conflict tends to result from disagreements on the street, or other such interpersonal conflict.

Of course, the aforementioned general dislike of working with female prisoners, irrespective of the officer's gender, may also encourage a more negative view of female prisoners – perhaps one inherent to correctional officer culture. This generalized dislike, including the view of female prisoners as more difficult to work with and emotional, led one female officer to explain that "a lot of people think I'm crazy" for enjoying working with female prisoners, and that this required some explanation, even justification. Indeed, officers who enjoy working with female prisoners are left in a potentially alienating position because of their occupational preference, yet they are part of an exclusive, small subgroup of staff with whom they can bond over their shared alienation and enjoyment of their occupational role. Overall, my findings illustrate that many of the realities that obtain for women outside of the correctional system as a result of societal perceptions of gendered embodiment also work to structure correctional officers' interpretations and perceptions of women who are incarcerated, as well as how female correctional officers are perceived by some colleagues.

5

The Male Correctional Officer

I don't come in here with the intention of changing every person I talk to. If I did that, I'd be doing more counselling or social work. Basically, we're here for protection. I'm a pretty open guy. I will talk to these guys: Like, say one guy, "Oh, I got a bad phone call from my girlfriend, man. She's cheatin' on me." "Hey man, if you want somebody to talk to, I'm here for you. I'm not going to hang you out to dry." But that's it ... Maybe later that day, maybe he wants to throw shit under the door. Then we've got to go into punishment mode. "We'll take you to seg. You want to be an asshole, I'll treat you like an asshole." And [I] take him to segregation – "there's your punishment." Rehabilitating in the morning; punishing at night time.

– Anonymous male officer describing his approach
to working with male prisoners

The officer role is shaped by ever-evolving vulnerabilities that emerge in light of policy, practice, and technological change, each of which demand that officers respond. Interviews with male correctional officers, as with their female counterparts, showed that these officers work within an occupational environment in which they experience and must respond to their vulnerabilities in order to mitigate risk.[1] Moreover, such responses are often achieved through a process of self-regulation that affirms and reaffirms their masculine identities. Ironically, this process, and the underlying gendered beliefs, are not entirely dissimilar from aspects of the "prisoner code," which, for instance, prizes masculine presentations of "toughness" and encourages risk avoidance and the creation of some semblance of safety for prisoners.

In this chapter, while I continue my focus on gender and how it shapes prison work, I shift my attention to male correctional officers and the strategies they use to navigate their occupational space. Such strategies are, as I have suggested above, shaped by understandings of masculinities (i.e., actively constructing the self as gendered, yet always within the context of power relations) that are then used to create masculine self-presentations. These self-presentations, as I reveal, are intended to be indicative of status, power, and ability, while overcoming or masking insecurities – physical, legal, or emotional – that are inherent in an officer's high-risk occupation. In this context, I argue that privilege and power are strengthened when vulnerabilities are successfully negotiated, but that when vulnerabilities are unsuccessfully maneuvered, the officer's gender status is reduced to an inferior position on this "hierarchy." Power relations, across all contexts, are structured such that he who holds the dominant position – that which is hegemonic in nature – must be understood as he who best overcomes his vulnerabilities. This is an indirect or direct response, whether the actor is aware or not, to the potential, actual, or perceived risks he faces within the prison work environment – the sources of vulnerabilities.

To make this argument, I begin by focusing on masculinities to bring to light how male correctional officers achieve and affirm their masculinities through gendered strategies of risk management at work, specifically in terms of strategies of muscularity and safekeeping. Next, I present two additional gendered strategies of risk mitigation, those based on positioning and those described as rooted in instinct. Finally, I discuss how risk is gendered and I draw from the interviews to reveal how this is experienced in prisons.

Gendering Risk and Self-Regulation

The self-presentation of identity as it is rooted in gender discourses, or, more tangibly, gendered conceptualizations, shapes individual agency, which always takes into account perceived uncertainties and corresponding vulnerabilities – perceived or potential risk. For example, with a focus on women, Stanko (1997) put forth that, in response to uncertainty, people need to engage in gendered processes of self-regulation that serve to mitigate risk. She describes how, for women,

> anticipating risk and danger is an active feature of self-regulation. What is essential is that safety itself for Woman/Women is embedded within and through femininities – socially-located, fluid, idealized, seemingly removed from any particular Woman/Women's circumstances. (1997, p. 488)

Here, "safekeeping" becomes the ongoing process of assessing risk, and includes interactive, mediated, or regulated representations of resistance to anticipated, experienced, or perceived risk. For example, using the case of violence against women, the dangerous "male other" would be representative of such risk. Self-regulation, or safekeeping, which are "performative" (Butler, 1990) practices embedded in respectable gender ideals, are structured by epitomes of dominating masculinities. By identifying the self as gendered, we see how the self becomes shaped within and by the different venues of gender exploration – always composed and situated within the vast and impressively progressive technological developments that shape risk society, an ever-evolving and advancing reality (Beck, 1992; Beck & Beck-Gernsheim, 1995; Giddens, 1994). Thus, how individuals learn to manage their self and risk – a gendered, culturally specific, and subjective process – becomes evident.

Rather recently, in conducting research to look at the affective nature of detention with staff and prisoners in a British immigration removal centre, Bosworth and Slade (2014) described prisons as "hyper-diverse" and noted that staff and prisoners experienced "status-insecurity" (p. 2) in their struggle for status recognition (Bosworth & Slade, 2014; cf. Fraser, 1997; see also Fraser, 2007; Honneth, 1996). Specifically, they found that the officers in their sample navigated cultural and professional understandings of gender when interacting with prisoners, while the detainees were found to assert a form of masculinity that served to resist subordination and misrecognition within their restrictive custodial environment. Such findings, while they fall outside the focus of this particular study, support the claim that gender is challenged, reproduced, and negotiated, and then renegotiated, by officers in light of the risk that shapes correctional work.

This gendering of risk has also been explored by Madriz (1997), who showed how women's narratives can express a shared "fear" of violent encounters with the "other." For the participants in Madriz's study, this "other" was often a respectable man or even a woman's intimate partner or someone in their support group. In light of these findings, Madriz (1997) concluded that women choose to situate themselves relative to their structural vulnerabilities. As evidenced in the transcripts of the women Madriz interviewed, women who exhibited any of the following characteristics were more fearful of being exploited or abused by the "other": a) not holding "official immigrant status"; b) having low-paying employment; c) not speaking English; or d) feeling overly vulnerable. Applying these ideas to correctional officers working in a prison environment, which is structured by the *risk* posed by prisoners to prisoners, staff, and society – where prisoners represent the "other" – encourages the understanding that officers must employ *gendered* self-regulatory processes to navigate risk, or what Stanko (1997) referred to as "safekeeping."

Not surprisingly, some international scholars have argued that correctional officer competence is mediated by gender (Boyd & Grant, 2005;
Britton, 2003; Farnworth, 1992), while others have noted how gendered
"organizational logic" shapes prisons (Britton, 1997, 1999), or have highlighted the relationship between gender and occupational stress (Dial,
Downey, & Goodlin, 2010; Hurst & Hurst, 1997; Lovrich & Stohr, 1993).
Such realities may shape the "working personality" (Liebling, 2008)
taken on by correctional officers. This working personality is then gendered – developed in what is arguably a hyper-masculine space – *and*
structured in the "low trust environments" (Crewe, 2011, p. 459) that
demark prisons, where officers need to manage life in high-risk spaces
(see also chapter 3).

The Workplace of Male Correctional Officers

Correctional officers' experiences working with adult populations of
different genders are riddled with varying challenges and familiarities
that are precipitated by the gender of both the officer and the prisoner.
Researchers, as well as prison policymakers, highlight the differences
in the formal and informal penal *structures* that shape how male versus
female prisoners "do time," which in practice then redefines the role
of correctional officers. These informal structures, again, include the
"prisoner code," or informal rules of penal living dictated by prisoner
culture that not only are found in prisons internationally, but that also
determine what type of conduct is and is not acceptable among prisoners (see Adams, 1992; Bandyopadhyay, 2006; Clemmer, 1940; Crewe,
2005, 2007; Einat & Einat, 2000; Grapendaal, 1990; Irwin, 1980, 2005;
Irwin & Cressey, 1962; Kaminski, 2003; Newton, 1994; Onojeharho &
Bloom, 1986; Ricciardelli, 2014a, 2014b; Ricciardelli, Maier, & Hannah-
Moffat, 2015; Maier & Ricciardelli, 2019; Sykes, 1958; Sykes & Messinger, 1960; Trammell, 2012). Such informal behavioural guidelines
are reinforced by prisoners, which have the latent function of teaching
this "code" to newly admitted prisoners, given that failing to adhere
to these rules may result in the perpetrator's physical, verbal, or social
violation.

The code was first defined by Sykes (1958) when he researched prisoners in the United States in the mid-twentieth century. However, the
lone study of the "prisoner code" in Canada revealed five predominant
elements of prison living for men, each demonstrating the determined
constitution of acceptable self-presentation and interactions for men in
prison: 1) never inform on another prisoner or be too friendly with staff;
2) "be dependable (not loyal)"; 3) follow day-to-day behaviour rules; 4)

pay no attention to the other prisoners' dealings; and 5) either be or appear "tough" (Ricciardelli, 2014a, p. 41). The possibility of a "prisoner code" among women has not received the same attention or investigation internationally; however, as noted in chapter 3, it is known that prison living for women is less about limiting contact with staff and more about the development of relationships between prisoners (Britton, 1999, 2003; Giallombardo, 1966; Pollack, 2009). Unlike their male counterparts, female prisoners do not focus on doing their "own time" to the same extent as male prisoners. Some have also argued that women in prison are more likely than men to engage in same-sex sexual relationships (see Gagnon & Simon, 1980; Pollock, 2002; Schmalleger & Smykla, 2005; Watterson, 1996).

Of course, many male correctional officers will not experience working on female prisoner units. As previously mentioned, although female correctional officers were integrated into service in male prisons over forty years ago, male correctional officers are not uniformly welcomed in female facilities or on units housing women across Canada. For example, male officers cannot be primary workers on female units in the federal correctional system and in many provinces and territories men cannot work as a correctional officer on a women's unit in *any* capacity. This fact corresponds to the ongoing concern surrounding policies that would allow male officers to supervise incarcerated women, specifically as the primary worker (i.e., in their living quarters). In Canada, men became eligible to supervise women in their living quarters in the federal system in 1989. Discussion around whether they *should* be allowed to do so often references a series of incidents at the Prison for Women (in Kingston, Ontario), which made national headlines in 1994, and specifically how the incarcerated women were treated by the institutional Emergency Response Team (Correctional Service Canada, 2013b). Several women's groups, including the Canadian Association of Elizabeth Fry Societies, the Women's Legal Education and Action Fund, Federally Sentenced Women, the National Association of Women and Law, and the Correctional Investigator, have expressed concerns over having male primary workers in female units (Correctional Service Canada, 2013b). The general consensus across these parties, as revealed in the *Cross Gender Monitoring Project 3rd and Final Annual Report* undertaken by Correctional Service Canada (2013b), is that males should not be primary workers in women's prisons, nor should they perform duties such as strip searches, bed checks, and other invasive procedures in light of concerns about the potential for sexual harassment or misconduct (Correctional Service Canada, 2013b). Many imprisoned women also have a history of trauma and abuse, and thus they require "a safe place" to heal, which may not be possible if they are incarcerated in an environment in which men hold direct positions of power and authority over them.

In sum, in provincial and territorial institutions, the regulations about if and in what capacity male officers are integrated into female prisons or units vary according to provincial and territorial mandates and agreements (e.g., males are not integrated as primary workers in Nova Scotia, British Columbia, and so on). Interviewed men in different provinces and territories discussed not "being allowed" to be primary workers (on the front lines) on units that house female prisoners. However, only in select provinces was this formally noted in easily accessible institutional policy.

Working with Men as Men

Correctional officers interviewed for this research explained that, whatever their role in the prison, they rely on their intellectual capacity (e.g., intelligence and experience) and "gut feelings" (e.g., involuntary instinctive understandings of environmental risk) to navigate actual and potential risk. They mitigate the risk tied to instances in which they "feel tension in the air when something is going to happen." Feeling physically vulnerable or being instinctively aware of possible threats that produce fear might suggest that one occupies a weak masculine subject position. Alternatively, however, when one draws on this instinctive awareness of possible risk, which is the source of fear and concerns of victimization, one can be seen as redefining the same emotional experiences and reading them in a way that suggests invulnerability rather than vulnerability. In this sense, men may refrain from disclosing instances of vulnerabilities by strategically presenting their "gut feelings" or environmental awareness as a way of using their instincts to avoid risk.

Some officers, for example, described thinking and acting quickly whenever prisoners seemed to be "out of sorts," too quiet, or if the tension "felt" too thick on the unit. They talked about maintaining their safety by "acting" preventatively – for example, by keeping their "back to the wall," which would allow them to observe prisoners' behaviours and reduce the possibility of anyone "sneaking up on them." In this context, they also talked about how it is important for officers to always ensure they have a clear view of the different prisoners in their custody, and to maintain constant eye contact with the other officer(s) working on the unit to ensure the person they are partnered with is safe and that they have "each other's backs" if necessary.

In this sense, men achieve masculinity(ies) by distancing themselves from "fear," which is culturally read as a feminine quality. This interpretation draws on the work of Lyng and Matthews (2007; see chapter 7 of this volume for additional discussion), who recognized that men (and women), when participating in activities that are culturally read as male-dominated, can and do express femininity. They argued that men, more than women, may be attracted to and "deal with risks in gender-specific ways," which requires the reconfiguration of gender – specifically, masculinities – to occur within this context (p. 75–6). In prison environments, then, officers engage in processes of self-regulation to manage their self-presentation such that they never expose their fears. They express their masculinity by disengaging with the notion of fear – a feminine quality – and instead adhering to a self-presentation that suggests they need not fear as they navigate risk. And, they pride themselves on their attention to such details. To illustrate, one male officer explained that when he goes to restaurants he chooses to face the door with his back to the wall: "'Cause you go to a restaurant, I'm facing myself to look at the door, [my] back to the wall. Same thing when I go to the unit, safety-wise you turn that on, you turn that [vigilance] on and you think a lot." Rather than recognizing this act as a sign of fear and vulnerability to possible threat, this officer saw himself as highly alert and responsive, and thus as more in control of any situation in which he perceived that danger might occur. Said another way, even paranoia, a quality that can be read as unfavourable, is redefined as a seemingly positive influence on officers that ensures they remain cautious and aware, keep their guard up, and not get too comfortable in the prison environment. This vigilance transcends their prison and social experiences. Officers thus present a rather stereotypically feminine quality, one that could be tied to more negative connotations (e.g., intuition and/or emotionality), as rather masculine in aptitude and favourability.

Intuition, specifically, was described as a developed skill or instinct – one never tied to mothering. Although always rooted in "gut feelings," for officers these feelings reflected safety, security, and threat negation. Intuition was an indicator of status and experience, a way to present masculine dominance via a gendered strategy employed to overcome uncertainty and unpredictability. In this sense, officers *can and do* express femininities even when engaging in male-dominated activities, in order to affirm their masculinity by redefining characteristics that typically are culturally read as feminine. The decision to exert, and then report, such exertions of personally regulated performances of masculinities are ways of reclaiming a gender position that is not framed by vulnerabilities. Being vulnerable is discouraged among officers, who must employ practices that fall within the boundaries of their occupational role.

Another way in which male officers mitigate risk is through presentations of male physical toughness. Muscularity, a long-standing indicator of masculinity, has been tied to representations of dominating and
dominant masculinities – varying over time and space. For example, in
the earlier decades of the twentieth century, men working in the fields
were of lower socio-economic status, and both tanned and muscular due
to the manual labour they performed under the sun. Conversely, wealthy
men lacked the same muscularity (and tan) and were not labourers. Now,
however, muscularity is often tied to wealth and status. Post industrializa-
tion, and even more so after the Second World War, people – especially
in the West – began a long history of obsession with muscularity, body
weight, and shape (see Pope, Phillips, & Olivardia, 2000, for an overview).
For some men, muscularity became central to their self-identification
as males, representing the masculinity they strove to embody. The reasons behind this trend put forth by scholars across disciplines are plenti-
ful and include how body ideals in society, beyond being tied to gender,
are representative of or associated with youthfulness – the firm, strong,
and healthy young body that is culturally read as "attractive" and "desirable" (see Ricciardelli, Clow, & White, 2010; Ricciardelli & Clow, 2009;
Ricciardelli, 2011; Ricciardelli & White, 2011).

Many of the younger male officers interviewed tended to be devoted
to acquiring a more muscular bodily presentation, though this was often
articulated as part of a health-and-safety discourse, which they achieved
by following a seemingly regimented fitness schedule. Officers frequently
described adhering to regimes that include rigorous combinations of
cardiovascular training and weightlifting. I was also witness to the extensive self-regulation and dedication of some officers to such regimes when
conducting interviews in prisons with integrated exercise facilities for
employees. Officers in these facilities explained that since they could
"get all the training we want," they felt they should all take advantage
of the opportunity. Some officers would arrive before the start of their
shifts to work out, or they would work out on breaks. It should be noted,
however, that I was unaware of any officer who stayed after his shift to go
to the gym; the desire to leave the prison as soon as possible after a shift
seemed to trump the desire to go to the gym, despite the commitment
to working out. Dedication to achieving muscularity or fitness was also
demonstrated among officers who spoke regularly about their diet and
nutrition, as well as their workout schedule and physical abilities. I was
frequently part of or aware of casual conversations among officers about
fitness, diet, and stamina. For example, I was told about the maximum
weight that different officers could bench press, or I received unsolicited
references to other indicators of an officer's physical fitness. In itself,

the desire for muscularity and fitness suggests that some correctional officers highly value muscularity as representative of embodied power, and, as such, they partake in demanding self-regulatory practices (e.g., the commitment to working out). Further, such structured workout patterns demonstrate the level of officers' commitment to a muscular bodily presentation, which they believed was necessary to ensure that prisoners recognized their authority and invulnerability.

The fact that interviewees discussed colleagues they felt were more respected, even idealized, for their physical abilities – men who some officers looked up to because of their muscular appearance – further reveals the emphasis correctional officers place on physicality, and its perceived importance as a strategy for achieving a gender position suggestive of power and authority. This is reinforced in how some officers lacking muscularity strive to obtain it, although they often framed their dedication as partaking in a valued practice because physicality assists them when they are required to handle or intervene in concerning situations. In this sense, *need* and *dedication* to physicality are tied to the occupational demands of being a correctional officer, instead of the personal lifestyle choice of working out and being fit or a desire for a specific bodily presentation.

To exemplify, an officer reported that his regular cardio and weight training were valued and necessary practices because he needed to be able to respond to incidents when required, as quickly as possible and with energy: "I'm not a big guy myself. But I've been around enough incidents. Obviously physical shape is definitely [nods to affirm its importance]." As this excerpt demonstrates, the strategic gender presentation of physical ability, constructed in light of occupational realities, was seen by officers as a requirement for the "safety" of staff and prisoners. Another officer, while noting that being "only five foot six and a buck seventy-five" meant he did not fit into the "big boys club," and thus he honed his communication skills to compensate, acknowledging that his lack of stature was "why I lift weights and drink my protein shakes." Clearly, many male staff see the strategic presentation of their gender and physicality as a requirement of their position.

Indeed, a commitment to physical fitness and muscularity is almost expected in this profession. It is virtually a requirement among officers – as much as the confines of the occupation's legal and social culture allows – that their colleagues be physically able to "have their back" if and/or when a situation arose:

> If I'm going to grab hold of a guy, I want somebody with me that's in decent shape too. Like, to me, you gotta be somewhat physically fit to be

good at this job. [If] I gotta run to an incident from one end of the jail to
[the] other, I'm no good to nobody if I get to the top tier, unit one, and I
can't even move. Like, if I'm gassed and I, you know, my legs are cramping
up, and, I mean, there are a lot of guys here that are like that [think like
that] too.

As this officer's comments reveal, the potential for vulnerability or
an increased personal sense of risk can also be shaped by one's fellow officers. In this sense, the hegemonic ideal in the prison context is reflective of embodied physicality, despite the fact that men
are unable to achieve this gendered self-presentation no matter
how much they try. Connell (1995), although in a different context,
explained that hegemonic masculinity is not the most common form
of masculinity (the dominant form), but instead is the most revered
form. In the prison context, this dominating form includes embodied
power as tied to muscularity and physical prowess. However, as shown
throughout this study, it is not just these qualities that are required to
navigate occupational risk; it also entails a culture where colleagues
must also embody power in order to offer protection and assist in
the surpassing of a wide range of vulnerabilities – essential for risk
avoidance. There is a pseudo group component to the construction
of safety, which, beyond requiring others in proximity to embody
strength and prowess, exists alongside the value accorded to personal
fitness and muscularity as a strategy to navigate risk while achieving
masculinity:

> It helps because we're *males*. They [prisoners] know we're more physically
> active, physically strong, so some of them will think twice about what they
> say or [whether to] try to wrestle or fight, because they know we don't back
> out from a fight, I won't back out from a fight.

As these words demonstrate, for officers to feel less vulnerable they need
to be able, or at least perceived as able, to "hold their own" – and better
yet, even to intimidate prisoners. This is something male interviewees
felt they should be able to accomplish as "men." Physical ability is understood as gendered, constructed in accordance with the occupational
nuances that serve to ensure the safety of staff, prisoners, and society. In
this context, muscularity creates a gender positioning that also affirms
a man's social position as dominant, dominating, or even subordinate.
Embodied muscularity in the context of correctional work is clearly tied
to the composition of a hegemonic ideal, one indicative of "power" and
"strength" that is also founded, as previously noted, in a *need*, rather than

being reduced to a desire, to draw on bodily strength when interventions are necessitated as a way to both construct and affirm their masculinity (Ricciardelli, 2016b).

Across such penal contexts, overall, it is evident that the focus falls on a variation of the "hegemonic ideal" that is founded on physical appearance – the ability to overcome physical experiences of vulnerabilities through embodied muscularity and physical prowess. Having dedication to extensive workout routines, even sometimes with the help of muscle-enhancing supplements, is one way that men strive to obtain a body that defies biology – a body that, as such, is not easily attainable (Davis, 2002; Pope et al., 2000). Understanding vulnerabilities as being tied to risk negotiation reveals how masculinities are achieved via muscularity (i.e., a gendered strategy of risk management) and the hegemonic ideal that emerges within such a context. A dialectical relationship becomes apparent as well, given that the successful embodiment of muscularity provides a relatively unachievable model of how the male body should look, which then creates new vulnerabilities for all those who cannot achieve it. This perpetuates the dialectical processes underlying hegemonic masculinity's evolution within the context of risk management.

Affirming Masculinity: Other Forms of Bodily Presentation

Interestingly, and worthy of some attention here, other forms of bodily presentation are also used to express invulnerability. For example, some officers equated tattoos with representations of masculinities. Tattoos were pretty common among officers interviewed. Some admitted to getting their first tattoo only after becoming an officer, or revealed that they were uninterested in tattoos prior to their employment. These men had acquired an interest in tattoos and were now on their way to extensive tattoo coverage (e.g., full sleeves, or half-legs, or back or chest tattoos, or a combination thereof). One officer explained:

Like, I had some beforehand, but when you see guys on shift, seeing any of your colleagues here working on full sleeves, it definitely impacts you. I started liking the full sleeves more and more. I love that and I'm working on it right now, actually [laughing]. Well, that's exposure to things. It doesn't mean that you want it because they have it. My significant other doesn't like it. My parents don't like it, but I like it. As long as you're respectful with the place you do it. Like, I'm not going for tattoos on my neck or my hands. But it's a full sleeve. It covers nicely. But overall, I'm still the same person. I still do the same things I did beforehand and I still have my priorities in line.

This excerpt shows how tattooing becomes a more idealized practice among officers over time, even shaping the perceived gender positioning of those around them. Essentially, there appears to be a link for some officers between tattooing and the achievement of a masculine subject position that produces a greater sense of occupational safety:

> When I first started off, it's not just the inmates that are intimidating; a lot of the staff here are big boys. And everybody's got tattoos. It's not an easy environment coming [in] as a rookie, that's for sure. Oddly enough, but it sounds stupid to say, a lot of the guys, they have big tattoos and stuff. The inmates are really interested in it. And they look at you as a person that's not so different from them. So they kind of latch on to those guys a lot.

Perhaps the historical tie of tattooing to "deviants" (see Adams, 2009, for an overview) and the long history of the criminal significance of tattoos (e.g., gang relations and criminality; e.g., see Phelan & Hunt, 1998; Irwin, 2003) impacts, at some level, the popularity and significance of the practice among officers. Tattooing may also represent an embodiment of masculinity – the signalling (see Maruna, 2012) of strength – for example, as a demonstration that one is tough enough to withstand the pain of the procedure as men engage in a "risky" process with pain and needles. Moreover, some officers valued prisoners' tattoos or the implications of the actual practice or art/image. Tattooing, then, may perhaps be used by officers to indirectly and thus discreetly present qualities of their personality, including their self-perceived "toughness," to prisoners. Body art, for some, appears to project a sense of self that can serve to mitigate risk and displace vulnerabilities.

Working with Male Colleagues

Male correctional officers not only work with men – that is, male prisoners on all-male units – but also with a cohort of male colleagues. Not surprisingly, interviewees described additional strategies of risk mitigation that were based on the different occupational roles an officer may occupy, different roles believed to offer different degrees of protection from or control over prisoners – some even minimizing direct contact with prisoners. These roles, or positions, are gendered. Some – for example, where the officer fails to exhibit any outright control in performing their occupational responsibilities – are linked to more subordinate (e.g., threatened rather than dominating) forms of masculinity. In such positions, officers appear to have little established authority and instead respond to the demands of their superiors. However, more often than not, as can be seen from some of the interview data presented above, much of what male officers do in terms of negotiating risk is directed at presenting a tough exterior for other male colleagues. Some of this posturing is oriented toward earning co-workers' respect by being seen as someone who can "have everyone's back" because one is physically, emotionally, and mentally capable of functioning in difficult, sometimes violent, circumstances.

Perhaps the ultimate symbol of being someone who has the "back" of their colleagues lies within other occupational positions that are tied to more dominating masculinities, given the officer holds overt authority and control over prisoners. Examples of these positions include membership on an Emergency Response Team (ERT)[2] – which is also referred to as the Institution Emergency Response Team (IERT) or Correctional Emergency Response Team (CERT) in different provinces, or the team who responses to "codes." It should be noted that not all provincial institutions are structured such that the ERT is composed of select members with a degree of exclusivity; instead, in some facilities, officers more generally suit up and respond to codes. The ERT, however, is often, but not always, a group of correctional officers – team members – that have undergone specialized training, including in crisis management, and that have access to equipment such as body armour, prisoner restraints, and weapons. These officers are relied on during situations that are deemed high risk, such as riots, cell extractions, and hostage takings, as well as when finding contraband and responding to incidents or altercations. For officers, such positions offer a means to achieve their desired masculinities, because in acquiring such a position some element of personal uncertainty, even insecurity, may be resolved. By being put on the ERT, for instance, the officer and his colleagues learn that someone in management considers them to be able, strong, and trustworthy, which may increase their self-confidence and garner additional respect from others in the prison.[3] Vulnerabilities, then, can be negated by occupying such positions, even if ambiguously constructed, that signify empowerment. Specifically, these officers must self-regulate their conduct in line with the expected behavioural norms associated with the position, like acting confident, capable, and embodying physical prowess, in order to achieve a more dominating form of masculinity while also having the opportunity to construct, even reaffirm, safety.

In this sense, ERT members display their masculinity when "suiting up" to intervene in a situation involving a prisoner or group of prisoners. Successful self-presentation in such situations includes never exposing vulnerabilities that may be (and often are) experienced when an officer is preparing for, entering, or actively intervening in a "situation."

It requires officers to maintain a bodily presentation and performance that suggests fearlessness, invincibility, powerfulness, and authority – the idea that they can handle any situation or prisoner they may face. When successful in their performance, these men embody an admirable and, for many, desirable position – one that is often dominating. Some interviewees thus described an aspiration to hold such positions: "I applied for the ERT, more or less to keep everything in order." Clearly, the ERT is thought to create order and safety. Further affirming the status attributed to the ERT is how some officers discussed who they would or, more importantly, would not want in the role. Male officers were direct in reporting that only *men* should hold positions on the team:

> I mean, definitely you get different opportunities [being a guy], [I] would say, especially when it comes to emergency response–type stuff. Like, normally, if you're going to do a cell extraction, normally you'd suit up all the guys so you get different opportunities. But I think the inmates respond better to the male staff than they do the female staff.

Again, as demonstrated above, some interviewees privileged masculinities – specifically, qualities that are culturally read as masculine – and, in response, men, because of the occupational opportunities provided exclusively to men. This gendered interpretation is not, therefore, a privilege rooted exclusively in biology, but instead is shaped by the prison culture. The belief that "inmates respond better to the male staff" evidences the superordinate positioning of masculinities – as both a sex (biologically) and gender (socially constructed). Further, it is more generally used as a blanket justification to explain why ERT membership is occupied generally, if not exclusively, by men. Being on the ERT is a way for men to construct a masculinity that is more dominating than dominant – not a common embodiment, but an empowered masculinity. The ERT, for example, responds to incidents in cases where it is essential for other officers working in the unit to maintain their safety by appearing unbiased and uninvolved:

> There're only two of my partners in there and the way it's supposed to work is that they're supposed to be unbiased in fights. That's why the codes teams gotta go in there and deal with the fight instead of those two officers that are gonna have a hands-off [policy].

As this excerpt reveals, the ERT provides a form of "backup" or protection for other officers by responding to situations when called upon. This represents another way officers can reshape and construct their masculinity as they integrate their occupational responsibilities into their persona. The role of the ERT enables members to occupy a position of power over other officers, who recognize that the ERT will at some point need to intervene in a precarious situation in which they are involved. In occupying such positions, officers are engaging in risk to negate risk. They face greater risk, thus have an increased likelihood of being harmed. Yet many, if not all, correctional officers subscribe to the perception of officers as problem-solvers and as fearless when in harm's way; these officers feel that safety is created and vulnerabilities conquered when risk is confronted in any circumstances, including those deemed most dangerous.

Officers' actions, and their desire for a position on the ERT, reveal their pride in being able to deal with conflict situations. For example, a group of ERT and non-ERT members from one facility talked at length and with pride about their role in ending a relatively recent riot. Some even showed me images of the different shanks and contraband they had confiscated. Others detailed the challenges inherent to intervening in these types of incidents, such as having weapons and drugs in circulation, as well as safety concerns in the specific prison in which they currently worked. These officers discussed frankly experiences where they were instrumental in subduing a prisoner who was engaging in misconduct, yet they always acknowledged the role and utility of the ERT:

> A couple of hours later I heard all this banging and banging and banging going on. I turn around, I look in, and I see all the inmates are looking at this guy's cell. And so I ran, trying to see what was going on, and I notice he's hitting the cell door window with something. The window was coming at me ... so I called a code and the codes team gets there and locks all the inmates up and stuff and we had to deal with this guy, and take him down to segregation. But he was looking to kill the young guy [the prisoner]. That's what he was yelling, that's what he wanted to [do]. He was looking to kill that young lad. That's what he was yelling.

As is evident from the quotation above, all correctional officers are called upon to deal with situations that might be fraught with risk. However, it is the ERT members that are mobilized to respond when a situation might escalate to a point beyond individual officers' ability to effectively and safely respond while also maintaining the safety of other prisoners on their unit. Moreover, ERT members are more readily exposed to such "risky" situations because they are called to respond to incidents that arise anywhere in the prison, not just on their unit. Thus, officers in these positions, through their ability to shape the outcome of prisoner

misconduct and their courageous self-presentation, confirm a dominating masculinity and gender position. Invoking imagery commonly
found in mass media, we might say they literally rush in to save the day,
affirming for themselves, and their audiences, a heroic, dominant male
self-presentation.

Other officers do elect to use different strategies tied to different occupational positions to mitigate risk. Often, it was the more experienced
interviewees with longer occupational tenure who sought out less visible roles in the prison, rather than choosing the more recognized and
visible role of ERT membership, to negotiate their safety. It should be
made clear, however, that officers who are not part of the ERT (where
applicable), or who occupy roles structured to primarily respond to situations thought to require intervention, are not thought to be lacking in
muscularity or instinct. These officers elect to affirm their masculinity
in a different way. In this case, they rely on their cognitive abilities and
occupational knowledge to do so, which is evidenced in how some interviewees drew with confidence on their prior experience when discussing
nuances in the prison environment. Interestingly, some officers in this
group, although they were no longer in direct contact with prisoners,
often held a position where they had control over the entire institution –
specifically those working in central control, where they were responsible for securing the entire facility.

I found that men working in these positions were confident and performed their occupational responsibilities in a consistent and effective
manner. They were happy to work "behind the scenes" in positions
integral to the functioning of the institution (e.g., more administrative
positions or in quieter areas of the prison). Often, these officers felt,
or were, older (not in their twenties or thirties) and referred to their
age as making them both softer and more open to calmer occupational
surroundings. They were always professional, appeared rather bright,
and presented their gender position as dominant yet subdued – they
never relied on muscularity, physical appearance, or high-profile occupational positioning to determine their masculinities. Their abilities and
demeanour, however, revealed that they were confident and comfortable in their job – able to negotiate safety and security while overcoming
uncertainties and vulnerabilities.

Working with Women as Colleagues

Another way in which masculinities are affirmed by male officers is the
adoption of a paternalistic obligation to *safeguard* the female officers on
their shift. Some officers described feeling that they had to be in top

physical form because they worked alongside women, including some female officers who were collectively considered physically weak (e.g., small frame, petite, thin). For some male officers working with women had the effect of elevating occupational stress because they felt responsible for the women's safety, as though they were personally supposed to protect the female officers. One officer stated that he'd "rather work with two guys than a woman," and this appeared to be for both safety and paternalistic reasons. Some officers revealed feeling *less* safe when working with female officers. One officer, for example, explained:

> Don't get me wrong! There are some girls here that can keep up with the best, but there's parts of the job where they can't do … And they got no intimidation, I guess you can call it – fear, intimidation – as far as bossing them [prisoners] around. "Go to your cell!" "Or what? You're going to call three guys to come, 'cause you're not doing it." The respect's not there. I don't like it [working with female officers]. They're not useful enough to benefit me; they're taking space away from someone [who] could protect me.

Similarly, another officer in a different facility, asked if he felt more comfortable with a partner who also works out (is "built"), answered yes. Like many male officers, his words reveal a preference for being partnered with a male rather than a female officer, and again, preferably a male who adheres to a fitness program. He reported:

> I'd rather work with two guys than a woman, but that's really safety-wise. And plus, it gives me another, like, I don't want you [notions toward me, a petite female interviewer] to get hurt. Even though I don't want my other partner, if it's a male, to get hurt; but for me a female is … I dunno … just more stressful. I feel too, like, I train [with] weights and it helps me [so] I don't have problems doing my job. So it works for me. But everybody's an individual, and [that] doesn't mean that they have to work out.

Yet, this is not to suggest that such perspectives are universal. Instead, select characteristics, culturally read as masculine (e.g., muscularity), are given status and value over qualities that are culturally read as feminine. It is not simply that men are superordinate to or valued over women. Some female officers were described as just as "tough" as any male. Referring to one particular female colleague, a male officer reported the following:

> She's bigger than I am. And she knows how to treat the inmates … and anybody who's been an inmate, that's been around our shift, at the time, they

know that they don't screw around with her. She'll put them in their place.
And even come to the physical part if she has to ... [Prisoners] know that,
they don't screw around with her.

This excerpt reveals that the gendered characteristic of "toughness,"
rather than the officer's biological sex, is highly valued. Said another
way, masculine characteristics or qualities are given superiority over
many feminine traits in the context of correctional work. This valuing of
"masculine" traits results in the positioning of these traits as superior to
those culturally read as feminine, and as a result, both male and female
officers who fail to embody such valued masculine characteristics are
deemed inferior – their self-regulated actions fall short when it comes to
embodying the required "masculine" presentation. This is not to suggest
that some feminine qualities are not valued by officers, as this is clearly
not the case; instead, the emphasis here is on the value awarded to stature, prowess, muscularity, and strength. The officer who holds a dominating gender position, then, likely needs to embody both muscularity
and physical ability.

I would also note, however, that in some instances officers (often those
with longer tenure and thus more experience) tended to value female
colleagues, in particular the communication skills of certain female officers, over the physical abilities of their male co-workers. As one prison
supervisor explained, "98 per cent of the time I'll take the girl over the
big 240-pound meathead, 'cause the girl can talk." In contrast, the male
officer with an attitude "has to be brought down a level; [you have] to
say 'put your brawn away and start opening your mouth. That's what's
going to work, not your big tough-guy attitude that's just going to get
you in trouble.' "

Conclusions

Masculinities have been subject to extensive theorization by scholars,
whose focus has ranged from men's personal (e.g., daily interactions) to
collective (e.g., power relations embedded in the gendered order) experiences, and everything in between. However defined, masculinities cannot be reduced to a single "type" or a simplistic understanding. They are
versatile social constructions, revealing many variations and subtypes.
This notwithstanding, it has been argued that a specific manifestation
of masculinity – hegemonic masculinity – will always prevail (Carrigan
et al., 1985; Connell, 1987, 1995). This dominant masculine subject position molds itself into different forms in response to the diverse vulnerabilities that each man faces, and this fact holds true for men working

as correctional officers. Thus, the male correctional officer best able to deal with his vulnerabilities is most able to embody hegemonic masculinity because little can threaten his status and positioning.

Masculinities are constituted in light of the environment(s) in which one interacts and by which one is surrounded, and where vulnerability and risk must be negotiated across all social positions. He who is able to best mitigate any perceived "weaknesses," through self-presentation, will occupy the dominating position in the relevant gendered space. What is counterhegemonic in this context, then, is anything that renders a man weak or vulnerable, anything that results in him being unable to successfully negotiate his social, cultural, and structural environment. Unfortunately, the dialectical underpinning of the concept demonstrates how, with each vulnerability an individual overcomes, new vulnerabilities are created that must then be overcome if one aspires to the hegemonic ideal. Thus, hegemonic masculinity, accounting for its complexities and spatial and temporal criteria, remains an unachievable ideal type. Its relational and legitimatizing aspects are always fundamental to the gendered risk demonstrated in correctional work, which can be understood as being rooted in risk that must be navigated as officers reaffirm their gender position.

Given that largely all-male prison environments are laced with potential risk, the fact that officers strive to create a sense of control by drawing on strategies of physical embodiment, positioning, and practices aimed at negating risk and ensuring safety is unsurprising. This includes the embodiment of muscularity, prowess, and agility, or appearing authoritative, assertive, and powerful when on duty, or taking an occupational role in the prison (e.g., ERT membership) where officers negate risk by confronting risk. Generally, officers affirm their gender positioning using a masculine performance that, whether overtly or discreetly, ensures they are respected and awarded status by their colleagues and prisoners.

As such, officers self-regulate their behaviours to manage the relationship between invulnerability and vulnerability, because, as is inherent to gendered strategies of risk avoidance, expressions of normatively feminine qualities (e.g., "gut instincts" or "intuition" about safety and well-being) can be redefined as masculine (e.g., as threat avoidance and environmental awareness), and thus as representative of masculine ability and dominance. Overall, common to all strategies of achieving masculinity for officers is an often subtle confidence in the embodiment of a gendered self that suggests that any possible vulnerability encountered, whether anticipated or experienced – such as being weak or unable to offer protection to a colleague – is in essence negligible in its effect. Hegemonic or dominating – and even some qualities tied to the

dominant – masculinities emerge as a constructed response to vulnerabilities that represents a gendered strategy of risk avoidance. In this
context, how vulnerabilities restructure, reinforce (even redefine), and
legitimize hierarchical gender relations, understandings, and achieve-
ments, as well as affirmations of masculinities, is evident. Privilege and
power is then reinforced by the successful negotiation of vulnerabilities,
as, in correctional work, the achievement and/or affirmation of masculinities is clearly founded in strategies used to reduce vulnerabilities.

6

Policing on the Inside: Foregrounding
Occupational Risk

I got staff on the unit locked up with the inmates and we're not gonna enter a
cell unless it's safe for us. So, I have buddies stashing up, and I got a fight on the
other end, [and a prisoner] saying, "First one to come in, I'll stab him."
                                  – Anonymous correctional officer describing workplace risks

Danger, risk, and the associated challenges of living in risk society make
the "problem of insecurity" utterly inescapable (Erickson, 1994, p. 168).
Prison work is embedded in uncertainties and vulnerabilities tied to risk
potential, including physical, emotional, and material threats that are
always evolving with society. Risk constitutes a source of prisoner and staff
insecurity, yet, in Canada, there remains a scarcity of research on correctional employment and risk, particularly at the provincial and territorial
levels. In the previous chapters, my primary focus was on the concept
of gender and how it structures various aspects of correctional officers'
working lives. Another recurring theme was the notion of risk, and, in
particular, the types of occupational risks that correctional officers face
and their responses to both real and perceived threat. In this chapter, I
foreground the notion of risk in order to delve deeper into the types of
physical, emotional, mental, and work-related vulnerabilities that officers
face. These vulnerabilities, rooted in understandings of risk or threat, as
I detail in the following pages, include not only risk from prisoners, but
also the risk resulting from the actions or inaction of other colleagues and
management. I also show that, for many correctional officers, these risks
may eventually seep into their life outside of their work environment.

Correctional Officers, Threat, and the Prison Environment

Although extensive variation exists in prison conditions across the United
States, researchers have tied the prison environment to the potential

worsening of officers' health and well-being over their occupational tenure. Bierie (2012), for example, showed how prison-level aggregates of
harsh conditions, even when required by policy (Finn, 1996), correlate
with a marked deterioration in the physical and psychological symp-
tomatology of officers. This included officers consuming more alcohol
and tobacco, experiencing reduced well-being, and having additional
financial concerns and physical problems (e.g., stomach aches, head-
aches, back pain), as well as taking longer and more frequent sick leaves
(Bierie, 2012).

Like their colleagues in the United States (Bierie, 2012; Finn, 1996),
Canadian correctional officers have been found to suffer from higher
rates of psychological distress and unfavourable psychosocial factors
than those working in other occupational groups (Bourbonnais, Malenfant, Vezina, Jauvin, & Brisson, 2005; see also Carleton et al., 2018a,
2018b, for results from the national study on the prevalence of mental
disorder caseness among correctional workers and public safety personnel more generally). Among the causes of psychological distress cited
by correctional officers employed in Quebec between 2002 and 2005
were job strain, low levels of autonomy at work, lack of social support
from supervisors and peers, experiences of intimidation or harassment,
and fewer financial or other benefits relative to other jobs (Bourbonnais
et al., 2005). Painting an even harsher picture is a study conducted by
Neil Boyd (2011), one of the few to focus exclusively on correctional officers in provincial institutions. In surveying two hundred officers, Boyd
found that they were susceptible to "credible threats of harm" from prisoners that included physical assault, being hit by faeces, blood, vomit,
urine, or spit, and other types of victimization. He also found that, over
time, officers had been exposed to more and more violence, and, as a
result, many reported high levels of stress (Boyd, 2011). The transient
nature of the provincial prison population, he suggested, is one factor
behind the degree of threat and violence in these institutions (Boyd,
2011). These findings also support the argument that overcrowding is
producing worsening prison conditions and is thus also a significant
factor in the deteriorating situation in many provincial and territorial
facilities.[1]

To be clear, though, Canadian researchers studying federal prison
samples have also reported similar results. In an older qualitative study of
federal correctional officers conducted by Seidman and Williams (1999),
researchers found that officers had been exposed to violent situations,
including hostage-takings. These officers reported associating feelings of "shock, anxiety, terror, frustration, vulnerability, powerlessness,
humiliation, and isolation" with these experiences (Seidman & Williams,

1999, p. 30). Moreover, some reported becoming hyper-vigilant on the job and developing sleep disorders, and over 50 per cent of the twenty-seven interviewees felt their personal lives were negatively affected by these incidents (Arnold, 2005; Seidman & Williams, 1999). Moreover, Merecz-Kot and Cębrzyńska (2008), supporting the findings of Seidman and Williams (1999), found that officers' experiences of violence included not only acts of violence originating among prisoners but also among colleagues and superiors. Perhaps not surprisingly, in discussing the results of a study on the relationship between working conditions and the health, safety, and well-being of federal officers, Samak (2003) observed that levels of harassment for officers were "alarmingly" high and that their occupational stress had "spilled over" into their private lives. In short, it appears that officers at both provincial and federal levels face myriad threats and that these extend well beyond those posed just by prisoners (Samak, 2003; see also Ricciardelli & Power, in press).

Contextualizing Risk within the Prison Environment

Threats, as expressed by interviewees, are always multifaceted and are largely attributable to diverse elements unique to the prison environment (and its associated deprivations). Not surprisingly, the majority – if not all – of interviewees described their occupational environment as being shaped by the potential threat or risk originating from the people in their custody (i.e., the prisoners), as well as from management (i.e., those dictating acceptable and obligatory behaviours) and their colleagues. The correctional officer's job, as discussed throughout this book, entails intervening in and de-escalating all sorts of situations, including those shaped by animosity and rage.[2] One officer, to exemplify, explained: "we've got to make sure they're [prisoners] not killing each other. We've also got to make sure that society kind of feels safe." He went on to explain that all officers *should* intervene if/when a situation arises – regardless of whether prisoners or staff or a combination of both are involved. Risk is ingrained in the correctional officer's occupational responsibilities, where, for example, a routine cell search has the potential to reveal contraband, such as needles, that if accidently touched by the officer searching the cell could result in the transmission of a potentially life-threatening infection (as discussed later in this chapter). More recently, the risk posed to officers by fentanyl or carfentanyl, including trace amounts in the air, is a source of increasing concern (for a discussion of the Canadian context, see McCormack, 2017).

Risk, Threat, and Vulnerabilities: The Prisoners

Throughout interviews, correctional officers stated that they felt that working in confined (often concrete) spaces, and in direct contact with physically and metaphorically encaged individuals who largely lack any genuine outlet for releasing their emotions, left them uniquely susceptible to physical or psychological harm and victimization. Officers spoke of this feeling of threat potentiality more uniformly in relation to working in remand or higher-security units, like the special handling unit or in administrative segregation, where prisoners are sent for infractions, including acts of violence in the unit. An officer explained that what made the special handling unit dangerous as a place of work, in his mind, was that it can hold individuals who are "gonna hurt other inmates or guards" because, "well, if prisoners completely screw up that's where they're at. They're only out an hour a day, basically." Another officer described his view of the segregation unit as follows: "We had psychiatric inmates who were in there ... They should've been in a hospital, [but] we had to house them ... It was unreal. People in there, so many psychos and nutcases there, it was unbelievable." Thus, officers who had worked in these types of environments reported that they felt at a heightened risk for violent attack and were constantly aware of the potentiality – and thus were on the lookout – for signs of aggressive behaviour. The perceived individual need to maintain a state of constant vigilance when working is reinforced by officers' training, particularly training in the use of force tactics, whereby they are taught to anticipate and be prepared for violence on duty. Training like this, however, may intentionally or unintentionally encourage violence – for example, by leaving an officer to (mis)interpret a prisoner's actions or words as threatening, thus encouraging an aggressive response from the officer, which may in turn trigger more aggression from the prisoner. I do note, however, that the argument that correctional officer training should have limited use-of-force training and should instead focus largely on de-escalation techniques is unbalanced, as both types of training are necessary. Omitting use-of-force training would leave officers feeling unprepared to manage violence on a unit and could impact staff and prisoner safety. Thus, such recommendations, although favourable in some circles, would likely create alternative challenges and may leave officers feeling less prepared to manage the scope of actions displayed by those in their custody.

Nonetheless, the feeling of omnipresent threat and the potentiality for aggression to trigger more aggression in light of this training is not unique to work in the special handling unit. Officers in other jobs also expressed feeling that they were potentially at risk "a hundred per cent" of the time.³ Indeed, managing risk is considered to be a core component of the correctional officer's work, as is the possibility of actual violence and being the recipient of that violence. One former officer described the job as "being assaulted and attacked. To me, it was part of my job. Some were fighting hard, you end up with a brawl." He further described a chaotic, violent environment in which prisoners can be "punching, kicking, biting, and spitting and everything like this ... [Sometimes] you [have to] give it to them just as much as they give to you, you can't take it easy on them. It just happens ... Sometimes you open the door and the inmate just suckers your face, nail[s] ya. You just don't know." Another retired correctional officer, speaking of his time in one unit, stated: "I remember being nervous. You always feel you've got to watch over your shoulder and stuff. After a while you still got to be careful because you can't really trust any of them because they are criminals."

Seasoned officers with longer tenure, including decades of occupational experience, also saw the threat of violent victimization as a customary part of the job. However, they also brought with them an institutional history that permitted them to place this violent victimization within the context of wider institutional and societal changes concerning the use of violence in prisons. They contrasted their experiences of victimization to changes in the levels of victimization experienced by prisoners, which have resulted from updated policies governing the disciplinary actions that can be used by correctional officers. Interviewed retirees and those officers nearing retirement related stories that suggested it was once within reason for correctional officers to abuse prisoners and that such actions were often justified as a form of deterrence. One officer provided the rationale for this behaviour:

> I'd bring a guy out 'cause he looked at me funny and I'd be around the corner slapping him around. And the inmate knew: "If I do anything this guy's going to kill me." You keep doing that to people back in the day. The minute they got the chance to get an officer ... when you went into the unit with thirty guys, and [if] I tried to turn my back to talk to somebody and they knew I wasn't looking, you'd have five inmates crawl up behind you and kick the crap out of you ... It's a common thing ... That's all orchestrated. It's science. And then you turn around [respondent hits chin], inmates are stabbing ...

This was contrasted to today's environment, about which one officer noted, "you would never see this [now]. Because we don't perpetuate violence ... we don't round [up], beat, and abuse them." Another officer similarly invoked deterrence as an excuse for prisoner beatings "back in the day." Yet another officer explained that the phrase "let's go get the mops" actually referred to the practice of taking a prisoner who "said anything" to the mop room, where "he might get a beating on him." The expression of such attitudes, even as justifications for the prevention of violence by prisoners, are no longer deemed appropriate within today's occupational culture, because, as another officer stated, "times have changed." To illustrate the nature of these changes he added, "it says in our policy: care, custody, and control – in that order. We are responsible for their safety and you can be held accountable."

Such a policy is also a result of the movement toward ensuring prisoner rights, and thus eliminating previously allowed practices that left prisoners feeling, and perhaps being, violated by officers. While these changes were lauded by some as being variously more humane or more professional, officers' tendency to link prisoner-on-prisoner beatings and officer attacks in stories about rising violence within prisons suggests that a select few officers continue to see more humane prisoner treatment as increasing their own potential for violent victimization. In support of that contention, I note here comments made by another officer, who admitted that if there is a situation on his unit, he responds to the offending prisoner with extra-legal violence as a "preventative" measure that affirms the officer's authority, just to "show them who's the boss."

For some officers, perceived risk is intensified by their knowledge of which prisoners have been accused or convicted of certain criminal acts, particularly those with "ugly" and/or cruel elements. An officer noted that "you would, one way or the other, find out [that] some of the details of those crimes were really, really ugly." As a result, it was opined, one gets "a stronger sense of how dangerous things can be in some places in society." This feeling was not, however, universal. Some officers said little about, and showed little interest in, the criminal history of the prisoners in their charge, while those who did admit such an interest reported that they tended to become less interested as they acquired more job experience. The general exception, though, could be seen when discussing select prisoners who either were involved in more incidents or arguments in the prison or who tended to be more notorious and, as such, had generated significant media attention. In the case of the former, officers felt these prisoners demanded more attention and they therefore wanted to learn about the person they felt they were constantly responding to and the possible threat they posed (e.g., legal, physical, social, psychological, medical). Regarding the latter, one officer sought to emphasize the general *dangerousness* of their occupation. Yet, in discussing such "dangerous" prisoners, correctional officers revealed sources of potential vulnerability and used these revelations, whether rooted in real or anticipated experiences, to emphasize the risky nature of their job. Vulnerabilities, it should be noted, can also intensify when officers are in direct contact with prisoners believed to be engaging in misconduct. Experiences of vulnerabilities, then, solidify the risky nature of correctional work, and yet such an experience is not permitted in the occupational role – officers should present as unassailable to ensure their safety because exposing their vulnerabilities would open them up to jeering and/or ridicule amongst their peers, superiors, and prisoners.

It has long been recognized within the literature on policing that police officers tell stories as a means of transmitting important lessons ("recipe rules") abstracted from experience, lessons intended to instruct less experienced officers about how to respond to certain situations they might face (Shearing & Ericson, 1991). Correctional officers have a similar oral tradition in which experiences are shared through storytelling. In many instances, officers used the medium of stories to provide the interviewer with salient facts and lessons learned through experience. The stories referenced here were mainly about how to identify, assess, and respond to risks faced on the job. Thus, for example, some spoke about how they had de-escalated a potentially grave situation with a prisoner or prisoners, or how they had managed their role in relation to regaining control of a prison that was occupied by a rioting population. Others told stories of being attacked, threatened, or harmed by a prisoner or prisoners and how they dealt with that experience. Regardless of their intended lesson, a theme underlying each of these stories was that prisoners, even those who were not directly aggressive, could pose a threat to officers under certain circumstances – a threat that would be intensified if the prisoners' attitudes included an openness to violence. One example comes from a story related by an officer who was attacked by prisoners: "When I got assaulted, one of the times I had to get taken out in a stretcher and they [the prisoners] saw. You'd think they'd killed me, they were all cheering as I was being taken out on the stretcher." It was in this sense that the prisoner was most clearly seen by interviewees as the "other." This was particularly evident in discussions put forth by officers who felt they genuinely needed to be wearing "stab vests" – a vest that offers protection because it cannot be penetrated by any sort of knife or homemade weapon.

In discussing threats within their work environment, some officers reported feeling that they were at increased risk relative to their counterparts working within the federal system. Such perceptions might surprise the general public, given that movies, television, and books on prison life typically portray prisons housing sentenced prisoners – albeit often those in the United States – as filled with prison gangs, murderers, serial killers, and so on. By way of contrast, depictions of provincial and territorial facilities are significantly more limited, and likely structured by the knowledge that these sites house those awaiting trial and/or individuals who have received lesser sentences (a maximum of two years minus a day). Thus, it may be believed that these facilities are not as "risky" as their federal counterparts. And yet, as one officer pointed out, the difference between provincial/territorial and federal prisoner populations is negligible, and prisoners are routinely transferred from provincial and territorial facilities to federal institutions. The difference, he noted, is in the relative degree of institutional precautions and safety devices available to officers within the different types of facilities. As he explained:

> What's the difference between provincial and federal? Buddy [the prisoner] murdered his wife, he spent twenty-eight months on remand for first-degree murder. I gotta deal with him face to face now, with no windows and without the bubble and stuff – no pepper spray, no vest, no nothing. Buddy gets a sentence for life, I can put a vest on me to lock myself in the van, put cuffs and chains on [the] guy, lock him up in a cage, put the lock on, and then drive up to [federal institution]. Uncuff him, hop back into the van, and drive back to [provincial], take the vest off, put it back into the closet. Why?

This officer was not alone in this view. Officers interviewed within provincial and territorial facilities expressed dissatisfaction over their belief that they are provided with fewer safety devices than their federal counterparts, despite working with individuals who pose the same level of risk. Thus, provincial and territorial officers perceive their level of vulnerability to prisoner violence as higher than that faced by their counterparts in federal facilities.

Risk, Threat, and Vulnerabilities: Co-workers

As noted in the previous chapter, correctional officers feel an obligation to ensure the safety of their co-workers, as is evidenced by the emphasis they placed on "having someone's back" or on a colleague having theirs. This obligation, however, also serves to underscore officers' preoccupations with risk and danger. A seasoned officer explained: "My main goal is safety and to secure the staff more than that I know my job is the safety of the community and the institution and the inmates. My main goal is to come and do work, and to leave healthy and with my co-workers healthy and not hurt." Although the obligation to protect others was frequently stated in relation to discussions of co-workers, I would note that this obligation is also extended to prisoners, albeit in terms of keeping them from hurting themselves or others in custody. "I don't want to see an inmate get hurt," an officer observed. Some also felt a sense of duty beyond the institution – that is, to protect the community at large: "I know my job is the safety of the community." Another officer phrased his obligation as follows: "my co-workers are my main safety [concern] ... but then basically it's kind of like 50/50 between the inmates and the public."

While the desire to protect others can in many respects be seen as noble, it is evident that such sentiments, when aimed at the protection of colleagues, also serve self-protective purposes that highlight perceptions of risk and danger. The same officer who stated that his co-workers were his primary safety concern also made clear that he saw this as a reciprocal arrangement: "I'll protect you, you protect me." This rationale also appeared in comments offered by another officer who discussed why officers were expected to get immediately involved if one of their colleagues got into an altercation with a prisoner: "It's about staying safe and keeping my co-workers safe. We gotta protect each other." The reasoning here is simply that officers need to be certain that when an officer is threatened or in danger, their colleagues will respond immediately. This represents an essential level of trust among colleagues if safety is to be prioritized.

Interview data also makes evident the fact that not all officers feel group solidarity and cohesion with all of their co-workers, a point also made apparent in the previous chapter (i.e., my discussion of some of the attitudes of male officers toward their female co-workers). Those who felt that such bonds of trust were lacking, or who were partnered with a colleague who did not share their approach to the job, perceived themselves as being at increased risk of threat or danger. Among such individuals, it was thought to be "tough to work with some folks [that] didn't seem to understand how to carry out the job." Officers avoided certain co-workers or wanted to be partnered with a colleague who would offer them protection in a threatening situation: "When you're working with somebody you want to know that somebody backs you up. I think you pick up a sense from people whether they would be there for you if things get a little rough." Still others, particularly female officers at some facilities, felt the existence of cliques from which they were excluded. One described her biggest source of occupational stress as "dealing with management or colleagues. Management here, it's all about the boys' club ... If you don't go out and get drunk with them every night, then

you're not part of the clique, so you're not getting shit in this institution
and that's how it is."

The types of situations that reportedly invoke the most fear are those
urgent situations in which an officer is potentially in harm's way or under
threat when responding to an incident – that is, when they are "calling
a code." Most officers felt that officers in such situations require immediate support from their co-workers, recognizing that a lot could happen to an officer in just a few seconds.[4] Despite the potential gravity of
these situations and the paramount importance attributed to responding to such calls for support, many officers spoke candidly about how
some of their colleagues did not respond to emergency situations *at all.*
Such individuals were described as either not showing up when called
or as failing to intervene when they arrived at an incident. One officer
was openly disgusted by the lack of support from individuals he termed
"spectators": "If problems arise or officers need assistance we'll hear a
code ... There's a lot of what we call 'spectators': they show up and they
do nothing ... That's the kind of response you get. I'm embarrassed to
tell you that, but that's what happens." To the extent that officers rely on
their colleagues to ensure they remain safe in a potentially dangerous
and volatile environment, these "spectators" and those who otherwise
fail to show up increase the risk inherent to a situation, and are thus perceived as representing legitimate threats to their co-workers. Moreover,
this non- (or inappropriate) response to "codes" was also attributed to
counterproductive institutional policies or weak institutional support,
which produce another source of vulnerability.

Risk, Threat, and Vulnerabilities: The Institution

The institution and its policies are also perceived as increasing the level
of potential risk that officers face. One factor cited was a real or perceived lack of institutional support for officers in situations that might be
subject to review. In relation to use-of-force situations, for example, some
openly cited fears of having their actions placed under investigation, a
practice mandatory in some jurisdictions "for every assault. I go up and I
put handcuffs on every inmate, we have to do a use-of-force assessment to
see if it was necessary; [there is then an] independent third-party assessment ... [where they] assess that we are using the appropriate amount
of force." In this instance, the risk is to the officers' livelihood, as an
investigation could result in significant repercussions, such as suspension, termination, or marred job-performance evaluations and reduced
opportunities for promotion. As a result, some officers stated that they
second-guessed their decisions and worried about how things might be

interpreted by internal or independent reviewers. "It's ridiculous. We're afraid to go to codes now. You have to describe why you took him in an arm bar to the ground. Why? It's hard to articulate that in a report. They'll [investigators] say it was excessive use of force." Some officers worried that prisoners would wield these types of institutional policies as a weapon against them. Prisoners, one said, "know how much they can get away with, nowadays." He elaborated:

> Inmate dynamics and mentality has changed that now. If staff ever so much as flick them, first thing they'll do is call the police. If you put on the cuffs, and they were struggling, and it made a mark on their wrists, they want to call the police and have pictures taken. So [we] just take extra steps. We have more cameras present [and we] make sure that the camera sees when we do the finger check to show that cuffs are not too tight. When they have to stay in cuffs and shackles for a period of time, we will go back, I think, every fifteen [minutes] to half-hour with a camera again to show "cuffs check, still okay." We need to protect ourselves.

Officers who had been suspended due to such investigative practices described having heightened anxiety on duty – they felt marked by their previous suspension and thus unable to perform their job as fully as before. For example, an officer noted, "I always have to watch what I'm doing." He likened his newly heightened anxieties around his job performance to "post-traumatic stress." "I'm always worried now," he fretted. "Am I going to get in trouble for this?" Another officer described in detail the incident for which he was suspended, following a report of inappropriate and aggressive behaviour toward a prisoner made by a nurse:

> I got suspended for six months. An inmate that was going to the hospital, we were watching [him]. He was a patient but he was all there, [and I got suspended] for beating him. He said that he wanted to try to hang himself, so he got on the bed and he was like, "You're not going to stop me." He wasn't handcuffed and usually we have to have them handcuffed, so we were like, "We have to do this." We tried stopping him from doing that and he started fighting back, [and] I gave him a few hits. We are taught to hit the pressure points, like on his neck, and his back. One of the nurses came in and she thought that that was patient abuse. I tried to defend myself: "He is in your care, but he is an inmate in this room. Yes, we're in a hospital." A lot of people don't realize that in the hospital that room becomes a cell. There are certain things that aren't allowed in there ... 'cause the inmate gets nothing. Like a knife, no sharp utensils, and they don't understand

that. When she came in and saw us hitting him – 'cause he tucked his arms
and we were trying to get his arms out to handcuff him to prevent him from
choking himself out and hitting us and attacking us – she thought that was
patient abuse, [and] called the cops. [They] didn't charge me, but [they]
charged my partner for excessive use of force. I had to go through court
and all that, [and] my partner was off for six weeks – he's still off for post-
traumatic stress. I was out for six months and they suspended me 'cause
they had to investigate me … They said, "Did you hit the inmate?" "No, I did
everything I had to do." "And did your partner hit the inmate and if he did,
did you see him?" Well, how could I see him when I was busy focusing on
what I was doing? I was not watching what my partner was doing. You're not
watching what they're doing; you're concentrating on trying to do what you
need to do to stop the inmate from hurting somebody else. Tunnel vision.
So they suspended me for six months and [then] thought: "Okay, maybe we
don't know the truth, here you can come back to work." Six months … It
changed my views on this job. I always have to watch what I'm doing.

This officer felt vulnerable due to the risk originating from prisoners
and management. He was concerned for his job, concerned about his
own behaviours and how they would be interpreted by prisoners and
staff, and he was concerned about the actions of prisoners. In this sense,
having policies in place to offer needed protection to prisoners is, in
some ways, taxing for officers who feel their agency on duty is hampered
and that their actions will be misconstrued as negative or excessive in
intention.

Officers also explained that certain institutional policies, like those
underlying the paramilitary organizational structure, abolished any possible "team atmosphere" among some co-workers. As a result, divisions
resulting from officers striving for promotion, as well as those caused
by interpersonal dynamics like "gossip" or personal frictions between
colleagues, were described as relatively common: "We spend an awful
lot of time with each other, new people versus old people, women versus men, [and] there's friction between races, friction between people
of different sexual orientations." The fact that officers spend so much
time together daily, that they must rely on each other, and have varying personalities, work ethics, ages, and political viewpoints, affects the
quality of the relationships developed between colleagues, or sometimes
ensures they do not develop at all. Select institutional policies, despite
being designed with positive intentions and to promote equality in the
work environment, were described as being "used [by some officers] as
weapons against each other, which is sad." As a result, allegations have
pitted some officers against each other, creating distrust and uncertainty,

which only works to intensify doubts about how quickly or even *if* select officers will have each other's backs in emergency situations.

A lack of available resources for prisoners creates further problems for officers, increasing the potential risks associated with their job. In essence, and as discussed in earlier chapters, many facilities lack a full range of available counselling services, as well as addictions, occupational, and other programming; thus, many prisoners, both male and female, and including those experiencing mental illness, the addicted, the physically disabled – and those with other complex physical, mental, and social needs – are placed into a high-stress situation – imprisonment – with few resources and fewer coping strategies. Speaking of the female facility in which she worked, one officer was clear: "It's been set in stone here pretty much that we are not a rehabilitation centre ... We don't have the resources for any of that." While she recognized there was a need for such services, as well as for the many prisoners dealing with mental illness, she also acknowledged being ill-equipped for dealing with all of these issues: "What can you do? There's only so much you can do. I wasn't trained in psychology."

Thus far, I have left unexamined a much less direct physical threat created by the nature of the institution and its policy: the fact that officers must work in conditions where bodily fluids can be spread, fluids that may contain Hepatitis C, HIV, and other blood-borne infections. Searches of cells and bunks open officers up to the possibility of accidentally sticking themselves on used needles. One officer described having to be "really careful when I search anything ... [to] never rub my hands anywhere. I always tap and look first. I've found needles." Another officer worried about acts of violence through which he could become infected with a serious disease. "Hepatitis, Hep-C. If I think about it, [shanks] are always in the back of your head, but if you go onto a range and you're wondering, 'Oh man, is this guy going to fucking shank me?' Does this guy have a needle tube?' Like, you can't have that in your mind. The job will eat you alive."

Dealing with hazardous waste is not unique to correctional workers. That said, it is a part of their job and one that has not drawn enough attention in terms of its potential health concerns. I would note that many officers self-reported what was described as a lack "adequate training, knowledge, and support [in how] to handle crises, and [when] we're in a crisis-type situation we [just] went in." He provided an example: "We were dealing with some hazardous materials and things like that ... [We] should have just stood at the door and refused, [but] we kept working through it, and exposing ourselves and everybody else." Moreover, when asked about the sources of his occupational stress, another officer said succinctly: "I've never been stressed because of an inmate. My stress is directly related to management and the way that management treats staff." In this and similar instances, such "treatment" includes requiring staff to deal with incidents involving hazardous waste materials that can carry infection and disease, including faeces, urine, vomit, bile, and blood, in some instances without proper training or safety precautions (for additional discussion, see Ricciardelli & Power, in press).

Risk, Threat, and Vulnerabilities: Government Policies

A significant source of institutionally induced anxiety is the set of issues surrounding overcrowding as a result of the increasing prison population. This is not to suggest that I am in support of government investment in processes that increase the capacity to incarcerate in Canada (and indeed, such arguments are outside the scope of this book). It remains clear, though, that the trend toward incarcerating more and more people for longer periods of time means that prisons are often well over capacity, with a low ratio of officers to prisoners, and more bodies tightly jammed into spaces, and thus greater potentiality for high-risk behaviours and activities to occur. The risks cited in interviews include the use of bodily fluids as weapons, increasing aggression, and rises in prisoner-on-prisoner violence and attacks against staff.

One officer described the problem as follows: "The thirty-to-one ratio [referring to the fact that there are thirty prisoners for every one officer in his unit] – that's basically one of my biggest concerns right now. Nobody has ever physically threatened me with anything, told me they're going to kill me, but just thirty to one?" An officer in another facility similarly emphasized the risks to officers associated with overcrowding: "The size of the unit makes me nervous sometimes, because, yeah, it's going to be like fifty inmates [on] each unit. So it's too much people for me, I think." He worried that, "if a riot's coming over, it's tough to do something with two officers in there. But fifty guys, even if you are three or four officers, what can you do? You're just there to make sure everything is going good – the routine is going on."

This problem is hardly unique to these two facilities. A female officer stated that the previous facility in which she worked "held 123 and we had 200." As a result,

> tensions were extremely high because you are throwing in an abundance of
> people in a small area. You're expecting all these personalities, and some-
> times you're dealing with mental health. Sometimes you're dealing with
> withdrawals. Sometimes you're dealing with people with bad blood from

the street ... So that creates so much tension within yourself because you're constantly on edge, saying, "Oh my God! [It's not] *if* something's going to happen, it's *when* is something going to happen?" And I find that the overcrowding just pops that up to an extreme amount.

To illustrate this point further: I visited a prison with a unit designed to house eight single-celled prisoners with two officers that was later converted to accommodate sixteen double-bunked prisoners, and which now houses up to twenty-four triple-bunked prisoners (two prisoners in bunks and one on a "mattress" on the floor). Despite the increased number of prisoners at that particular facility, the number of officers remained the same (two officers per unit). At yet another provincial institution, which one officer described as presenting workers with "a brand new challenge every time you come in on duty," an officer noted that

> the place was fit for fifty-seven inmates and you got to come [into work] with ninety-two. Then the next thing you know, sheriff comes in with three guys. They have to sleep in the gym or phone room, where there's not enough room to put a single mattress on the floor. They gotta spend a whole weekend there. And it's hot in there, it's filthy, it's gross, people spit on the walls and snot.

Beyond the poor living conditions, including poor hygiene and lack of private space, which impacts both prisoners and officers, officers saw this level of overcrowding as a threat to their own safety:

> Oh, it affected everybody. Everybody was involved in it. When you have, instead of ten, thirty in each area and one officer outside and one officer inside, it's a big difference. Where you got thirty, you've got problems. You have a problem with thirty, not a problem with ten. At times it was [frightening]. I was involved in riots and stuff where they refused to come in from the yard and you have to go in, fight them, and bring them back in.

Stresses caused by overcrowding are felt by both officers and prisoners, creating what one interviewee described as a "pressure cooker." At his facility, which housed only sentenced individuals, the numbers of adult male prisoners would "spike" to the point at which "we had all four units with twenty-five on each, and we had thirty men at the gym. It was crazy. You couldn't move; everything just sucked."

It appeared to rarely be the case that only some units in a prison were overcrowded. Instead, officers felt – and I often saw for myself – that most if not all units within a facility would be over capacity, including some that were home to high-profile prisoners who might be targeted, as well as those with histories of serious criminal violence that left them susceptible to victimization. These types of prison spaces were considered particularly dangerous work environments that, as such, intensified perceived threats to officer occupational safety. Although officers on any unit might report feeling anxious or nervous on duty, and thus a need to be cautious, such feelings were particularly strong among officers working on units classified as maximum security or that housed specific prisoner populations. An officer who "remember[ed] being nervous" talked about what he described as "the 'heavy range.' And what I mean by that, the heavy range in jail, is the tough guys; it could be bikers, could be gang leaders, murderers, cop murderers." When this officer first walked into this unit, "they scoped me out right away, because I was the new one, right? It was intimidating, yeah. Murderers and ... you have to learn who they are quickly." His words show just how officers can experience different levels of vulnerability or risk on different units. While some specific units – such as the special-handling unit and the "heavy range" – are generally considered more unsafe than others by virtue of the population they house, officers are keenly aware that an otherwise peaceful atmosphere in any one unit can, as a result of overcrowding, quickly turn into a charged atmosphere, rendering it immediately unsafe for staff and prisoners alike.

Officers thus felt they had to be hyper-vigilant when it came to subtle changes in the atmosphere in a unit, particularly those cues that might signal something was about to transpire between prisoners or that a prisoner was preparing to harm an officer. Others spoke of having to take special precautions when interacting with certain prisoners in situations where they believed officers were more prone to being attacked. For example, an officer explained: "If you're dealing with an inmate or a guy that's just very agitated [because an officer's] been ordering him around all day and he doesn't like authority ... he'll come up from behind you and pop you in the head or whatever." Another scenario was provided: "A guy that's got a murder beef and he knows he's being sent away for the rest of his life ... and doesn't want to go to wherever. That's one of their things. The inmates, they don't care. They'll fight you." Another officer described working in an institution in which "the people that were in there were so nuts to tell you the truth. They were just terrible. They shouldn't have been in there ... the extremely dangerous ones ... murderers, rapists, ones who couldn't get along with the inmates in jail, you had to be very, very careful and sometimes we had [to have] three or four officers every time we open[ed] the door."

In each of the stories told, we can see officer threat tied to diverse conditions of confinement (e.g., in segregation units) and different types of
prisoners (e.g., those suffering from mental illness or with known extensive criminality). Officers explained that, given their role is to ensure
the safety of all prisoners living on all units, they were obliged through
their occupational responsibilities to navigate any threat posed when on
duty. Of course, the degree of risk posed to the officer varies according
to some conditions – like prison structure, officer personalities, and the
overall penal climate or atmosphere – which increases perceptions of
risk. Moreover, the manner in which the prison context and environment is viewed suggests that the officers feel that these institutions fail
to provide them with a sense of safety. As a researcher, I have had, per
institutional policy, to wear a stab vest onsite because of the escalating
number of prisoners-on-officer attacks in select facilities. This and other
similar experiences show the undeniable occupational hazard underpinning correctional work.

Other government imposed policies, while perhaps well intentioned,
can inadvertently increase the potential for violence within facilities.
An excellent example of this are those policies aimed at desegregating
prisoner populations in order to integrate persons convicted or accused
of different types of crimes (e.g., sex offenders) into the greater prison
population. An officer working in an institution that was ordered to integrate prisoners said bluntly that "it just didn't work" because racial and
ethnic divides led to power struggles within units. Although he felt "the
government got what they wanted ... they [government] were so much
against segregating prisoners – like you can't have the black inmates in
this unit, the Vietnamese and Chinese in this unit, and the whites in this
unit." After the integration, he said, "that's when I seen some of the nas-
ties, with guys coming out of their units with pencils sticking out of their
heads."

Beyond the Workplace: Risk, Threat, and Vulnerabilities

The threats perceived by correctional officers extended beyond the
prison walls, seeping into their personal lives and in some cases impacting their families. For instance, it was not uncommon for interviewees
to describe feelings of threat when they were not on duty, sometimes
in public encounters with former prisoners.[5] As a result of phone calls
to his home by either former prisoners or their affiliates, one officer
advised his wife and children that if they encountered one of his former
prisoners in public, they were to run into a bathroom while he called
the police: "If this happens, you ... just run there and I'll take care of

it and call the police." Colleagues working at the same institution, the officer said, would get threatening phone calls at their homes that "they couldn't deal with." Although such incidents were reported infrequently, the thought of this occurring (i.e., how easily the boundaries between an officer's personal and work life could be crossed) was enough to instil concern into the lives of some officers.

While conducting interviews onsite, I observed an instance in which an officer abruptly left work (with support from colleagues) after receiving a phone call from their partner, who had reported feeling "scared" that someone was looking into the windows at their home. I also heard of other instances where officers were concerned about someone at their front door or someone who had approached them in a way that made them uncomfortable. It is perhaps noteworthy that such concerns, although each must be taken seriously, never to my knowledge resulted in any detectable source of foul play or physical violence directed toward the officer or their loved one. Motivating an officer's fears was a concern that a former prisoner or their associate would seek revenge against the officer and his or her family. To explain such fears, some officers noted they had been "followed before" or had experienced awkward or threatening encounters outside of work. One officer had taken his family to a Santa Claus parade when he came across a couple of former prisoners from his jail: "I'm walking with my wife and my little girl and my father-in-law and my brother-in-law and these guys said, 'Well, you're not in uniform. We can kick the crap out of you.' " The officer continued walking with his daughter, but they continued following for some time. This exchange occurred, he said, "in front of my two-year-old daughter." The threats described by participants indicate that they could not always leave their work, or the feelings of threat associated with the risky nature of their employment, behind during off-hours. As a result of their direct experience, or the experiences of colleagues, many had become more cautious over time, avoiding certain areas and making plans to ensure their family would not be victimized.

Some officers also consciously believed that prisoners sought out "weak" officers whose bearing or behaviours might suggest vulnerability, and as a result they made sure to avoid being perceived as weak or vulnerable on the job to evade any threats at home or in their personal life (i.e., the threat of being exploited). The fact that their work could negatively impact their family was worrisome for officers and largely problematic. Also of note, some officers explained that they were not just concerned that a former prisoner would want to cause them harm for personal reasons, but that they might be targeted because, in their employment, they represented the justice system. Not surprisingly, many officers had reportedly curtailed their public activities and avoided certain public spaces known to be frequented by former prisoners.

Conclusions

The correctional officer occupation is shaped by risks that in their intensity surpass most risks experienced in free society. This in turn shapes officers' actions and reactions when on duty and extends into their personal lives. The prison environment is thought to be structured by the potentiality for violence that is intensified by factors like overcrowding and prisoners' stresses and deprivations. Correctional work is most often normative, even mundane, yet it is also ripe with the potential for different types of physical, emotional, mental, and work-related vulnerabilities. For officers, these vulnerabilities, which are rooted in understandings of risk or threat, stem from prisoners, the actions and inactions of colleagues, and management. As a result, violence is all too easily viewed as largely unavoidable, and officers become increasingly wary, on guard, and primed to respond to any perceived threats. The perhaps inadvertent result is that officers may exacerbate an already potentially volatile situation. Some interviewees mentioned specific times when they were concerned for their safety and felt under threat. In essence, then, showing how male correctional officers experience risk and negotiate vulnerabilities within the penal environment may reveal how the self, and its many components, is achieved and affirmed on duty.

7

Correctional Officers as Occupational Edgeworkers?

People don't understand ... My mom, she asked me: "Segregation, what's this? What type of inmate stays here?" She was all paranoid. I've been doing it for five years; I don't mind doing it for another ten. She got all scared, because she didn't understand, she'd never been in a jail.

– Anonymous correctional officer detailing "outsider" reactions to her line of work

Much of what has been presented in this book thus far reveals a collective portrait of individuals who construct myriad ways to mitigate risk while occupying what they, and many others, see as an inherently risk-laden occupation. In chapter 2, I unpacked some of the motivations expressed by correctional officers for undertaking this occupational role, including financial, family, and/or career-related reasons – regardless of the risk involved. In this chapter, I similarly foreground the subject of risk, but do so in an attempt to move beyond these explanations to explore the extent to which some officers might be drawn to the work *because* of its risky nature or the perception of it being a "high risk" job.[1] It is manifestly true that while some people are highly risk-averse, others embrace any number of activities or occupations that might potentially place them in situations that could result in adverse physical, mental, or emotional outcomes – that is, they want to embrace danger. Following a line of inquiry established by other scholars who have explored how and why some people actively choose to engage in *risky* lifestyles or behaviours, I consider whether the potential for danger may serve to attract some individuals who enter correctional work. My focus in this chapter is on male correctional officers working largely in maximum security, classified men's prison units. To this end, I pose the following question: Can the correctional officer be understood as a type of edgeworker?

To explore this idea, I employ the concept of edgework (Lyng, 1990) to examine how risk is interpreted and negotiated and to look at the social contexts in which risk experiences emerge. An "edge," it may be recalled, is the boundary between safety and disaster, a boundary that is negotiated by individuals who are drawn to the excitement of high-risk situations. Lyng and Matthews (2007), for example, explain that individuals are drawn to high-risk activities by the "seductive power of the experience ... [that is derived] from the attraction of a clear and vitally consequential boundary line – an 'edge,' as it were – which must be negotiated by the individual risk taker" (p. 78). Such engagement with risk cannot be reduced to the concept of actors trying to satisfy urges (e.g., personality or intrinsic motivations) (Lyng, 1990), or to attain rewards (e.g., cost-benefit analyses) (Heimer, 1988). Instead, edgework is a life trajectory, one that often crosses boundaries between traditional practice and modern choices as actors negotiate the edge (Lyng & Matthews, 2007). They push to be as close as possible to the object boundary of perceived risk without ever crossing the line.

In this chapter, I explore edgework in the context of the correctional officer occupation, detailing a concrete preliminary objective boundary and the resulting revised interpretation of the officer role. I first present the various personal and environmental factors that support how the correctional officer occupation can be understood as a form of edgework. Next, I reveal the constitution of objectively defined primary and secondary edges in this particular field, with the former being at the point of any encounter prone to escalation and the latter within the space between criminal and civil behaviours that are occupationally sanctioned. Finally, I explore how officers revealed their empowered position as edgeworkers.[2]

Correctional Officers as Edgeworkers: Constructing Edges

Although correctional work is repetitive, even boring, the majority of correctional officers interviewed – particularly those working in higher-security institutions – identified their occupation as high risk and potentially dangerous. Those who did not initially do so, when I probed for more information, were in agreement with this characterization (see chapter 6). The correctional officer role is certainly potentially unsafe and that leaves individuals susceptible to some degree of risk that varies in intensity based on a variety of factors (e.g., prison, climate, context, and personality). Occupational realities indicate that correctional work represents a variation of arguably *voluntary risk-taking*. For some officers, though not all, this voluntary dimension is tied to the choice to enter an occupation that both insiders (correctional workers) and outsiders (general society) view, whether correctly or incorrectly, as unsafe (see also chapter 2).

Analyses of officer transcripts provide detailed insights into officers' perceptions of their occupational safety within prison environments, spaces in which officers work alongside prisoners in "hazardous conditions." Officers characterized these conditions as follows:

> [Shanks] concern me ... Spitting is not going to kill you, punching is not going to kill you, kicking ... but [shanking], that's life ending ... You know they're there.

> We have strong, big, burly guys that work here that can be antagonizing, that will try to push buttons and make the situation worse. I'm out there trying to de-escalate the inmates, and I have a guy behind me saying, "What are you going to do about it?" Well, it's not what I need right now. Just sit there ... Don't make it worse.

As these excerpts, and others within this book, demonstrate, interviewees described feeling unprotected as a result of prison policies, poor prisoner adherence to conduct regulations, including those around possessing contraband, and the behaviours and attitudes of their co-workers. Indeed, I have outlined in prior chapters these and other potential threats – ranging from economic and career threats to physical dangers – in the form of the actions of co-workers and the operation of institutional policies that place officers in greater risk and under greater scrutiny. Thus, it is of little surprise that all officers interviewed saw their work as "dangerous" and saw themselves as putting their lives on the line in their work life. This sentiment was expressed most clearly by an officer who contrasted his work to that of a police officer: "Our job is more dangerous than a police officer's. We don't have weapons! I have zero weapons, and I'm locked in a room with convicted felons." Another emphasized the uniquely dangerous aspects of his work, asking, "how many people [at work] have a chance that they could get assaulted, or even taken hostage, or killed in the course of their twelve-hour shift?" He then concluded, "it's a very high-risk, dangerous job."

Some officers' pride in their occupational role was tied to their perceived status – the seduction of the occupation – which was thought to come from having first-hand knowledge of or experience with criminals that attract public attention. Some officers revealed being intrigued by certain types of crimes and select notorious criminals. They invoked media imagery or cinematic depictions in their accounts of their work.

For example, one officer noted that his job involved being "surrounded by them [prisoners]." Before that he explained that he described his work to outsiders by referencing a movie:

> I usually say, have you ever seen the movie *Blow?* With Johnny Depp? [From] '98, 2000, something like that. When he was in jail, he went in there, he said [it was with] a "BA in crime," in, like, [selling] marijuana. Then he came out with a "PhD in how to sell it …"

Others referenced the notorious individuals who had been in their custody, bringing attention to these prisoners' public persona and perceived "dangerousness." Having authority and control over such "dangerous" men, who are feared by the public, gave some officers a sense of pride and allowed them to generate a favourable social status among individuals in their personal network, who admired their willingness to take the risks associated with protecting society from such dangerous people. This supported the officers' feeling that, in their occupational role, they can offer "protection" to society and perform a public service via their awareness of and encounters with prisoners, and, as such, can even offer some retribution to victims. Such perceptions evince the emotional sensations that accompany the correctional officer role. For example, one officer spoke with noticeable pride when discussing how he described his work to "outsiders":

> It's a good job. It's a dangerous job. It's a dirty job. I'll be like, "Why am I even doing it?" But like I said, I like the excitement. If someone was like, "What do you do?" "I'm a guard." "Oh, fuck, that's cool! You must have some stories and I'll be interested in hearing them." And, like, "Holy shit, really?" The stories I can tell, in what happened in a day shift on any given day, would blow some people's minds!

Like many of his colleagues, this officer viewed the job as shaped by the potentiality for danger. Correctional officers are, then, self-defined risk-takers who come into close contact with, and indeed survive encounters with, individuals they (and many others) perceived as dangerous.

As may be recalled from earlier discussions of edgework (see chapter 1), according to Lyng (1990), this type of work is characterized by powerful emotional sensations that accompany risk-taking behaviours – the seductive power of risk-taking – and a clearly defined "edge." Some interviews with officers, particularly those earlier in their careers or working in detention centres, reveal the presence of both criteria. Emotional sensations underlie correctional officers' accounts of their on-duty experiences, perhaps in the earlier days of an officer's career, a derivative of curiosity about prison to some extent. Further, there is also an objective primary edge constituted at the point where the correctional officer responds to an event, in cases of rioting, conflict, disobedience, or poor temperament (e.g., voluntarily entering a situation despite knowing one may be harmed rather than "opting not" to respond). Within this context, I limit my analysis to the correctional officers who described such events with excitement, anxiety, and anticipation. These elements can be seen, for example, in the following excerpt from an interview with an officer who described being called up for a "shit show":

> There's a riot, so you got a police escort. You're driving 180 on the highway. You get [there] and there's that much water in the unit. They're popping sprinklers, throwing toilets through the bubble!

In recounting the story, the officer was visibly excited: "Was it bad? Was it crazy? Yes!" Similarly, another interviewee explained the edgework inherent to the job:

> I think people [correctional officers] are underappreciated, underpaid. I don't think people understand what goes on in here and how difficult this job can be, and how dangerous this job is! ... So it's a very high-risk, dangerous job.

As evinced above, although different officers described how correctional work is "dangerous," some did so with excited energy as they recounted their experiences at the "edge." This was in stark contrast to officers who recounted similar experiences but with apparent angst or stress, or with frustration because of how the situation was managed. Those who expressed excitement, rather than angst, felt that being called to respond to *any* escalating situation solidified the objective boundaries that constitute the edge. This was further evidenced when interviewing onsite, as some men located and played video footage of a riot they had "worked," presented photos of shanks and other contraband they had removed from prisoners, or even drew diagrams to contextualize a particular experience. The obvious desire of some select participants to discuss "dangerous encounters" further supported the emotional sensations they experienced in relation to their job. There was a clear aura of excitement, one that was most evident when they were reflecting on these high-risk experiences or when even mentioning men with high-profile cases that were or had been held in their custody.

In medium and lower security facilities, in which the emergency response tactics were less common (i.e., where incidents were rarely daily occurrences and codes tended not to be called multiple times a day), some interviewees would ask if I had heard about incidents that had occurred while I was onsite interviewing or had seen them "suited up" in protective gear earlier in the day (preparing to use force to end a situation), events that left an undeniable energy, neither positive nor negative, in the atmosphere. In detention centres and maximum security units, the energy was a mix of anticipation, excitement, and quasi-annoyance – incidents were too constant – while in less-secure facilities, the energy was more limited to anticipation and, for some, excitement. Overall, however, some officers' experiences appeared to be laced with emotions; their occupational trajectory might place them in harm's way, but they live and relive the emotionality provided by their experiences when telling stories about such incidents. The desire to discuss these dangerous encounters, often in significant detail, and the animation with which they did so, evidences not only these officers' pride in their work, but also the excitement some experience in relation to real or perceived high-risk activities on the job.

Further constituting a second objectively defined edge is how correctional officers' obligatory occupational practices cross the boundary between criminal action and heroism, further creating new emotional sensations. Correctional officer accounts here reveal that the practices one *must* perform (e.g., cell extractions, responding to prisoner non-compliance) would be viewed as criminal in a different context. As noted earlier, A correctional officer, under justified conditions as per policy and protocol, can use force that results in bodily injury, and yet in an alternate situation, outside the prison context, the same behaviour could result in criminal charges (e.g., for assault). As well, the occupational practices officers must engage in, such as removing personal property from a cell – an act paralleling theft – and reading prisoners' mail – in free society, constituting an illegal act – among others, can represent prohibited, and even criminal, practices in society that are legitimized when officers are on duty. Officers, then, constitute a second objective edge as they are empowered to use prohibited actions – in essence breaching the Criminal Code – in a legal and expected fashion when on duty. Interestingly, failing to perform such duties would be a violation of their occupational responsibility and would therefore subject them to reprimand. They invade a prisoner's private realm in a scenario prone to escalation that is laced with emotional sensations derived from risk-taking, and always obligatory, behaviours. Moreover, correctional officers are subject to disciplinary action, as journalist Donovan Vincent (2014) reported, after reviewing documents obtained under the Canadian Access to Information Act, finding that "the number of penalties received by guards working in this country's 43 federal institutions soared from 47 in 2009–2010 to 337 in 2012–13." Edgework is clearly highlighted in this case, in that officers navigate the boundaries of what is "just" when acting in ways that in another context could land them in prison.

Correctional officers thus navigate the space between normative living (i.e., that of law-abiding citizens in the community) and that reserved for deviant rule-breakers (e.g., prisoners). Living in this occupational space provides each officer with the opportunity to negotiate the *edge* by becoming engaged with perceived risk without crossing the line (i.e., they remain law abiders) (see Lyng & Matthews, 2007). They navigate concerns and excitement about potential threats while trying to remain cognizant of their greater public image and gender position; being scared is inappropriate. Edgework, for these officers, also plays a role in identity construction.

Empowered Edgeworkers

Perceptions of the risk and danger underlying the correctional officer role were made visible in select officers' descriptions of the prisoners in their charge – specifically the more negative descriptions. Officers who vocalized more adverse views of prisoners linked negative characteristics, such as being untrustworthy and manipulative, with prisoners' identities. To exemplify, one officer reported that "inmates take advantage of correctional officers that try to 'save' them," while another explained that prisoners have too many privileges in prison given the "crimes they commit." These excerpts demonstrate the select negative views, and even the lack of sympathy, that some correctional officers hold toward prisoners. This was most notable in reference to repeat "offenders," whose life choices, some officers felt, ensured they cycled through the "revolving door" of prison. Aside from some officers describing these prisoners as men who "should be in jail," these prisoners were also thought to lack remorse and pose an undisputable threat to society. Such views of prisoners allow these officers to affirm their empowered position over prisoners, which they can assert in encounters when they feel necessary. Moreover, this further reveals inherent tensions embedded in the "us" versus "them" dichotomy that too often underpins the penal system – staff and prisoners are in many ways pitted against one another rather than together being oriented toward "rehabilitation." In this sense, the dichotomy reflects the general cultural critique of those who "do bad things" and society's ambiguous views on what to do with the "correctional system" or the "penal system": is the objective to rehabilitate or penalize? Nonetheless, having negative views of prisoners can further inform officers' perceptions, and thus their presentations, of the "dangers" shaping their occupational role. This, in turn, intensifies the object boundary of the edge.

In discussing "dangerous" prisoners, officers create a more profound edge *and* expose potential vulnerability. Cautioning about prisoners (or talking about them within the context of risk), then, serves the latent function of highlighting their self-perceived "weaknesses" or "inferiorities," the nuanced realities shaping correctional officers' vulnerabilities, which may intensify in direct encounters with prisoners thought to be engaging in misconduct. To counteract the potential for this experience of vulnerability, some officers presented authoritatively, and select others spoke of how they would inflict their own punishment (e.g., retribution) on prisoners when outside of the camera's view:

> Say somebody wants to be a little prick and stuff like that and then you got
> to suit up for him. Well, once in a while, there might be a little punch in
> the ribs, just to show them we're boss and you're not going to fuck around
> every day.

This excerpt reveals how the decision to exert and then report such exertions of power is a strategy some officers use to claim their superiority while suppressing any feelings of vulnerability, vulnerabilities that are arguably discouraged and unacceptable for any occupational edgeworker. In this way, correctional officers solidify the risky nature of their occupation and, simultaneously, offer an overt performance of their power that is presented as a necessary aspect their job – representing the antithesis of their perceptions of prisoners. For example, a correctional officer must be intelligent and able to protect himself and his colleagues from the demands, ploys, and manipulations of prisoners. To further demonstrate their status, some correctional officers interviewed had established a subtle confidence in themselves that indicated that any potential source of vulnerability, like feeling unable to offer protection, was negligible in its effect. These officers did not feel prisoners posed a threat, and they claimed to be able to "see through" manipulation, expressing comfort in their occupational position. Some also asserted a confidence founded in their occupational responsibilities to the men in their custody – the prisoners – and to society more generally. This confidence was visible in their recognition of each prisoner's individuality. As mentioned in chapter 3, prisoners were not homogenously perceived as "bad people at heart"; rather, they were viewed by some officers as men who had made "mistakes," while some were described as "unlucky" or "broken," and others had reportedly struggled to change but lived with "bad circumstances" or without "positive opportunities." To this end, some correctional officers suggested a vocational need to be "fair and consistent with inmates" and to care, because only by caring could they do their job and aid a prisoner.

These men expressed their status by presenting themselves as able to change prisoners. As discussed above, and as put forth by Lyng and Matthew (2007), men participating in male-dominated activities (generalized here to include occupations) can, and do, express femininity. Correctional officers, via their positive perceptions of, and work "caring" for, prisoners, express more emotive traits, which are culturally read as representative of femininities, alongside their masculinity; they express compassion, warmth, or understanding toward prisoners – albeit while still viewing them as "dangerous men" – and thus reaffirm their strength, fearlessness, courage, maturity, professionalism, and intellect. They positively affirm their status through their occupational presentation – as protectors, in control and confident. And they achieve their position by conquering their vulnerabilities and taking control – most evidently when they are toeing the edge.

These officers, in contrast to those who told stories of on-duty dramas and dangerous prisoners, did not strive to prove their dominance or status. Although aware that some prisoners had committed disturbing crimes, they did not focus on these men to intensify the perceived riskiness of their occupation. Instead, they elected not to learn about these prisoners' crimes in order to protect against a tendency to treat any prisoner differently from another: "I never check their file so that I [do] not judge the prisoners." These men were quick to state that they did not determine a prisoner's, or enforce any personal, punishment – that was "the judge's responsibility." They revealed their power through their self-confidence – they could handle themselves – which enabled them to pity rather than glamorize criminality or be intimidated by prisoners. The nature of edgework for these officers was affirmed by how they presented the occupation as requiring heroic acts of all varieties, from enforcement to caring.

Conclusions

In reflecting on Miller's (1991) critique of edgework as being empirically based on white male pursuits and, as such, located within patriarchal understandings, in this chapter I consider the role of correctional officers (a white-male-dominated occupation; see appendices) in largely maximum security classified, adult men's prison facilities. As edgeworkers within a self-identified population of white officers, these men revealed the riskiness of their occupation, the objective edges they negotiated, and the strategies they employed to achieve or affirm their status or position within the institution. Officers could and did express qualities culturally read as feminine alongside or even instead of masculinities, yet these "feminine" qualities were presented such that each furthered a position of empowerment over prisoners. Correctional officers, in their views of the occupation itself, including how they understood their responsibilities and described their obligations – to society, their colleagues, and the prisoners – revealed the existence of a primary and secondary *edge* to be negotiated.

Interviewees described their public duty to protect civilians from offenders and to protect offenders from each other by highlighting the *dangerous* nature of prisoners – how the nature of their occupation opened them up to diverse risks. In doing so, they further intensified the riskiness of their occupation. These officers created a primary edge located in any on-duty encounter in light of the constant possibility that interactions could escalate into altercations. Per Lyng (2005), it is the objective nature of risk in edgework that clarifies why edgework is alluring for participants; the encounter with an objectivity of consequential edges in edgework can be a powerful experience with lasting emotional responses, evidenced among the correctional officers in the stories they told, videos they showed, and photos they presented. For officers, being called to respond to an escalating situation among prisoners, whether a riot or an irate prisoner, is the objective encountering of this edge – the moment of threat, encountered intentionality or unintentionality, in which outcomes are unpredictable despite all precautions taken. Moreover, perceptions of the occupation are structured by a desire to engage in risk-taking behaviours, a way to experience deviance while taking a "moral" high road.

Risk, in actuality, is recognized as an expected and natural occupational hazard, one intensified by the complexities of the correctional officer's job requirements; as such, it is a representation of occupational edgework. Interviewees revealed their empowered position in their construction of the riskiness of their edgework – in their presentation when bordering the edge – which was always structured within the hyper-masculine context of the prison environment. For example, they defined their role as officers as necessitating characteristics such as being authoritative, assertive, and powerful, while also being laced with heroic undertones, as they helped to "change" prisoners. Stereotypical feminine characterizations such as "caring" and "helping" were

reframed as valued skills for officers, skills that simultaneously characterized their dominance. Traits culturally read as feminine were again
redefined as masculine realities and purchased into by officers. Further, arguably controversial behaviours were reconstituted as acceptable in the prison environment, where objectively defined edges are
created.

Conclusion

He was a big, big guy. And we caught him [acting inappropriately] ... and she [a female correctional officer] pulled this guy out of his cell at night time, which was a no-no ... He was about six foot two and he had no shirt on and he was built. And this guy here was, like, you could see him shaking. And I thought, "oh my God ... him and I are going to fight. And there's probably not a good chance for me here 'cause he's a big dude." But, he didn't. He chilled out and went back to his cell. That was probably one of the most, the scaredest I've ever been ... 'cause, I mean, he's capable of murdering and we knew that, we knew that he was guilty.

– Anonymous male correctional officer working on
a male unit with a female partner

In the Canadian provincial and territorial correctional systems, correctional officers are responsible for ensuring the safety and well-being of the prisoners in their custody – and for doing so without prejudice or discrimination. Their occupational responsibilities are largely contradictory in that they must "provide for" prisoners in a controlled space, while simultaneously navigating the risk posed by prisoners to staff and to their fellow prisoners, as well as to society more generally (Cornelius, 2010; Klofas & Toch, 1982). For example, the Correctional Service Canada officer job profile explicitly states that employed officers are to encourage and assist prisoners in becoming "law-abiding citizens" by "monitoring, supervising, and interacting with" them (Correctional Service Canada, 2012c). The words of correctional officers interviewed, however, suggest this is not necessarily possible within the confines of their provincial and territorial occupational responsibilities as understood in the current prison structures. As such, my aim in this book is largely to put forth how correctional officers understand their occupational responsibilities, the prisoners in their custody, and their own lived experiences in light of their occupation, gender, and the gender of those in their custody.

History has demonstrated that prisons, in Canada and even internationally, have been designed with largely punitive intentions (even disturbingly so), rather than prisoner "rehabilitation" – they are arguably punitive in nature, even when created with conditions of penitence in mind (Gallo & Ruggiero, 1991). Indeed, to have a prison environment that is truly geared toward prisoner "rehabilitation," there is an undeniable need for citizens to want to invest in prisoners and prisons; to ask government to spend public funds to improve conditions of confinement and available programming for prisoners. Until this time, in modern society, the need for a rehabilitative penal environment will continue to be recognized by prison scholars, yet the organization and structure of prisons will remain criticized as generally running contrary to this rehabilitative intention, despite correctional officers being designated as "peace officers" (Correctional Service Canada, 1992).

This concluding chapter serves two important functions. It allows me to conclude this book by, first, offering a summation of my main points and the central objectives of this book. One objective has been to bring insight to the latent and manifest essence of gender in shaping how an individual chooses to act as well as self-present when serving as a correctional officer, both positively and negatively – recognizing that gender is shaped by and shapes identity, life experience, opportunities, and contextual factors. Second, this book has been aimed at unpacking, at the individual and structural levels, how correctional officers' perceptions, attitudes, and beliefs about their occupational responsibilities and toward prisoners influence their work practices. The other principal objective has been to present some of the realities that shape working in provincial and territorial closed-custody spaces, including, more specifically, the experiences of both male and female officers working with male and female prisoner populations. In doing so, I have strived with this research to inform readers about prisons and prison work, and to do so despite changes in correctional work – often accompanying changes in legislation, prison policy, and practice – as there remains a pervasive and omnipresent potentiality of risk that shapes carceral work experiences. Correctional services remains the area of justice that can change most with political change and pressures, for better or worse, impacting both prisoners and staff.

Perhaps more importantly, though, I use this conclusion as an opportunity to provide a possible vision of the future of provincial and territorial prison work, one abstracted from the empirical analysis presented here. I contend that the current political climate, which is shaped by advocacy for new penal policies and practices – such as the almost forty-year effort at the federal and later provincial levels to promote direct or dynamic security within the institutions, alongside still increasing incarceration rates – may imply that Canadians must be cautious: as a nation we seem to be slowly losing the battle against punitive practices.

I begin this closing chapter with a final discussion of risk and gender in relations to correctional work. Next, I speak to the orientations of correctional officers toward prisoners and the factors shaping such orientations. I theorize the need for a therapeutic (or working) alliance between officers and prisoners, yet also acknowledge the factors hindering the development of this alliance. Finally, I present some limitations of the current work and suggest future directions before concluding the book with some more general reflections.

Risk, Gender, and Prison Work

Prison work, like contemporary society more generally, is shaped by calculable yet unpredictable and unfamiliar risk – it is a fluid and flexible process that includes personal insecurity and unpredictability (Beck, 2002). This risk, a result of development, globalization, and the consequential disbanding of traditions, norms, and values, weakens previously static structures of gender and class (Beck, 1992; Giddens, 1990), both in society and prison. Within regimes of risk are systems designed to prosecute, punish, and confine citizens (i.e., the system of justice), systems that discipline *and* protect citizens from potential threat if people practise conformity to rules (i.e., laws) (Hannah-Moffat & O'Malley, 2007). Rule-breakers, to be held accountable for their violations, must be punished accordingly. If the sanctioned punishment includes confinement, these individuals are then placed under the supervision of correctional officers (Hannah-Moffat & O'Malley, 2007). Taking from Hannah-Moffat's explanation (1999, p. 89) of risk as "linked to a wide range of strategies and techniques aimed at governing offenders as well as the wider law-abiding population," and the fact that the "impact and meaning of risk is often contingent upon the objective of governing," it can be understood that how correctional officers mitigate the risk tied to their occupational realities is very much a process of adapting to risk that can be either stable or fluid, consistent or unpredictable, and grave or comforting. Hannah-Moffat (2004a, 2004b) later put forth that how risk is managed, which is often tied to seemingly objective categories that in actuality are based on actuarial – not personalized – data about prisoners, along with personally acquired knowledge of these risks, structures how individuals choose to act (i.e., their agency). Although this was in reference to the "offender," her words also describe the experiences of correctional officers, whose actions, too, are shaped, at least in part, by prison structures and the risk classification of the prisoner, unit, and facility. In this sense, officers, just like prisoners, become responsible for how they manage their self and risk, which is a gendered, culturally specific, and subjective process. Of course, such practices are heavily limited in terms of how a correctional officer can engage within the confines of prison work, yet may still be carefully scrutinized by the governing bodies or authorities. Gendered understandings, it should be noted, also shape edgework more broadly, and within the occupational structures of correctional services.

My intention here was simply to start the processes of filling the lacuna in scholarly and qualitative knowledge about how gender influences officers' attitudes toward prisoners of diverse genders. For example, how Cook (2012) found significant differences in the attitudes of male and female officers when it came to victim blaming and questioning the credibility of prisoners – not a surprising finding, given the structural, cultural, and other differences between male and female prisons. Indeed, very few researchers have examined officer gender outside of specific circumstances or qualitatively (e.g., Crewe, 2006; Easley, 1990), rather than using gender as an independent variable in statistical analyses.

Correctional Work: Perspectives and Attitudes toward Prisoners

The humane element of prison is always arguable to an extent, as some prisons maintain a strict, heavily monitored, and controlling orientation toward prisoners, while others are more "welfare-oriented" (Crewe & Liebling, 2012; Garland, 1985; Pratt, 2008a). Underlying these variations, it has been suggested, are practitioners and policymakers' orientations to corrections. Such orientations provide insights into the penal culture among correctional professionals that then becomes reflected in policy and in the penal environment (Cavadino & Dignan, 2006; Pratt, 2008a) – further impacting the persons in officers' custody by shaping the conditions of daily living (see Cavadino & Dignan, 2006; Crewe & Liebling, 2012; Pratt, 2008b). It is under the governance of correctional officers in direct contact with prisoners that the behavioural conditions and formal regulations of the prison environment come to be developed. As previously noted (see chapter 1), some scholars have investigated or worked to create a typology outlining the diverse orientations of correctional officers (e.g., Allaire & Firsirotu, 1984; Farkas, 2000; Kaufman, 1988; Klofas & Toch, 1982; Ricciardelli, 2016a).

Many correctional officers, certainly the overwhelming majority in my sample, align their values to some degree with liberal-humanitarian positioning. Of course, this is more so the case for some officers, in comparison to the extent of the orientation presented by other officers, but it has been found to be optimal for officer-prisoner relationships and the prison atmosphere more generally (Crewe & Liebling, 2011). The applied practise of liberal-humanitarian values, however, is at least partially inhibited in different prison environments, due to the prisoner code, institutional structures, and other tensions. The few officers with more negative orientations toward prisoners may tarnish the reputations of all officers, and they can also create a negative atmosphere on or across units. Interactions with said officers create tensions and concerns for other officers on their shift, who must mitigate the tensions and discontent caused by these more negative attitudes and behaviours, further compromising their sense of safety. The fact that some officers have more negative orientations is not remarkable when we recall that officers' attitudes, and thus behaviours, are further impacted by the unpredictability, uncertainty, and potential for violence in their occupational space (e.g., Lahm, 2009a, 2009b; Lambert et al., 2009; Lambert et al., 2010); indeed, officers are "also serving time."

Such knowledge of officer perspectives can only be complemented by more knowledge about the views that prisoners hold of correctional officers. Knowledge of these, perhaps juxtaposing, views are fundamental for understanding the underlying dynamics in the penal environment. The challenges inherent to "rehabilitative" practices in corrections, specifically, in developing a working alliance between officers and prisoners that assist with post-incarceration reintegration and creating trust between prisoners and authority figures (e.g., correctional officers and other correctional staff) can be better understood with greater bidirectional insight into these perspectives.

Indeed, nearly four decades ago Jurik (1985) argued that "rehabilitative" programming for prisoners is more successful when officers hold positive attitudes toward prisoners. The fact that not all officers hold such positive attitudes or are recognized as doing so by the prisoners further hinders the development of trust and any belief in the assistance officers can provide – officers being the very persons whose responsibility it is to protect prisoners in their care. Whatever the source of officers' attitudes, these attitudes have been described as a fundamental factor in the cultivation and perpetuation of criminal behaviours among those who are incarcerated (e.g., Chang & Zastrow, 1976; Guenther & Guenther, 1974; Jackson & Ammen, 1996; Simourd, 1997). Creating more opportunities for prisoners and officers to interact, such as movements toward dynamic or direct supervision (also referred to as open custody), is one way that officer attitudes toward prisoners (and prisoner attitudes toward officers) could be positively affected. Increased officer-prisoner interactions can help officers bulid relationships with, and thus, perhaps, provide support to, prisoners. Such movements represent a strategy aimed at buliding working alliances, which are deemed central to successful communication (Horvath & Marx, 1991; Horvath & Symonds, 1991) between prisoners and correctional officers. The principles underlying working alliances – also referred to as therapeutic alliances – are largely structured to reflect effective *and* empirically validated strategies of intervention intentioned to enhance the potentiality of prisoner reintegration.[1] This focus on reintegration is tied to the fact that the working or therapeutic alliance has received attention in the community correctional literature but significantly less in prison scholarship.

In 2004, Dowden and Andrews clarified that only with open, warm, and enthusiastic communication between service providers and service recipients can the interpersonal persuasion exercised by staff be maximized. Applying their work to the prison context, the problem arises when the willingness of prisoners to go to correctional officers for emotional support and assistance is found to be hampered in prisons, at least among male prisoners. Specifically, Hobbs and Greg (2000) used data from 187 prisoners in a male maximum security facility to find that prisoners were more willing to seek practical help rather than emotional support from officers, and this was consistently found despite the history of the prisoner (e.g., those with a history of self-harm versus those without). Barriers to alliance building are thus particularly salient in men's prisons. Just as Sykes (1958) in his classic study outlined the five tenets of a "prisoner code" that structures prison conduct and enforces the rules of prison living, others also contended that a conduct code shapes officers' behaviours. Although a conduct code did not clearly emerge across my interviewees, Griffiths (2010) described a code that emphasizes officers protecting each other, refraining from becoming friendly with prisoners, and never talking behind the backs of their colleagues. Interviewees in my sample, instead, spoke about the officer they preferred to work with, rather than a conduct code, describing this officer as someone who would be there if an incident were to arise, did not disclose personal information to the prisoners, and was consistent in their actions. However, interviewees also spoke openly about their colleagues who did not behave in such manners. Thus, the question of whether a clearly tenable conduct code exists among officers, beyond the formal occupational guidelines within each provincial and territorial penal system, requires additional investigation. What is apparent, however, is that both officers and male prisoners refrain from interacting with each other, a fact that makes relationship building between prisoners and officers – at least in male units – rather difficult, if not seemingly impossible.

In the realm of programs, those that are not sustained through a working alliance can still be effective, but the success of programming outcomes can always be improved with strong relationships between the service provider – too often the correctional officer in provincial and territorial facilities – and prisoner. Prison officials view "rehabilitative" programming or treatment as indispensable for institutional management because such programming, ideally, reduces prisoner idleness and dissatisfaction, and assists prisoners as they adjust to the realities of incarceration, while simultaneously providing an incentive to motivate good behaviour and communication between prisoners and staff (Cullen, Latessa, Burton, & Lombardo, 1993; Dilulio, 1987, 1991).

Recognizing the value of working alliances between prisoners and correctional staff is not a new suggestion, and presenting it as such would be disingenuous. However, it is both fair and appropriate to put forth that efforts aimed at creating opportunities for building such alliances have been less successful than hoped in penal spaces. Perhaps this is without surprise, since how can officers play a role in prisoner "rehabilitation" or future desistance from crime without the ability to consistently interact and build relationships with those in their custody? How are officers to decrease the uncertainty and unpredictable nature of correctional work without insight into the persons in their custody? Knowing the prisoners as individuals rather than as part of a collective is crucial to such insight, as the latter would suggest the potentiality for a seemingly us-versus-them mentality. As such, enabling the creation of a respectful, open, and communicative relationship between prisoners and officers should provide an opportunity for correctional officers to effectively employ "rehabilitative" oriented penal practices. To this end, efforts to change the penal environment into a more communicative and open space remain necessary areas of focus.

Limitations

First, I will reiterate that the interviews were lengthy, and beyond the interviews, I spent days and nights in prisons with the different officers. I passed time in control rooms and bubbles. I visited different areas of facilities, and spent time in staff rooms and in shared spaces, or just hung out for meals. This allowed me the opportunity to get to know many of the different officers and exchange stories in more informal settings. Although these stories are not included in the data, they did provide important context and information that helped me better understand correctional officers' descriptions of their occupational work. In the end, I am very grateful to the many officers who were so welcoming and willing to share their stories. My hope is that the insight they have provided also helps with improving their working conditions in Canada and perhaps even beyond. Thus, while recognizing that, as with any research, there are some limitations in this study, I propose that the benefits and insight provided by this research far outweigh any limitations.

Like any research project, then, there are limitations in the data and gaps in knowledge that can only be filled with more interviews and follow-up interviews, more analyses, policy reviews, analyses of training criteria across provinces and territories, and more time spent writing and in the field. Nonetheless, a few central limitations that lace the current research project include, first, that the point of my research was not to explain why prisons exist in our society or if they should continue to exist. Thus, I chose not to speak to the history of prisons or correctional work, or include scholarship on the abolition or future of the prison in any form. Instead, I have provided insight into the experiences of officers in provincial and territorial prisons as they currently exist, and I explicitly chose not to compare correctional work across provinces and territories or the federal prison system. This choice was founded in multiple reasons, most importantly the need to maintain the confidentiality and anonymity of the institutions and people participating in this study.

Consistent with any interview-based study, interviewees may struggle with recall, and I cannot say for certain if any officers were hesitant to reveal any aspect of their work experiences for whatever reason. While the semi-structured and open-ended nature of the interview process helped to safeguard against this possibility, there is no way to know if an interviewee refrained from disclosing something of relevance. The number of men and women interviewed, the many places they had worked, and their years of experience gives me some confidence that the sample puts forth a fair understanding of correctional officer experiences. Yet, like all qualitative research, caution is advised when considering the representativeness of the findings or when generalizing from them.

Finally, it must always be recognized that the perspectives of prisoners were not the basis of this inquiry. The focus instead was on how the officers perceived themselves, their colleagues, and the prisoners in their care, how they viewed their occupational role, and what such interpretations can reveal about their work experiences. Thus, while another limitation is that prisoners were not interviewed for this study, that is an area of inquiry reserved for future study.

Future Directions

The men and women who shared their stories with me contributed to creating more knowledge about provincial and territorial prison work experiences. There remains a need for future researchers to continue to explore the realities of correctional work more directly across provinces and territories and comparatively within the federal system. Moreover, attention must be directed toward unpacking diversities in the training that correctional officers receive, which varies across provinces, territories, and even institutions. Training can thus differ depending on when or where an officer started in their corrections-related position, and in light of their prior employment experiences and education, as well as due to other factors. It can involve classes, touch on practical and/ or applied aspects, and may or may not be done "in-house." Further, in some provinces and territories, candidates are paid or compensated for their training, while in others they are not. Given the variations in training, not to mention in curriculum (involving written, lecture, and demonstrative content), and the profound impact that training can have on how correctional officers approach their occupational work, there is a need for future researchers to focus on how training impacts officer orientations to their work and to prisoners. Comparative work in this area, across jurisdictions that have variations in their training practices and curriculum, might lend invaluable insight into best training practices and evidence-based approaches in ways that can better optimize outcomes. Such a research focus was outside of the scope of the current project, where access to training curriculum and practices (e.g., written materials, classes, lectures, testing, and "demonstrative" aspects) was entirely random (i.e., unintended and unplanned).

Another limitation stems from the fact that what constitutes successful "prison work" is nearly impossible to operationalize. In the short term, many correctional officers described a shift without incident as a "good day" – a success. However, longer-term understandings of "success" are more ambiguous, and could be measured in a variety of different ways, with some centring on the actions of the officers or of the prisoners, or on systemic/institutional factors. For example, success can be found in a reduction of incidents on a unit, in reduced numbers of persons being incarcerated, in a reduction in the number of persons returning to prison post release (increases in desistance from crime), or in process-oriented changes that reduce the overall need for correctional officers. Thus, an additional recommendation for future researchers is to unpack how officers operationalize success – occupational success or being successful at work – and in what circumstances they feel successful.

Perhaps such an area of inquiry would lend itself to an analysis of how correctional work can be better understood by citizens as a care-based profession.

Liberal-humanitarian values can and do complement understandings of correctional work as a care-based profession. Corrections, however, has yet to be recognized or grouped with nursing, teaching, or even social work as an equivalent "care" or "assistance" oriented occupation. The contradiction evident within the occupation of correctional officer – the need to care, while also supervising and applying consequences – is also inherent to professions like teaching and nursing. Across these occupations, professionals must supervise, monitor, and interact with their charges, while also enforcing negative sanctions where needed (e.g., a misbehaving child goes to the principal's office, while a prisoner may be administratively segregated). Yet, the tie between nursing, teaching, and other such professions and correctional services remains largely unnoticed by citizens and some scholars. Given that many officers strive toward the positive treatment of prisoners and to recognize each individual's unique identity and self-worth, these officers are deserving and should be awarded status and respect similar to that experienced by others in care-oriented positions. Moreover, such an interpretation of the correctional officer occupation (i.e., as a form of care-based work) would create a space for examinations of caretaker burnout, fatigue, and other related occupational stress injuries among correctional employees. Reflecting once more on research directed toward officer training, it would be pertinent to examine and appropriate – where empirical evidence supports positive outcomes – diverse training, practices, or policies from other care-oriented occupations that could serve correctional officers well in their occupational pursuits.

Finally, I ask: How can punitive orientations toward prisoners or correctional work more generally be eliminated among officers? Research that focuses on the views officers hold of prisoners *prior* to their employment in corrections, with the inclusion of follow-up interviews after training, might help unpack how correctional work impacts officers over time. Conducting a longitudinal study with additional intermittent interviews during officers' probationary period and across years of work experience – noting any changes in the aforementioned views – might shed light on how orientations develop with occupational experience, and thus help to eliminate or reduce punitive orientations among officers. Without more liberal-humanitarian orientations toward prisoners, the possibility for any semblance of a working alliance to develop between prisoners and officers is rather non-existent. Moreover, a longitudinal study of this type would provide needed insight into how the occupation itself may affect officers over time, which is invaluable knowledge for helping to inform processes aimed at improving the well-being of people working and living in prison.

Another factor likely to impact the development of more negative orientations to prisoners is officers' stress levels. Officers need to be trained to recognize if or when they become stressed or negative on the job, and at these times perhaps officers should be moved into positions with more limited contact with prisoners (e.g., in control rooms). Such movements, however, should not be viewed as "failures" or "demotions," but instead must be recognized as occupational needs that are bound to arise given the actualities of this, and any, stressful occupation. Correctional work is undeniably stressful. Recently, Carleton and colleagues, in their study of the prevalence of mental disorders among public-safety personnel, found that correctional employees – largely employed by Correctional Service Canada – reported symptoms consistent with post-traumatic stress disorder at a frequency of 29.1 per cent, while 31.1 per cent reported symptoms consistent with major depressive disorder, 23.6 per cent reported symptoms of generalized anxiety disorder, and 54.6 per cent had symptoms of one major mental disorder. It should be noted that the sample was not only made up of correctional officers. Instead, the sample included correctional staff working in administrative roles, as well as community and institutional roles. Thus, it can be hypothesized rather soundly that correctional officers, particularly those in correctional centres with remand prisoners, will report high levels of mental disorders. Additional research looking specifically at the mental health and well-being of correctional officers working federally, provincially, and territorially is thus necessary and encouraged.

Final Words

My intention across this book was to shed light on the realities of correctional work, specifically the work of correctional officers across genders employed in the Canadian provincial and territorial prison systems working with incarcerated individuals. The perspectives and words of officers shaped the pages, which reflect how orientations *and* attitudes toward the job and those in custody are interconnected yet also inform officer work experiences as well as prisoners lived experiences. The occupational role of correctional officers is conflicting, even contradictory, in its expectation and scope; officers are to support prisoner "rehabilitation" and yet uphold societal expectations of prisoner "accountability" by ensuring they experience deprivations and the "pains of imprisonment." Moreover, officer gender and prisoner gender, as well as the

hierarchical structure of prison management and positioning, shape
correctional officers' occupational role, responsibilities, and daily
experiences. As such, there is no singular "type" of correctional officer.
Officers are neither inherently "punitive" nor "caring" in nature; their
morals, ethics, and values vary, as do their person and priorities. Perhaps
such realities help account for Liebling's (2008) findings, enhancing
prior work by Skolnick (1966), that correctional officers continue to put
forth a "working personality" that reveals their responsibilities toward
public safety, yet which is shaped, Liebling suggests, by "cynicism and
pessimism, due to the hard-nosed nature of their work, to be suspicious,
conservative, macho, internally cohesive, and pragmatic" (p. 106).
Nonetheless, changes in prison culture, which often include variations
tied to institutional security classification or the level of occupational
autonomy held by an officer, provide insight into the extent to which
a correctional officer takes on their "working personality" – whatever it
may be (Liebling, 2008).

What is undeniable is that over time correctional work, including
experiences faced on the job and the prisoners encountered, shapes
and impacts officers. These occupational dynamics can create stress and
harm, and are riddled with risk that, at times, is posed, perceived, threatened, and/or experienced. The realities shaping correctional work are
vast, leaving officers to navigate different dynamics depending on the
population they hold in their custody. Like prisoners, correctional officers must learn to cope with the nuances of the prison environment in
order to survive in their occupational role – indeed, to survive their own
experience of "doing time."

The effects of these experiences on correctional officers in terms of
their well-being, expectations, occupational health, and safety requires
more attention and more research. Like prisoners, correctional officers
spend a large portion of their time in prison. They are affected by barriers to services, constrained by limited resources and policies, scrutinized
by colleagues, management, and the public, and often feel overburdened
with occupational responsibilities that, arguably, fall outside their job
description. Correctional officers are public safety personnel. They serve
the public by keeping "society" safe, yet they risk their own safety to do so.
They work within a mundane, yet tension-laced, environment – as tense
as any situation would be where adults are being involuntarily confined
as punishment for their transgressions. As such, I argue, should not their
work environment be prioritized when political or operational decisions
are being made about prisons and, more generally, criminal justice tied
to penality? Without a doubt, a movement toward making prison a more
humane environment would benefit all – prisoners, staff, and society.

Acknowledgments

Many persons and organization made possible the research on which this book is based.

Thanks must go, first and foremost, to the formerly federally incarcerated men who suggested I learn about the provincial and territorial correctional officer population. If not for those many lengthy conversations and exchanges I never would have expanded my research to include prison staff and those employed within the institutions. I cannot thank these men enough. They set me on a path on which I have spent years trying to navigate the space in which men and women both live and work, where human beings are in many ways posed against each other, yet also share experiences, vulnerabilities, and realities – some more connected than others. Indeed, I have seen prisoners whose relatives are officers working within the same facility (never unit); I have learned of officers serving in the institutions side by side, completely unaware that they both are veterans with a shared history too similar to be comprehendible but each kept private from the other – yet both aware of the veterans in their custody. Learning to navigate all these interrelationships may be difficult. I find it challenging to interpret intellectually. I also recognize that I, unlike prisoners or some employees, choose to do this work and be in this space. I can always "go home" and choose when or if to return.

I must also extend a heartfelt thank you to the many men and women whom I interviewed, spent time with, was welcomed by, and just hung out with over the course of this research. I was fortunate to meet many amazing people. It is in prisons, between interviews, that I was able to get new dance shoes for my eldest daughter, watch shows, eat meals, and just share a lot of laughs. I was included in tactical and classification meetings, was able to sit in control, different units, and see diverse facility designs. I was able to visit brand new institutions and old institutions that, in my view, should likely be historical museums, not functioning facilities. I had a lot of great conversations and have kept in touch with many inspiring people. I feel fortunate to be able to call some of these individuals friends. I appreciate each person's story. I hope that they, too, enjoyed sharing their story with me, and I look forward to seeing everyone again in the future.

I would like to thank the Social Sciences and Humanities Council of Canada (SSHRC) for funding the research through an Insight Development Grant awarded in 2011, as well as Memorial University for the (SSHRC) Vice President's Research Grant awarded in 2014.

I would like to thank the blind reviewers for their comprehensive reviews and attention to detail. I appreciate their reading of the original manuscript and willingness to give the revision a chance. I also would like to thank my colleague Dr. Huey, who assisted with the restructuring of the book after the revisions. Most of all, however, my thanks goes to my family, and especially my four amazing children – Sadie for being such a creative inspiration, Nate for his honesty, Johny for his uniqueness, and Paige for her uninhibited sense of justice and her belief in me. Paige has in many ways been a unique part of this journey, always accompanying me along the way. Writing this book has also served a therapeutic purpose: it was the manuscript I drafted while witnessing cancer take the life of a family member too soon and much too young. And, of course, a special thanks goes to Stephen, as without his seemingly everlasting support and belief in me, this project would not have been possible.

APPENDIX A: METHODOLOGY

Methods: Inclusion Criteria

The research I present in this book is restricted to experiences of male and female correctional officers working with adult male and female prisoners. I focus exclusively on adult prisoners because adult male and female prisoners are governed under the same Criminal Code *and* over-arching body of correctional legislation – the Correction and Community Release Act of 1992 – whereas youth in closed custody fall under a different legislation, the Youth Criminal Justice Act (Bala, Carrington, & Roberts, 2008). Thus, youth are sentenced under a different set of pro-cesses, and, in some provinces, youth custody and adult custody are governed by different ministries or departments (e.g., Department of Youth, Department of Child, Youth and Family Services for youth correc-tions versus Departments of Justice or Public Safety for adults). Youths in custody also follow different regulations in comparison to adults; they are to be single bunked, have more access to programming, and *must* attend school until they earn their high school diploma or its equivalent. Youth facilities are not as deprived of comforts as some adult institutions (e.g., youth may have gaming systems, activities, and sports) and youth have more visitation privileges. Thus, the experiences of officers working with youth are not comparable to those of officers working with adult prisoners.

The Correctional Officers

Between October 2011 and September 2014, I conducted interviews with over 130 correctional officers, either in person, or, for four interviews, by telephone, in different provinces and correctional facilities across the country. The first 100 of these interviews make up the data for this book.

Participant recruitment varied depending on whether or not the pro-vincial ministry was able to support the research project. Word-of-mouth recruitment was the primary means of participant recruitment; this was particularly effective when I was onsite (i.e., I became familiar with the prison staff and gained trust), but this also took place in the commu-nity among correctional officers who heard about the study from their colleagues (current or retired) and contacted the interviewer to partici-pate. Where there was ministerial support, an advertisement about the study and details about when the interviewer would be onsite (if avail-able) was circulated to all officers employed in the specific prison via the staff email LISTSERV. The sample, then, was purposive, yet included elements of both convenience and snowball sampling. All participation was voluntarily. It should be noted that participants increasingly came forward to participate as I spent time in each prison. The interest in participation was great enough that I was never able to speak to all interested participants within the limited time I was at each facility. Further, in provinces with supportive ministries of justice or public safety, after confirming approval and solidifying a research agreement, I was able to add an ethnographic component to my research by conducting interviews onsite with staff in participating facilities. Being onsite provided me with an opportunity to become familiar with different prison layouts, the general atmosphere on different shifts, and the dynamics on different units, in that I was able to reflect on differences across facilities, available services for prisoners, and staff areas, and learn how the different institutions functioned. I witnessed the intersection between conditions of confinement and conditions of employment.

Both prisoners and officers spend endless hours on units, which are often windowless, and have questionable air quality and diverse degrees of sanitization. Segregation units were observed to leave officers more detached from prisoners – they were often partitioned by a physical barrier (interacting through a slot in a door). The admission and holding units tended to require more direct contact between officers and prisoners, as they were busier, while female and male units, even in the *same* prison, were structurally different. For example, at the time when I was conducting interviews in one prison in Atlantic Canada that did not have direct supervision throughout the units, male units had a one-way floor-to- ceiling shatter-proof "glass wall" dividing the control bubble (i.e., the area in which officers observe prisoners) from the prisoner living area. The "glass wall" on the female unit, however, stopped halfway between the floor and ceiling, making officers accessible to prisoners at all times. Almost ironically, because there is only one women's unit in the facility, the unit is classified as maximum security, although the unit's structure is less secure than that of a unit housing men classified as minimum security in the same institution. The inherent problem here is that the physical structure and design of prisons should correspond to the safety and security classification of the prisoners, which does not hold true for incarcerated women.

Many provincial facilities are built as maximum security institutions, with high levels of surveillance and control. Maximum security prisons, especially newer facilities, are architecturally designed and internally upgraded to ensure the movements and activities of prisoners are monitored at all times. These facilities tend to have cameras in select cells and intercoms that allow for officers in the control bubble to listen to prisoners in their cells – offering staff unrestrained surveillance of prisoners.

In provincial and territorial facilities, the physical structure of a unit may not correspond to the security classification of those housed in it – the unit is designed as maximum security with restricted freedoms and heavy surveillance. Thus, to create the "illusion" of a less-secure unit that falls in line with the security requirements of prisoners with a minimum security classification, there may be "rewards" and incentives offered to prisoners (e.g., a coffee pot, or more time in the gym). Minimum security placement is often earned by following institutional rules and refraining from violence or misconduct. Prisoner classification is re-evaluated during classification meetings and is made more complex in larger facilities, where prisoners may have more unsettled disputes with other incarcerated persons from their time on the streets. The priority during classification is to ensure the safety of prisoners and staff by disambiguating a housing arrangement that does not provoke conflict between prisoners. The challenges with prisoner classification are systematic and rooted in the structure of prisons, which obligate prison staff to classify prisoners in ways recognized as suboptimal, even damaging, to prisoner rehabilitation and healing, but that are nonetheless required for safety within the current structure. Not surprisingly, researchers have found that when prisoners are classified, their needs, as determined through risk and need assessment, are neglected and safety concerns are prioritized (Farr, 2000; MacKenzie, 1989; MacKenzie, Posey, & Rapaport, 1988; Van Voorhis, 1993). This is a valid criticism tied to the indisputable complexities underlying prisoner classification.

The Interviews: The Process

Few officers – approximately 2 per cent of the sample – were retired or no longer working in corrections when interviewed. Nonetheless a similar process was used during all interviews. A semi-structured interview guide – a list of open-ended questions I constructed – was available during interviews, but was often only used as a sort of checklist to ensure that conversational paths included select topics. These five topics were gender experiences and understandings; orientation toward and interactions with prisoners; negotiations and constructions of safety, risk, and vulnerability; understandings of the occupational structure; and motivation for entering the field. The conversation tended to be determined by the interviewee because my objective was to hear what was on each participant's mind, what stood out in his or her experiences, and how he or she interpreted the correctional officer role. Although I rarely directed conversation, I did at points ask interviewees for clarification or for more detail.

The interviews were in depth and as such permit a more profound understanding of the realities that officers experience. On average, interviews were about an hour in duration, although some lasted up to three hours – the length of the interview depended on the talkativeness of the interviewee, their experiences, and the rapport we developed. Although confidentiality is maintained in the data and the interviewees are anonymous, when interviewing onsite, it was not possible to ensure participant anonymity because interviews were conducted on shift. This means that not only did another officer have to cover for the officer being interviewed, but we were also on camera, and thus who was where and when could be tracked through swipe cards and central control. Since dozens and dozens of people agreed to an interview in nearly every institution I visited (although as noted, time limitations left me unable to interview all willing officers), this did not seem to pose a problem. Informed consent was obtained before each interview, and the interviews ended with questions about demographics and employment history. Field notes were also recorded.

The Analyses

Each interview was conducted in English, digitally recorded, and then transcribed. Across the data, my desire was to reveal the trends – similarities and differences – across the experiences reported by correctional officers. To this end, interview transcripts were thematically coded, using an approach that pulls from Strauss and Corbin (1990). I used a rigorous process of data analysis that systematically allows conceptual themes to emerge from the data. The basis of this coding process is drawn from a strategy first illuminated by Glaser and Strauss (1967), who advised scholars to "use *any* materials bearing on [their] area that [they] can discover" when analyzing data (p. 169; emphasis in original). However, I furthered the process by using a *constructed approach* that is both driven by data and attentive to existing theory (Charmaz, 2006). As such, I approached the data with neither preconceived ideas of what themes would arise nor how the themes were to be theoretically analysed; instead themes emerged *from* the data. I also did not discard my own prior knowledge or learning.

I started this process by reading each transcript and assigning codes (consistent with Strauss and Corbin's open codes) to the sections of data that captured the emergent theme in question. Next, I reflected on the similarities and differences across the officers' diverse discussions, always looking for shared patterns, relationships, or reported experiences that constituted *central* organizing themes (consistent with Strauss and Corbin's axial coding). Central themes emerged when multiple respondents described similar perspectives, experiences, and understandings of a specific topic, while major recurrent themes were constituted by similarities in officers' experiences across participants. If few participants reported a specific experience, although it was invaluable as a lived reality and impactful for these individuals, the experience did not constitute an emergent theme and was removed from the analyses. Further, my primary concern was to maintain the context of every experience reported *and* to stay true to the voices of all those who were willing to share their stories. Direct quotes, however, have been edited for speech fillers and grammar to assist with flow and comprehensibility, although participants' vernacular, including the use of profanity and slang, remain untouched. All references to participants in the text have been fully anonymized; pseudonyms are used and different quotes on different topics – if coming from the same respondent – are not tied together with an identifier to further protect participant anonymity. The sheer number of interviewees and the removal of any identifiable information provides a safeguard to ensure findings cannot be tied back to any person.

APPENDIX B: SNAPSHOTS OF PROVINCIAL AND TERRITORIAL PRISON FACILITIES ACROSS CANADA

During the interviews, it became increasingly clear that occupational realities for correctional officers, including the rate of pay, employment structure, working conditions, and prison environment, vary greatly by province and territory and the exact penal facility in which one is employed. Although I did not undertake research in each of the provinces and territories, the importance of location to one's working environment was confirmed by interviewees, who, collectively, had worked in nearly every province and territory in Canada.

Within this appendix, I provide a "snapshot" of provincial and territorial prison systems in order to examine how they might vary across the country, and what these variations mean for the working lives of the officers interviewed.

Provincial and Territorial Corrections: Localized Realities

Newfoundland and Labrador

Newfoundland and Labrador is not home to any federal prisons, but there are five adult correctional facilities and two detention centres in the province (Statistics Canada, 2014a).[1] Further, in 2008, the province employed 232 correctional officers, of which 187 (81 per cent) were men and 45 (19 per cent) women, all overseen by a superintendent of prisons (Poirier, Brown, & Carlson, 2008). Of these employees, 151 held permanent positions and 81 casual positions, with more women employed in casual in comparison to permanent positions. Women made up 30 per cent of senior management and only 3 per cent of middle managers, and thus they were under-represented in Newfoundland and Labrador correctional services. Officers in the province are unionized (NAPE, Newfoundland and Labrador Association of Public and Private Employees) and their salaries, as of 1 November 2013, varied from $39,103 for a new recruit with less than six months experience to $63,203 for an officer with over three years of experience.

Nova Scotia

Nova Scotia is home to five provincial prisons at the time of writing, although a new facility, the Northeast Nova Scotia Correctional Facility, intended to replace the "aging" Antigonish and Cumberland facilities, is under construction near Priestville, Pictou County (this facility should be open and functioning as this book goes to press; Northeast Nova Scotia Correctional Facility; Priestville, Pictou County, 2013). Officers in the province are held to a "code of professional conduct" (see Correctional Services, 2007), and are unionized with salaries starting at $41,162 for entry-level positions. There are no casual employees.

New Brunswick

The Department of Public Safety is the governing body of provincial corrections in New Brunswick. Home to many federal prisons, the province also houses five provincial facilities, one of which confines adult female and youth prisoners. In 2014, 399 correctional officers worked across these facilities (New Brunswick Department of Public Safety, personal communication, 26 June 2014). Of these employees 267 (67 per cent) were full time, 28 (7 per cent) held permanent part-time positions (i.e., had job stability, however only worked part-time hours), 37 (9 per cent) were term employees, and 67 (17 per cent) were casual (i.e., lacked job stability or security) as of June 2014 (Department of Public Safety Community and Correctional Services, 2014). Provincial officers do not have a signed collective agreement at the time of writing and have some of the most precarious positions in terms of occupational security if the officer is employed as a casual.

Prince Edward Island

In Prince Edward Island there are two adult correctional facilities, one of which is dual-designated (i.e., houses both adults and youths), with a combined capacity of 132 beds for prisoners (Department of Environment, 2009). Although information was unavailable from the dual-designated facility, the Provincial Correctional Centre, in 2014, employed an estimated 67 correctional officers, of which 75 per cent ($n = 50$) were male and 25 per cent ($n = 17$) female. Of these officers, 52 held permanent positions (75 per cent were held by males) and 15 were employed in temporary or casual positions. Among senior management, 84 per cent were male and 16 per cent female (information provided from personal communication with staff, 12 November 2014).

Officers are required to either have a diploma in corrections, criminology, or child-and-youth care from a recognized community college, or a degree in the social sciences, along with a class-four driver's licence (Department of Environment, 2011). Correctional officers are part of a public-sector employees' union, and have starting salaries ranging from $19.24 to $21.85 an hour for casual employees in adult facilities. In 2013, officer salaries started around $37,920 (entry level) to $58,283 (upper level), according to the collective agreement. Among correctional staff, officers are paid less than nurses, social workers, and probation officers, and are within one dollar of the hourly wage of cooks and administrative staff (Roy, 2010).

Quebec

In Quebec, the 23 adult institutions are referred to as *detention facilities*, with each reportedly devoted to "ensur[ing] the safekeeping of these people while promoting reintegration" (Ministère de la Sécurité Publique, 2014). The facilities admit, on average, 40,000 adults annually, of which approximately half, as reported by the Ministry of Public Security of Quebec (Ministère de la Sécurité Publique), are remanded into custody. In 2012–13, 42,720 individuals were admitted, representing a 2.3 per cent increase since 2011–12 and an increase of 4.7 per cent since 2007–8 (Ministère de la Sécurité Publique, 2013). The ministry's published "prospective analysis of the prison population in detention facilities in Quebec from 2010–2011 to 2020–2021" projects a need to house an additional 612 to 1,884 prisoners (depending on the predictive model used) in the already overcrowded facilities over the next five years (Chene, 2013).

Available statistics from the census of 2006 report 5,250 persons working in federal and provincial prisons in Quebec. Women hold 33 per cent of the jobs – a proportion that has increased by 17 per cent since 1991 – and the majority of officers (54 per cent) are between 25 and 44 years of age (Correctional Service Canada, 2013a). Overall, 94 per cent of employees work full time and 6 per cent part time, with an average annual income of $50,871. Twenty per cent of officers also have a bachelor's degree and 53 per cent have a post-secondary degree (now a required accreditation for the occupational position) (Correctional Service Canada, 2013a). All correctional officers are unionized in the province.

Ontario

The large number of prisoners in Ontario are housed in, at the time of writing, twenty-six provincial adult correctional facilities that include correctional, treatment, and detention centres and jails (see Ontario Ministry of Community Safety and Corrections, 2010). Although data on the number of officers employed across these facilities is not easy to locate in public documents, they are part of the Ontario Public Service Employees Union, and entry-level officers earn an hourly wage of $24.02, with ample room for promotion and higher earning potential.

Manitoba

In Manitoba, there are seven adult facilities that purportedly offer prisoners vocational training, work experience, counselling, educational opportunities, and rehabilitation programs (see Manitoba Justice, 2015). Although data is limited, 1,152 adults were in provincial custody between 2008 and 2009, and these rates of incarceration increased 25 per cent in 2012–13 (Office of the Auditor General, 2014). Officers are part of the Manitoba Government and General Employees' Union, and, from March 2013 to February 2014, entry-level salaries were around $53,000 ($25 to $30 per hour).

Saskatchewan

In Saskatchewan, the Custody, Supervision and Rehabilitation Services Division is responsible for youth and adults in the provincial correctional system. The division tries to balance rehabilitation and supervision in correctional practice with the goal of encouraging "offenders to contribute positively to their communities" (Ministry of Justice, 2012). The Saskatchewan Ministry of Justice reports that, at any given time, approximately 1,200 adults are held in one of the 11 adult correctional facilities in the province (see Ministry of Justice, 2012, "frequently asked questions"). Some of these facilities are classified as multi-level, others as "Camp" – a Saskatchewan-specific official label (it is used unofficially in many provinces) for minimum security correctional facilities. Although data across prisons is not available, through telephone communication on 9 November 2014, I learned that the Prince Albert Correctional Centre employs 220 permanent and 80 part-time officers, who are held to a "code of professional conduct" and "code of professional ethics" (Ministry of Justice, 2012), and that all officers are members of the Saskatchewan General Employees Union.

Alberta

In Alberta, the Correctional Service Division is responsible for the 9 adult correctional centres, one of which is operated by an Indigenous organization, while another is the $580 million Edmonton Remand Centre that opened in April 2013.[2] These 9 facilities house prisoners in remand custody, those who are provincially sentenced, or federal prisoners that are detained by Correctional Service Canada or the Canada Boarder Services Agency (Alberta Justice and Solicitor General, 2014a). The technological innovations in the Edmonton Remand Centre include 60 public video visitation booths that can be used for video conferencing to connect prisoners with their friends and family (Alberta Justice and Solicitor General, 2014c).

The division reports that between 2005–6 and 2009–10, the average daily prisoner population increased by 22.5 per cent – although Indigenous admissions remained relatively unchanged, making up approximately 35.6 per cent of prisoners (Alberta Justice and Solicitor General, 2014b). Further, the adult custody division of corrections employs 2,174 correctional officers, of whom 1,480 are male versus 694 females. Officers are part of the Alberta Union of Provincial Employees, and their entry-level salaries are among the highest in the country, starting around $49,000, with a typical salary range between $49,000 and $61,000 (Alberta Justice and Solicitor General, 2014d).

British Columbia

British Columbia is, at the time of writing, home to nine adult provincial correctional facilities that are currently undergoing a $185 billion capital expansion, with future projects approved. The prisoner population has also increased 40 per cent since 2002 (Ministry of Justice, 2014).

The British Columbia Ministry of Justice reports that adult corrections employs 1,568 people across its facilities, of which 55 per cent are male and 45 per cent female; this number includes people working in correctional facilities, community corrections, and corporate program divisions (Ministry of Justice, 2013b). The chain of command in the adult custody division places correctional officers at the very bottom of the hierarchy, with officers reporting to the correctional supervisor, who then reports to the assistant deputy warden, deputy warden, warden, deputy provincial director, and, at the top of the hierarchy, the provincial director (Ministry of Justice, 2013a). Officers are unionized and entry-level salaries begin around $41,000 to $48,000, according to the collective agreement.

The Yukon

The Community and Correctional Services Branch of the Department of Justice oversees the sole adult correctional facility, the Whitehouse Correctional Centre, in the Yukon. The facility houses both federal and provincial prisoners – including those who are on remand, on immigration holds, found not criminally responsible by order of the Yukon Review Board, or on parole violations (Department of Justice, 2014). It opened in March 2012, is classified as a maximum security facility with special handling units and a healing room, and has the capacity to hold 190 prisoners (Department of Justice, 2013b). Officers in the Yukon must have at least a grade 12 education, and preferably have the qualification training offered at Yukon College. Officers are members of the Union of Canadian Correctional Officers and earn between $43,600 and $80,200 per year, with an average salary of $51,600. Personal communication in 2018 revealed that 115 persons work in institutional and community correctional services in the Yukon.

Northwest Territories

Correctional Services, under the Department of Justice, purports the use of a transparent holistic and culturally relevant approach to adult corrections in the Northwest Territories (Northwest Territories Justice, 2015). There are three adult facilities, one of which is dual-designated. Officers are members of the Union of Northern Workers. The Department of Justice awards a medal, the Corrections Exemplary Service Medal, to employees with at least twenty years of experience who have "contributed to enhancing the profession" (Northwest Territories Justice, 2015).

Nunavut

Corrections in Nunavut include closed- and open-custody facilities and on-the-land camp operations (Department of Justice, 2013a). The adult correctional facilities in the province include the notorious Baffin Correctional Centre (BCC) in Iqaluit, which Gabriel Zarate, in 2010, described as "hell for inmates and staff alike … At any time, a guard might be spat upon, bitten and bled upon" (Zarate, 2010). Kim Roth, the BCC manager, explained that "it's really hard to attract people to work here. People have quit after their first shift." Howard Sapers (former correctional investigator), after visiting the facility with Dr. Ivan Zinger (former Executive Director and General Counsel, and the current Correctional Investigator), noted that the conditions in this facility are "certainly as bad as any" he has seen elsewhere, including the United States, as well as China, South Korea, the Czech Republic, and Singapore (Rennie, 2014). In his "watchdog" report, Sapers wrote that "the current state of disrepair and crowding are nothing short of appalling, and negatively impact both inmates and staff" (Sapers, 2013, p. 6). Among his many concerns about the prison, he listed the following: the presence of mold and bad odours; poor air quality; fire hazards; lack of heat; unhygienic conditions; compromised static (locked doors, control posts) and dynamic (pro-social interactions, direct supervision) security; and holes in the exterior walls made by prisoners to bring drugs into the facility, which indicates an unsecure perimeter.

In March 2015, Rennie cited a memo written by Nunavut's deputy minister of justice, Elizabeth Sanderson, to her colleagues in which she highlighted "serious constitutional and legal concerns associated with the ongoing use of the Baffin Correctional Centre" (Rennie, 2015). The government, at the time of writing, is investing $76 million to renovate, rebuild, and rebrand the facility as the Qikiqtani Correctional Healing Centre.

At the time of writing, an estimated 83 correctional officers are employed in Nunavut facilities, including 72 males and 11 females. The priority in hiring is given to Nunavut Land Claim Beneficiaries, in order to better understand and serve the needs of Nunavummiut. The officers are members of the Nunavut Employees Union, and earn starting salaries – as advertised in a job posting for three positions closing 23 May 2014 – of $66,008.00 per year, plus a Northern Allowance of $15,016.00 per year.

Table C.1. Average counts of adults in correctional services, by jurisdiction, 2014–15

Jurisdiction	Custody[a]		Per cent change in incarceration rate from 2013–14 to 2014–15[e]	Community supervision[b]		Per cent change in community supervision rate from 2013–14 to 2014–15[f]	Total correctional services[c]		Per cent change in total rate from 2013–14 to 2014–15[c]	Per cent change in total rate from 2010–11 to 2014–15[c]
	Number	Rate[d]		Number	Rate[d]		Number	Rate[d]		
Newfoundland and Labrador	314	72	10	1,647	379	–5	1,960	451	–3	–13
Prince Edward Island	105	89	–12	875	742	–2	979	831	–3	0
Nova Scotia	506	65	–4	..	..	..	..	..	..	..
New Brunswick	408	66	–3	..	..	..	..	..	..	..
Quebec	5,179	77	–1	13,713	205	–4	18,892	282	–3	–7
Ontario	7,785	71	–7	46,802	425	–10	54,587	496	–9	–23
Manitoba	2,387	240	–1	7,515	757	–5	9,902	997	–4	3
Saskatchewan	1,702	195	0	5,540	636	2	7,241	832	2	–6
Alberta	3,291	102	..	..	..	..	..	..	..	..
British Columbia	2,404	63	–2	12,530	330	–5	14,934	393	–5	–18
Yukon	76	261	–7	361	1,236	1	437	1,497	0	8
Northwest Territories	174	533	–29	443	1,355	8	617	1,888	–6	–28

Nunavut	125	534	–6	...	846	3,624	–13	...	971	4,158	–12	...	–21
Provincial and territorial total[c]	24,455	85	–4		90,271	376	–7		110,521	461	–6		–16
Federal[g]	15,168	53	–1		7,895	28	0		23,062	81	–1		–3
Total	39,623	138	...		...	...	...		...	...	...		...

Statistics Canada, Canadian Centre for Justice Statistics, Adult Corrections Key Indicator Report, 2014–15.

Note: Counts are based on the average number of adults in correctional services on any given day. Figures may not add up due to rounding.

.. not available for a specific reference period

. . . not applicable

[a] Total custody includes sentenced custody (including intermittent sentences), remand, and other temporary detention.

[b] Total community supervision includes probation, conditional sentences, provincial parole, full parole, day parole, statutory release, and long-term supervision. The data excludes other types of community supervision and inmates on temporary absence. Community supervision data excludes Nova Scotia, New Brunswick, and Alberta due to the unavailability of data.

[c] The total number and rate of adults in correctional services in 2014–15 excludes adults in Nova Scotia, New Brunswick, and Alberta. For this reason, total custody plus total community supervision do not amount to the total correctional services. The per cent change in total rate from 2010–11 to 2014–15 excludes Nova Scotia, New Brunswick, and Alberta.

[d] Rates are calculated per 100,000 adult population (18 years and over) using revised annual 1 July population estimates from Statistics Canada, Demography Division. Rates may not match those previously published in other reports.

[e] The per cent change in the incarceration rate from 2013–14 to 2014–15 excludes Alberta. The per cent change in total rate from 2010–11 to 2014–15 excludes Nova Scotia, New Brunswick, and Alberta.

[f] The per cent change in the community supervision rate from 2013–14 to 2014–15 excludes Nova Scotia, New Brunswick, and Alberta.

[g] As of 2013–14, federal offenders on temporary absences are counted in custody counts rather than in community counts. Comparisons to previous years should be made with caution.

Table C.2. Average counts of adults under correctional supervision, by type of supervision and jurisdiction, 2014–15

Jurisdiction	Sentenced custody[a]			Remand			Probation		
	Number	Rate[b]	Per cent change in rate from 2013–14	Number	Rate[b]	Per cent change in rate from 2013–14	Number	Rate[b]	Per cent change in rate from 2013–14
Newfoundland and Labrador	213	49	9	100	23	11	1,491	343	−5
Prince Edward Island	84	72	−10	17	14	−21	866	735	−2
Nova Scotia	156	20	−10	328	42	−1	...	...	...
New Brunswick	261	42	−8	147	24	8	...	...	...
Quebec	2,826	42	0	2,353	35	−1	10,702	160	−2
Ontario	2,675	24	−11	4,862	44	−4	43,948	400	−9
Manitoba	845	85	−6	1,542	155	2	6,827	688	−5
Saskatchewan	1,038	119	−4	664	76	7	4,329	497	4
Alberta	1,056	33	...	2,101	65	...	...	...	...
British Columbia	1,012	27	−13	1,361	36	7	11,008	290	−3
Yukon	31	108	−7	45	153	−7	328	1,125	3
Northwest Territories	99	302	−35	75	230	−20	421	1,287	10
Nunavut	67	288	−4	55	234	−9	785	3,363	−13

Provincial and territorial[c]	10,364	36	−7			13,650	48	−1	..	
Federal[d]	15,168	53	−1		..	..	..	80,705	336	−6	..	..

Statistics Canada, Canadian Centre for Justice Statistics, Adult Corrections Key Indicator Report, 2014–15.

Note: Counts are based on the average number of adults in correctional services on any given day. Figures may not add up due to rounding.

.. not available for a specific reference period

... not applicable

[a] Sentenced custody counts for the provinces/territories include offenders on intermittent sentences (when in) and offenders serving federal sentences where applicable.

[b] Rates are calculated per 100,000 adult population (18 years and over) using revised annual 1 July population estimates from Statistics Canada, Demography Division.

[c] The provincial and territorial probation data excludes Nova Scotia, New Brunswick, and Alberta. Per cent change in rate from 2013–14 excludes Alberta for sentenced custody and remand.

[d] As of 2013–14, federal offenders on temporary absences are counted in custody counts rather than in community counts. Comparisons to previous years should be made with caution.

Notes

Introduction: Provincial and Territorial Prisons in Canada

1 Despite any decrease in rates, new and bigger prison facilities are being funded, built, or renovated in different provinces and territories – however, conditions of confinement remain riddled with problems of overcrowding and violence. In Canada, federal and provincial/territorial corrections are increasingly adopting the strategy of direct supervision (also referred to as dynamic security), particularly with new facilities built over the last quarter-century. Such adoption would suggest that, in select cases and to varying degrees, officers would have more input into the casework process. Officers would also have more opportunities, potentially, to interact and create relationships with prisoners and thus make strides toward aiding prisoners in their "rehabilitative" journey. This finding, however, is not supported in many of my interviews to date, perhaps because many prisons either did not include direct supervision or direct supervision had only been recently introduced (e.g., in rather new facilities). In addition (see tables 1.1 and C.1), the number of prisoners in remand is tremendously high in Canada, and this has a significant impact on correctional centres, prisoner movement, and the work experiences of correctional officers (Weinrath, 2009, 2016; Weinrath & Coles, 2003).

1 Setting the Stage

1 Bill C-10 is also known in Parliament as "An Act to enact the Justice for Victims of Terrorism Act and to amend the State Immunity Act, the Criminal Code, the Controlled Drugs and Substances Act, the Corrections and Conditional Release Act, the Youth Criminal Justice Act, the Immigration and Refugee Protection Act and other Acts" (First Session, Forty-first Parliament, 60–61 Elizabeth II, 2012–2012, Statues of Canada 2012, Assented to 13 March 2012).

2 Aspects of this section come from: Ricciardelli, R. (2016a). Prisoners' perceptions of correctional officer orientations to their occupational responsibility: Liberal humanitarian versus neo-liberal persuasions. *Journal of Crime and Justice, 39*(2), 324–43. http://dx.doi.org/10.1080/0735648X.2014.972430.

3 This broader typology will frame the current analysis, in light of emergent themes in the data.

4 It is recognized that scholars have developed typologies of correctional officers (see, for example, Crawley, 2004; Farkas, 2000), however the focus here is on the typology that Crewe and Liebling (2012) first constructed in light of the correctional managers' orientations.

5 It should be noted that Braithwaite (1994) referred to a "materialist" orientation, where the individual, due to prior experience of economic or physical insecurity, focuses on order and stability in hopes of preventing the repeat of such experiences in the future. "Post-materialists," however, include those with higher moral values, which are also thought to develop in response to their past experiences.

2 Pathways: Who Are Correctional Officers and How Did They Get There?

1 Diverse content and findings from this chapter can be found in Ricciardelli, R., & Martin, K. (2017). Why corrections? Motivations for becoming a Canadian provincial or territorial correctional officer. *Journal of Criminological Research, Policy and Practice, 3*(4), 274–86. https://doi.org/10.1108/JCRPP-01-2017-0001.

2 In 1996, Shaffer surveyed 740 employees of the Pennsylvania Department of Corrections, finding that almost 90 per cent of male and female employees cited "economic considerations" as an important motivator underlying their occupational entry. Other important, yet less frequently cited, reasons for their occupational entry included: "career growth" (60 per cent), "military orientation" (34 per cent), and, to a lesser extent, having family and friends employed in corrections or a past personal experience with the law. Economic considerations, then, were an overwhelmingly dominant factor influencing occupational trajectories.

3 Dating back as far as the 1960s, when police and correctional officers were comprised predominantly of white men, researchers have suggested that police recruits are motivated to enter policing due to the perceived job security (Westley, 1970), the opportunity to help people (Cumming, Cumming, & Edell, 1965; Westley, 1970), the desire to enforce the law (Cumming, Cumming, & Edell, 1965), and wanting to work in a profession perceived as important and adventurous (Harris, 1973). Recently, scholars

have found that reasons for entering the field of policing have remained relatively stable (Foley, Guarneri, & Kelly, 2008; Lester, 1983).

3 "99 Per Cent Boredom, 1 Per Cent Sheer Terror"

1 I would like to thank the anonymous reviewer who first drew this analogy.
2 Maguire (2004), in surveying staff in the Oregon Department of Corrections, found that among correctional officers, years of service, gender, education, and job position were significantly correlated to belief in the prisoner's ability to change.
3 Micucci and Monster (2004, p. 515), in their study of prisoners, correctional officers, and treatment providers at a Canadian provincial facility, found that conditions such as "economy of scale, prison location, facility design, conditional sentencing and trans-institutionalization, [and] correctional officer work orientations" impact the effectiveness of rehabilitative programming or intentions in such facilities.
4 Of course, history has long shown that involuntary removal from any life situation has more negative than positive outcomes over the long term.
5 Identification of whether someone was experiencing vicarious trauma or burnout was not performed in any way, nor did I volunteer such labels or introduce them into the conversation, although officers did highlight their own diagnoses, or self-reported mental health, and led such conversational paths. Nuances in such discussions are beyond the scope of the research I conducted and my expertise.

4 The Female Correctional Officer

1 Women are allowed products that could easily be considered "potential weapons" in men's facilities.
2 Moreover, turning the discussion to male officers working on female prisoner units, Britton found that some male officers described themselves as needing to be "on guard against accusations of sexual harassment by female inmates, who are often perceived to make false claims when their advances are rejected" (1995, p. 227). Again, this suggests that female prisoners rather than male officers pose a threat.
3 This was also dominant in discussions about working with male prisoners.
4 Although it is rather absurd that such work was ever creditable, Katharina Dalton (1961), in a peer-reviewed journal article, argued that menstruation was a causal factor in female criminality, which she "supported" in a study of newly convicted women.
5 Some scholars have argued that incarcerated women may create "pseudo-families" in which different women play masculine and feminine roles as

well as those of children, something for which I have not seen empirical support, although I have seen strong family-like bonds develop between incarcerated women.

5 The Male Correctional Officer

1 Aspects of this chapter have been taken from Ricciardelli, R. (2016b). Canadian provincial correctional officers: Gendered strategies of achieving and affirming masculinities. *Journal of Men's Studies*, 25(1), 3–24. doi:10.1177/1060826515624389.
2 Given the degree of provincial variation in information and websites, please see www.csc-scc.gc.ca/text/plcy/cdshtm/600-cde-eng.shtml for general information about CERTs at the federal level of corrections.
3 Participants were not questioned about whether they had ever desired positions on the ERT, or if they had been passed up for promotion or specialized training and the associated occupational position – although some discussed such realities. Thus, it cannot be known for certain how many interviewees elected to assume this alternative occupational position by choice or as a response to a lack of other options.

6 Policing on the Inside: Foregrounding Occupational Risk

1 Although statistics are not available at the provincial level, upward trends are expected in light of the current climate with overcrowding and other legislative changes following Bill C-10.
2 Correctional officer training ranges; it is diverse and thus inconsistent across institutions, provinces, and territories. My purpose here is not to access training and how training varies by institution, nor how training prepares or does not prepare officers for the job, or if it primes them for violence or de-escalation. Although, I recommend that researchers in the future put forth a province-by-province-by-territory comparison of training processes, outcomes, and consistencies versus inconsistencies.
3 Again, some interviewees mentioned specific times when they were concerned for their safety or felt under threat, but they rarely directly admitted experiencing fear.
4 In this context, some officers described feeling less safe working in larger prisons because response times to codes were longer (given the distance to be travelled by responding colleagues), which could result in greater harm and even their or another's death.
5 Encounters with former prisoners can be positive as well as negative or seemingly driven by threat.

7 Correctional Officers as Occupational Edgeworkers?

1 Class dimensions are thought to shape who is employed in dangerous occupations. For example, many dangerous occupations (e.g., commercial fishing) are populated by individuals at the lower end of the class structure; nonetheless, in their analyses, scholars have cautiously examined whether correctional officers' job choices reflect a lack of alternative options for (relatively) well-paid work. Thus, the argument put forth is that edgework is a valid and reliable "part" of the correctional officer occupational experience and viewed as a rewarding aspect of a job, as presented in the results.

2 Recognizing that officers' perceptions of prisoners at a general level are tied to their conception of occupational riskiness, and that this study is limited to an adult male officer population, it would be beneficial to understand how female officers negotiate risk – as well as gender – to achieve status, and how such understandings are contextualized or understood based on their experiences in a hyper-masculine environment. Female officers may or may not construct their occupation as edgework in the same way that males do. Moreover, given that the officers interviewed were exclusively white, inquiries into diversities in risk perception and edgework in light of ethnic identification juxtaposed with gender, as well as the security level of the prison, are suggested. As the security classification of the prison decreases, so, too, will the inherent riskiness of the occupation, and thus edgework may no longer be apparent in the same form. Overall, although the results are telling, future research is essential to fully understand the realities of edgeworkers' attempts to achieve gender. In recognizing the officer occupation as edgework, more insight into occupational stresses and realities can be drawn. Further, gender achievement is an underpinning reality that, whether we are aware of it or not, shapes lived experiences. Achieving gender is a way to positively impact officer well-being and safety while further navigating the *edge*.

Conclusion

1 The concept of a therapeutic relationship was put forth in scholarship discussing the five dimensions of core correctional practice by Andrews and Kiessling (1980). These five dimensions are: 1) the efficient and constructive use of authority (e.g., the staff maintaining a just, yet always firm, position in prisoner-staff communications and interfaces); 2) staff, or service providers, "modeling and reinforcing anti-criminal attitudes and behaviors through direct, positive and/or negative reinforcement" (p. 451);

3) an approach to problem-solving rooted in community, interpersonal, recreational, personal, and emotional influences (e.g., a moral approach to finding solutions to potential "problems"); 4) the effective employment of community resources (e.g., employment referrals and pre-employment training programming, information seminars, and drop-in offices); and 5) *relationship factors*, specifically factors shaping the relationship between staff and prisoners, or the *therapeutic alliance* (e.g., mutual respect developing between parties).

Appendix B: Snapshots of Provincial and Territorial Prison Facilities across Canada

1 Federal prisoners in Newfoundland and Labrador, Nunavut, Prince Edward Island, Yukon, and the Northwest Territories are more likely to be housed in local provincial/territorial facilities, because to transfer a prisoner from any of these locations to an out-of-province federal facility would be removing them from their community, family, and even culture. Being able to visit with family has been found to reinforce family relationships and prisoner self-esteem, and, most notably, assist with post-release community reintegration. In this way, prisoners are able to maintain community ties and relationships with their supports in the community – all factors tied to lower rates of recidivism (Bales & Mears, 2008).
2 See introductory chapter for specifics regarding bail. Also, recent documentation suggests a maximum of fifteen days in segregation for prisoners. See www.un.org/apps/news/story.asp?NewsID=40097#. VpHYnvkrLIU, or www.fifteendays.org/act/.

References

Adams, J. (2009). Marked difference: Tattooing and its association with deviance in the United States. *Deviant Behavior, 30*(3), 266–92.

Adams, K. (1992). Adjusting to prison life. *Crime and Justice, 16,* 275–359. doi:10.1086/449208

Alberta Justice and Solicitor General. (2014a). *Adult Centre operations.* Retrieved from www.solgps.alberta.ca/programs_and_services/correctional_services/adult_centre_operations/Pages/default.aspx

Alberta Justice and Solicitor General. (2014b). *Correctional and Remand Centres.* Retrieved from www.solgps.alberta.ca/programs_and_services/correctional_services/adult_centre_operations/correctional_and_remand_centres/Pages/default.aspx

Alberta Justice and Solicitor General. (2014c). *Edmonton Remand Centre.* Retrieved from www.solgps.alberta.ca/programs_and_services/correctional_services/adult_centre_operations/nerc/Pages/new_edmonton_remand_centre.aspx

Alberta Justice and Solicitor General. (2014d). *Research careers and calculate pay & benefits.* Retrieved from www.jobs.alberta.ca/explore/research.html

Allaire, Y., & Firsirotu, M.E. (1984). Theories of organizational culture. *Organization Studies, 5,* 193–226.

Andrews, D.A., & Kiessling, J.J. (1980). Program structure and effective correctional practice. In R.R. Ross & P. Gendreau (Eds.), *Effective correctional treatment.* Toronto: Butterworth.

Antonio, M., Young, J., & Wingeard, L. (2009). When actions and attitude count most: Assessing perceived level of responsibility and support for inmate treatment and rehabilitation programs among correctional employees. *The Prison Journal, 89*(4), 363–82.

Arnold, H. (2005). The effects of prison work. In A. Liebling & S. Maruna (Eds.), *The effects of imprisonment* (pp. 391–420). New York: Routledge.

Bala, N., Carrington, P.J., & Roberts, J.V. (2008). Evaluating the Youth Criminal Justice Act after five years: A qualified success. *Canadian Journal of Criminology and Criminal Justice, 5*(2), 131–67.

Bales, W.D., & Mears, D.P. (2008). Inmate social ties and the transition to society: Does visitation reduce recidivism? *Journal of Research in Crime and Delinquency, 45*(3), 287–321.

Bandyopadhyay, M. (2006). Competing masculinities in a prison. *Men and Masculinities, 9*(2), 186–203. doi:10.1177/1097184x06287765

Barnett, L., Dupuis, T., Krikby, C., Mackay, R., Nicol, J., & Bechard, J. (2012). *Legislative summary: Bill C-10: An act to enact the Justice for Victims of Terrorism Act and to amend the State Immunity Act, the criminal code, the Controlled Drugs and Substances Act, the Corrections and Conditional Release Act, the Youth Criminal Justice Act, the Immigration and Refugee Protection Act and other acts* (41-1-C10-E). Ottawa: Library of Parliament.

Beasley, C. (2008). Rethinking hegemonic masculinity in a globalizing world. *Men and Masculinities, 11*(1), 86–103. doi:10.1177/1097184X08315102

Beck, U. (1992). *Risk society: Towards a new modernity*. London: Sage.

Beck, U. (1999). *World risk society*. Cambridge, UK: Polity Press.

Beck, U. (2002). *The silence of words and political dynamics in world risk society*. Retrieved from http://logosonline.home.igc.org/beck.htm

Beck, U., & Beck-Gernsheim, E. (1995). *Ecological politics in an age of risk*. Cambridge, UK: Polity Press.

Beck, U., & Beck-Gernsheim, E. (2002). *Individualization: Institutionalized individualism and its social and political consequences*. London: Sage Publications Ltd.

Beck, U., Giddens, A., & Nash, S. (1994). *Reflexive modernity: Politics, tradition and aesthetics in the modern social order*. Cambridge, UK: Polity Press.

Bensimon, P. (2005). Correctional officers and their first year: An empirical investigation. *Correctional Service Canada*. Retrieved from www.csc-scc.gc.ca/research/r179-eng.shtml

Bierie, D. (2012). The impact of prison conditions on staff well-being. *International Journal of Offender Therapy and Comparative Criminology, 56*(1), 81–95.

Blaze Carlson, K. (2014, 12 June). Sister of Justin Bourque speaks of his troubled life, paranoia. *Globe and Mail*. Retrieved from www.theglobeand mail.com/news/national/sister-of-justin-bourque-speaks-of-his-troubled-life-growing-paranoia/article19131608/

Bosworth, M., & Carrabine, E. (2001). Reassessing resistance: Race, gender, and sexuality in prison. *Punishment & Society, 3*, 501–15.

Bosworth, M., & Slade, G. (2014). In search of recognition: Gender and staff-detainee relations in a British immigration removal centre. *Punishment & Society, 16*(2), 169–86.

Bottoms, A. (1995). The philosophy and politics of punishment and sentencing. In C. Clarkson & R. Morgan (eds.), *The politics of sentencing reform* (pp. 17–49). Oxford: Oxford University Press.

Bourbonnais, R., Malenfant, R., Vezina, M., Jauvin, N., & Brisson, I. (2005). Work characteristics and health of correctional officers. *Revue d'Epidémiologie et de Santé Publique, 53*, 127–42.

Bowersox, M.S. (1981). Women in corrections: Competence, competition, and the social responsibility norm. *Criminal Justice & Behavior, 8*, 491–9.

Boyd, E., & Grant, T. (2005). Is gender a factor in perceived prison officer competence male prisoners perceptions in an English dispersal prison. *Criminal Behavior and Mental Health, 15*(1), 65–74.

Boyd, N. (2011). *Correctional officers in British Columbia, 2011: Abnormal working conditions.* Victoria, BC: Ministry of Public Safety & Solicitor General.

Braithwaite, V. (1994). Beyond Rokeach's equality-freedom model: Two-dimensional values in a one-dimensional world. *Journal of Social Issues, 50*(4), 67–94.

Braithwaite, V. (1998a). Communal and exchange trust norms: Their value base and relevant to institutional trust. In V. Braithwaite & M. Levi (Eds.), *Trust and governance.* New York: Russell Sage Foundation.

Braithwaite, V. (1998b). The value balance of political evaluations. *British Journal of Psychology, 89*, 223–47.

Britton, D.M. (1995). *Sex, violence, and supervision: A study of the prison as a gendered organization* (PhD). University of Texas, Austin, TX.

Britton, D.M. (1997). Perceptions of the work environment among correctional officers: Do race and sex matter? *Criminology, 35*(1), 85–105.

Britton, D.M. (1999). Cat fights and gang fights: Preference for work in a male-dominated organization. *Sociological Quarterly, 40*, 455–74.

Britton, D.M. (2003). *At work in the iron cage: The prison as gendered organization.* New York: New York University Press.

Brosnahan, M. (2013, 25 November). *Canada's prison population at all-time high: Number of visible minority inmates increased by 75% in past decade.* Retrieved from www.cbc.ca/news/canada-s-prison-population-at-all-time-high-1.2440039

Butler, J. (1990). *Gender trouble: Feminism and the subversion of identity.* New York and London: Routledge.

Byrd, T., Cochran, J., Silverman, I., & Blount, W. (2000). Behind bars: An assessment of the effects of job satisfaction, job-related stress, and anxiety of jail employees inclinations to quit. *Journal of Crime and Criminal Justice, 23*, 69–89.

Camp, S.D. (1994). Assessing the effects of organizational commitment and job satisfaction on turnover: An event history approach. *The Prison Journal, 74*(3), 279–305.

Canadian Bar Association. (2011). *Submission on bill C-10: Safe Streets and Communities Act.* Ottawa: Canadian Bar Association.

Carleton, R.N., Afifi, T.O., Turner, S., Taillieu, T., Duranceau, S., LeBouthillier, D.M., & Asmundson, G.J.G. (2018). Mental disorder symptoms among public safety personnel in Canada. *The Canadian Journal of Psychiatry, 63*(1), 54–64. doi:10.1177/0706743717723825

Carleton, R.N., Afifi, T.O., Turner, S., Taillieu, T., LeBouthillier, D.M., Duranceau, S., & Groll, D. (2018). Suicidal ideation, plans, and attempts among public safety personnel in Canada. *Canadian Psychology/Psychologie Canadienne, 59*(3), 220–31. doi: org/10.1037/cap0000136

Carrigan, T., Connell, R.W., & Lee, J. (1985). Towards a new sociology of masculinity. *Theory and Society, 14*(5), 551–604.

Cavadino, M., & Dignan, J. (2006). Penal policy and political economy. *Journal of Criminology and Criminal Justice, 6*(4), 435–56.

CBC News. (2012, 26 January). Corrections union opposes bill C-10. Politics: The pulse. Retrieved from www.huffingtonpost.ca/2012/01/26/omnibus-crime-bill-canada_n_1236224.html

CBC News. (2014, 31 October). Justin Bourque gets 5 life sentences, no chance of parole for 75 years. Retrieved from www.cbc.ca/news/canada/new-brunswick/justin-bourque-gets-5-life-sentences-no-chance-of-parole-for-75-years-1.2818516

Chang, D., & Zastrow, C. (1976). Inmates' and security guards' perceptions of themselves and each other: A comparative study. *International Journal of Criminology and Penology, 1*, 89–98.

Charmaz, K. (2006). *Constructing grounded theory.* London: Sage Publications.

Chene, B. (2013). *Analyse prospective de la population carcérale adulte des établissements de détention du Québec de 2010–2011 à 2020–2021.* Quebec: Ministère de la Sécurité publique.

Clemmer, D. (1940). *The prison community.* Boston: Christopher Publishing.

Collins, P., Iannacchione, B., Hudson, M., Stohr, M.K., & Hemmens, C. (2013). A comparison of jail inmate and staff correctional goal orientations: Results from across the line. *Journal of Crime and Justice, 36*(1), 100–15.

Connell, R.W. (1987). *Gender and power: Society, the person and sexual politics.* Stanford, CA: Stanford University Press.

Connell, R.W. (1990). A whole new world: Remaking masculinity in the context of the environmental movement. *Gender & Society, 4*(4), 452–78.

Connell, R.W. (1992). A very straight gay: Masculinity, homosexual experience, and the dynamics of gender. *American Sociological Review, 57*(6), 735–51.

Connell, R.W. (1993). The big picture: Masculinities in recent world history. *Theory and Society, 22*(5), 597–623.

Connell, R.W. (1995). *Masculinities.* Cambridge, UK: Polity Press.

Connell, R.W. (1998). Masculinities and globalization. *Men and Masculinities, 1*(1), 3–23.

Connell, R.W. (2002). *Gender.* Cambridge, UK: Polity Press.

Connell, R.W. (2005). *Masculinities* (2nd ed.). Los Angeles: University of California Press.

Connell, R.W., & Wood, J. (2005). Globalization and business masculinities. *Men and Masculinities, 7*(4), 347–64.

Cook, C. (2012). Examining differences in attitudes about sexual victimization among a sample of jail officers: The importance of officer gender and perceived inmate characteristics. *Criminal Justice Review, 37*(1), 191–213.

Cornelius, G.F. (2010). *The correctional officer: A practical guide.* Durham, NC: Carolina Academic Press.

Correctional Service Canada. (1992). *Commissioner's directives: Peace officer designations* (003). Ottawa: Correctional Service Canada. Retrieved from www.csc-scc.gc.ca/policy-and-legislation/003-cde-eng.shtml

Correctional Service Canada. (2001). *Correctional officer retention figures.* Ottawa: Government of Canada.

Correctional Service Canada. (2010). *Corrections in Canada: An interactive timeline.* Retrieved from www.csc-scc.gc.ca/hist/1900/index-eng.shtml

Correctional Service Canada. (2012a). *Bill C-10: Safe Streets and Communities Act.* Retrieved from www.csc-scc.gc.ca/victims/003006-1002-eng.shtml

Correctional Service Canada. (2012b, 22 October). *Correctional Service Canada: About us.* Retrieved from www.csc-scc.gc.ca/about-us/index-eng.shtml

Correctional Service Canada. (2012c). *Correctional officer – group & level CX-01.* Retrieved from www.csc-scc.gc.ca/text/carinf/correctional-eng.shtml

Correctional Service Canada. (2013a,). *Correctional service officers: Service Canada, people serving people.* Retrieved from www.servicecanada.gc.ca/eng/qc/job_futures/statistics/6462.shtml

Correctional Service Canada. (2013b). *The cross gender monitoring project 3rd and final annual report.* Ottawa: Correctional Service Canada. Retrieved from www.csc-scc.gc.ca/publications/fsw/gender3/cg-02-eng.shtml

Correctional Service Program. (2015). *Statistics Canada: Adult correctional statistics in Canada. 2013/2014.* Ottawa. Retrieved from www.statcan.gc.ca/pub/85-002-x/2015001/article/14163-eng.htm

Correctional Services Nova Scotia. (2007). *Code of professional conduct: Correctional services.* Halifax: Province of Nova Scotia. Retrieved from http://novascotia.ca/just/corrections/_docs/CodeofProfessionalConduct-2007.pdf

Correctional Services Nova Scotia. (2014). *Careers in correctional services: One industry. Three exciting paths* (p. 7). Halifax, NS: Department of Justice.

Crawley, E. (2004). Emotion and performance. *Punishment & Society, 6*(4), 411–27.

Crawley, E. (2013). *Doing prison work.* Milton, UK: Willan Publishing.

Crewe, B. (2005). Prisoner society in the era of hard drugs. *Punishment & Society, 7*(4), 457–81. doi:10.1177/1462474505057122

Crewe, B. (2006). Male prisoners' orientations toward female officers in an English prison. *Punishment & Society, 8*(4), 395–421. doi:10.1177/1462474506067565

Crewe, B. (2007). Power, adaptation and resistance in a late-modern men's prison. *British Journal of Criminology, 47*, 256–75. doi:10.1093/bjc/azl044

Crewe, B. (2009). *The prisoner society: Power, adaptation and social life in an English prison.* Oxford: Oxford University Press.

Crewe, B. (2011). Depth, weight, tightness: Revisiting the pains of imprisonment. *Punishment & Society, 13*(5), 509–29. doi:10.1177/1462474511422172

Crewe, B., & Liebling, A. (2011). Are liberal humanitarian penal values and practices exceptional? In T. Ugelvik, J. Dullum, & T. Mathiesen (Eds.), *Nordic prison practice and policy – exception or not? Exploring penal exceptionalism in the Nordic context(s).* Cullompton, UK: Willan Publishing.

Crewe, B., & Liebling, A. (2012). Are liberal humanitarian penal values and practices exceptional. In T. Ugelvik & J. Dullum (Eds.), *Penal exceptionalism? Nordic prison policy and practice* (pp. 175–98). Abingdon, UK: Routledge.

Crichton, H., & Ricciardelli, R. (2016). Shifting grounds: Experiences of Canadian provincial correctional officers. *Criminal Justice Review, 41*(4), 427–45. doi: 10.1177/0734016816669981

Crouch, B.M. (1980). *The keepers: Prison guards and contemporary corrections.* Springfield, IL: Thomas.

Cullen, F.T., Clark, G.A., & Wozniak, J.F. (1985). Explaining the get tough movement: Can the public be blamed? *Federal Probation, 49*, 16–24.

Cullen, F.T., Latessa, E.J., Burton, V.S., & Lombardo, X.L. (1993). The correctional orientation of prison wardens: Is the rehabilitative ideal supported. *Criminology, 31*(1), 69–92.

Cullen, F.T., Link, B.G., Wolfe, N.T., & Frank, J. (1985). The social dimensions of correctional officer stress. *Justice Quarterly, 2*(4), 505–33.

Cullen, F.T., Lutze, F.E., Link, B.G., & Wolfe, N.T. (1989). The correctional orientation of prison guards: Do officers support rehabilitation? *Federal Probation, 53*(1), 33–42.

Cumming, E., Cumming, I., & Edell, L. (1965). Policemen as philosopher, guide and friend. *Social Problems, 12*(3), 276–86.

Dalton, K. (1961, 30 December). Menstruation and crime. *British Medical Journal, 1752–3.*

Davis, K. (2002). "A dubious equality": Men, women and cosmetic surgery. *Body & Society, 8*(1), 49–65.

Deci, E.L. and Ryan, R.M. (1985). Intrinsic motivation and self-determination in human behavior. New York: Plenum Press.

Department of Environment, L. a. J. (2009). *Correctional services.* Retrieved from www.gov.pe.ca/jps/index.php3?number=1027251&lang=E_

Department of Environment, L. a. J. (2011). *Job opportunities in community and correctional services division.* Retrieved from www.gov.pe.ca/jps/index. php3?number=1038490&lang=E

Department of Justice. (2013a). *Corrections.* Whitehorse, YK: Government of Yukon.

Department of Justice. (2013b). *Information on the Correctional Centre building and supervision style.* Retrieved from www.justice.gov.yk.ca/prog/cor/wcc/correctional_building.html

Department of Justice. (2014). *Corrections.* Retrieved from www.justice.gov. yk.ca/prog/cor/

Department of Justice and Public Safety. (2014a). *Corrections: Institutional services.* Retrieved from www.justice.gov.nl.ca/just/corrections/institutional_services.html

Department of Justice and Public Safety. (2014b). *Youth secure custody (Newfoundland and Labrador Youth Centre).* Retrieved from www.justice.gov. nl.ca/just/department/branches/division/division_youth_secure_custody. html

Department of Public Safety Community and Correctional Services. (2014). *Human resources.* Fredericton: Government of New Brunswick.

Dial, K.C., Downey, R.A., & Goodlin, W.E. (2010). The job in the joint: The impact of generation and gender on work stress in prison. *Journal of Criminal Justice, 38*(4), 609–15. doi:10.1016/j.jcrimjus.2010.04.033

Dignam, J., & Fagan, T.J. (1996). Workplace violence in correctional settings: A comprehensive approach to critical incident stress management. In G.R. VandenBos & E.Q. Bulatao (Eds.), *Violence on the job: Identifying risks and developing solutions* (pp. 367–84). Washington, DC: American Psychological Association.

Dilulio, J.J. (1987). *Governing prisons: A comparative study of correctional management.* New York: Free Press.

Dilulio, J.J. (1991). *No escape: The future of American corrections.* New York: Basic Books.

Ditchfield, J., & Harries, R. (1996). Assaults on staff in male local prisons and remand centres. *Home Office Research and Statistics Directorate Research Bulletin, 38*, 15–20.

Doucette, K. (2014, 10 September). Overtime, sick days cost N.S. government $38 million last year. *The Canadian Press.* Retrieved from http://atlantic.ctvnews.ca/overtime-sick-days-cost-n-s-government-38-million-last-year-1.2000429

Dowden, C., & Andrews, D. A. (2004). The importance of staff practice in delivering effective correctional treatment: A meta-analytic review of core correctional practice. *Journal of Offender Therapy and Comparative Criminology, 48*(2), 203–14.

Easley, C.A. (1990). *A descriptive study of Alaskan correctional officers and their attitudes toward inmates* (MA Thesis). University of Alaska, Anchorage.

Einat, T., & Einat, H. (2000). Inmate Argot as an expression of prison subculture: The Israeli case. *The Prison Journal, 80*(3), 309–25.

Ekberg, M. (2007). The parameters of the risk society: A review and exploration. *Current Sociology, 55,* 343–68.

Erickson, R. (1994). The division of expert knowledge in policing and security. *British Journal of Criminology, 45,* 149–75.

Farkas, M. (2000). A typology of correctional officers. *International Journal of Offender Therapy and Comparative Criminology, 44*(4), 431–49.

Farmer, R.E. (1977). Cynicism: A factor in corrections work. *Journal of Criminal Justice, 5,* 237–46.

Farnworth, L. (1992). Women doing a man's job: Female prison officers working in a male prison. *Australian & New Zealand Journal of Criminology, 25,* 278–96.

Farr, K.A. (2000). Classification for inmates: Moving forward. *Crime & Delinquency, 46*(1), 3–17.

Ferrell, J., Milovanovic, D., & Lyng, S. (2001). Edgework, media practices, and the elongation of meaning: A theoretical ethnography of the Bridge Day event. *Theoretical Criminology, 5*(2), 177–202.

Figley, C.R. (1995). *Compassion fatigue: Coping with secondary traumatic stress disorder in those who treat the traumatized.* Bristol, PA: Brunner/Mazel.

Finn, P. (1996). No-frills prisons and jails: A movement in flux. *Federal Probation, 6,* 35–44.

Foley, P.F., Guarneri, C., & Kelly, M.E. (2008). Reasons for choosing a police career: Changes over two decades. *International Journal of Police Science and Management, 10*(1), 2–8.

Forum on Corrections Research. (2014). *Exposure to critical incidents: What are the effects on Canadian correctional officers?* Retrieved from www.csc-scc.gc.ca/research/forum/e041/e041m-eng.shtml

Foucault, M. (1981). The order of discourse. In R. Young (Ed.), *Untying the text: A post-structuralist reader* (pp. 48–78). Boston: Routledge & Kegan Paul.

Foucault, M., & Sheridan, A. (1972). *The archaeology of knowledge.* New York: Pantheon Books.

Fox, J.P. (1984). Women's prison policy, prisoner activism, and the impact of the contemporary feminist movement: A case study. *The Prison Journal, 63,* 12–26.

Fraser, N. (1997). *Justice interruptus: Critical reflections on the "Postsocialist" condition.* New York: Routledge.

Fraser, N. (2007). Feminist politics in the age of recognition: A two-dimensional approach to gender justice. *Studies in Social Justice, 1*(1), 23–35.

Freedman, E. (1981). *Their sister's keepers: Women prison reform in America, 1830–1930.* Ann Arbor, MI: University of Michigan Press.

Gagnon, J.H., & Simon, W. (1980). The social meaning of prison homosexuality. In D. Peterson & C. Thomas (Eds.), *Corrections: Problems and prospects.* Englewood Cliffs, NJ: Prentice Hall.

Gallo, E., & Ruggiero, V. (1991). The "immaterial" prison: Custody as a factory for the manufacture of handicaps. *International Journal of the Sociology of Law, 19*(3), 273–91.

Garcia, R.M. (2008). *Individual and institutional demographic and organizational climate correlates of perceived danger among federal correctional officers* (PhD). Temple University, Philadelphia, PA.

Gardner, D. (2009). *Risk: The science and politics of fear.* New York: McClelland & Stewart.

Garland, D. (1985). *Punishment and welfare: A history of penal strategies.* Aldershot, UK: Heinemann/Gower.

Garland, D. (2001). *The culture of control: Crime and social order in contemporary society.* Chicago: University of Chicago Press.

Giallombardo, R. (1966). *Society of women: A study of a women's prison.* New York: John Wiley.

Giddens, A. (1990). *The consequences of modernity.* Cambridge, MA: Polity Press.

Giddens, A. (1994). Living in a post-traditional society. In U. Beck, A. Giddens, & S. Lash (Eds.), *Reflexive modernization: Politics, tradition and aesthetics in the modern social order.* Cambridge, UK: Polity Press.

Gilman, E. (1991, Summer). Implementing key indicators: Adopting innovation in the BOP. *Federal Prisons Journal, 49*–56.

Glaser, B.G., & Strauss, A.L. (1967). *The discovery of grounded theory: Strategies for qualitative research.* Chicago: Aldine Publishing Company.

Grapendaal, M. (1990). The inmate subculture in Dutch prisons. *British Journal of Criminology, 30*(3), 341–57.

Griffin, M.L. (2005). Women as breadwinners: The gendered nature of side-bets and their influence on correctional officers' commitment to the organization. *Women & Criminal Justice, 17*(1), 1–25.

Griffiths, C.T. (2010). *Canadian corrections* (3rd ed.). Toronto: Nelson Thomson Learning.

Grossi, E., & Berg, B. (1991). Stress and job satisfaction among correctional officers: An unexpected finding. *International Journal of Offenders Therapy and Comparative Criminology, 35*, 73–81.

Guenther, A.L., & Guenther, M. (1974). Screws vs. thugs. *Society, 11*(5), 42–50.

Haney, C. (2011). The perversions of prison: On the origins of hypermasculinity and sexual violence in confinement. *American Criminal Law Review, 48*(1), 121–41.

Haney, C., Banks, C., & Zimbardo, P. (1973). Interpersonal dynamics in a simulated prison. *International Journal of Criminology and Penology, 11*, 69–97.

Hannah-Moffat, K. (1999). Moral agent or actuarial subject: Risk and Canadian women's imprisonment. *Theoretical Criminology, 3*(1), 71–94.

Hannah-Moffat, K. (2004a). Losing ground: Gendered knowledges, parole risk, and responsibility. *Social Politics: International Studies in Gender, State & Society, 11*(3), 363–85. doi:10.1093/sp/jxh041

Hannah-Moffat, K. (2004b). V. Gendering risk at what cost: Negotiations of gender and risk in Canadian women's prisons. *Feminism & Psychology, 14*(2), 243–249. doi:10.1177/0959-353504042178

Hannah-Moffat, K., & O'Malley, P. (2007). *Gendered risks*. London: Routledge Cavendish.

Harris, A. (1973). *Deviant identity, rational choice, and cognitive simplification* (PhD). Princeton University, Princeton, NJ.

Hayes, W.S. (1985). *Assault, battery & injury of Correctional Officers by inmates: An occupational health study* (PhD). John Hopkins University, Baltimore, MD.

Heimer, C. (1988). Social structure, psychology and the estimation of risk. *Annual Review of Sociology, 14*, 495–519.

Hepburn, J.R., & Knepper, P.E. (1993). Correctional officers as human services workers: The effect on job satisfaction. *Justice Quarterly, 10*(2), 315–35.

Hobbs, G.S., & Greg, E. (2000). Prisoners' perceptions of prison officers as sources of support. *Journal of Offender Rehabilitation, 31*(1/2), 127–42.

Hochschild, A. (1983). *The managed heart*. Berkeley: University of California Press.

Hochschild, A. (1998). The sociology of emotion as a way of seeing. In G. Bendelow & S.J. Williams (Eds.), *Emotions in social life* (pp. 28–52). London: Routledge.

Honneth, A. (1996). *The struggle for recognition: The moral grammar of social conflicts*. Cambridge, MA: MIT Press.

Horvath, A.O., & Marx, R.W. (1991). The development and decay of the working alliance during time-limited counseling. *Canadian Journal of Counseling, 24*(4), 240–59.

Horvath, A.O., & Symonds, B.D. (1991). Relation between working alliance and outcome in psychotherapy: A meta-analysis. *Journal of Counseling Psychology, 38*(2), 139–49.

Hurst, T.E., & Hurst, M.M. (1997). Gender differences in mediation of severe occupational stress among correctional officers. *American Journal of Criminal Justice, 22*(1), 121–37.

Irwin, J. (1980). *Prisons in turmoil*. Boston: Little, Brown.

Irwin, J. (2005). *The warehouse prison: Disposal of the new dangerous class*. Los Angeles: Roxbury Publishing Company.

Irwin, J., & Cressey, D.R. (1962). Thieves, convicts, and the inmate subculture. *Social Problems, 10*(2), 142–55.

Irwin, K. (2003). Saints and sinners: Elite Tattoo collectors and tattooists as positive and negative deviants. *Sociological Spectrum, 23*(1), 27–57. doi:10.1080/02732170309206

Jackson, J.E., & Ammen, S. (1996). Race and correctional officers' punitive attitudes toward treatment programs for inmates. *Journal of Criminal Justice, 24*, 153–66.

Jacobs, J., & Kraft, L.J. (1978). Integrating the keepers: A comparison of Black and White prison guards in Illinois. *Social Problems, 25*(3), 304–18.

Jacobs, J., & Retsky, H. (1980). Prison guard. In B. Crouch (Ed.), *The keepers: Prison guards and contemporary corrections* (pp. 183–206). Springfield, IL: Charles C. Thomas.

Jurik, N.C. (1985). Individual and organizational determinants of correctional officer attitudes toward inmates. *Criminology, 23*(3), 523–40.

Jurik, N.C. (1988). Striking a balance: Female correctional officers, gender role stereotypes, and male prisons. *Sociological Inquiry, 58*, 291–305.

Jurik, N.C., & Halemba, G.J. (1984). Gender, working conditions, and the job satisfaction of women in a non-traditional occupation: Female correctional officers in male prisons. *Sociological Quarterly, 25*, 551–66.

Jurik, N.C., Halemba, G.J., Musheno, M.C., & Boyle, B.V. (1987). Educational attainment, job satisfaction, and the professionalization of correctional officers. *Work and Occupations, 14*(1), 106–25.

Jurik, N.C., & Musheno, M.C. (1986). The internal crisis of corrections: Professionalization and the work environment. *Justice Quarterly, 3*, 457–80.

Jurik, N.C., & Winn, R. (1987). Describing correctional-security dropouts and rejects. *Criminal Justice and Behavior, 14*(1), 5–25.

Kaminski, M.M. (2003). Games prisoners play: Allocation of social roles in a total institution. *Rationality and Society, 15*, 188–217.

Kaufman, M. (1988). *Prison officers and their world.* Cambridge, MA: Harvard University Press.

Kaufman, M. (1994). Men, feminism, and men's contradictory experiences of power. In H. Brod & M. Kaufman (Eds.), *Theorizing masculinities*, (pp. 142–64). Thousand Oaks, CA: Sage.

Kiekbus, R., Price, W., & Theis, J. (2003). Turnover predictors: Causes of employee turnover in sheriff operated jails. *Criminal Justice Studies, 16*(2), 67–76.

Kjelsberg, E., Skoglund, T.H., & Rustad, A.B. (2007). Attitudes towards prisoners, as reported by prison inmates, prison employees and college students. *BMC Public Health, 7*(147), 71.

Klofas, J., & Toch, H. (1982). The guard subculture. *Journal of Research in Crime and Delinquency, 19*, 238–54.

Koff, E., & Rierdan, J. (1995). Early adolescent girls' understanding of menstruation. *Women & Health, 22*(4), 1–19. doi:10.1300/J013v22n04_01

Kong, R., & Peters, V. (2008). *Remand in adult corrections and sentencing patterns.* Ottawa: Statistics Canada. Retrieved from www.statcan.gc.ca/pub/85-002-x/2008009/article/10706-eng.htm

Kropp, P., Cox, D., Roesch, R., & Eaves, D. (1989). The perceptions of correctional officers toward mentally disordered offenders. *International Journal of Law and Psychiatry, 12,* 181–8.

Kruttschnitt, C., & Gartner, R. (2005). *Marking time in the golden state: Women's imprisonment in California.* Cambridge: Cambridge University Press.

Lahm, K.F. (2009a). Inmate assaults on prison staff: A multilevel examination of an overlooked form of prison violence. *The Prison Journal, 89*(2), 131–50. doi:10.1177/0032885509334743

Lahm, K.F. (2009b). Physical and property victimization behind bars: A multilevel examination. *International Journal of Offender Therapy and Comparative Criminology, 53*(3), 348–65. doi:10.1177/0306624X08316504

Lambert, E.G. (2006). I want to leave: A test of a model of turnover intent among correctional staff. *Applied Psychology in Criminal Justice, 2*(1), 57–83.

Lambert, E.G., Altheimer, I., & Hogan, N.L. (2010). Exploring the relationship between social support and job burnout among correctional staff. *Criminal Justice and Behavior, 37,* 1217–36.

Lambert, E.G., & Hogan, N.L. (2009). The importance of job satisfaction and organizational commitment in shaping turnover intent: A test of a causal model. *Criminal Justice Review, 34,* 96–118.

Lambert, E.G., Hogan, N.L., Altheimer, I., & Wareham, J. (2010). The effects of different aspects of supervision among female and male correctional staff: A preliminary study. *Criminal Justice Review, 35*(4), 492–513. doi:10.1177/0734016810372068

Lambert, E.G., Hogan, N.L., & Barton, S.M. (2002). Satisfied correctional staff: A review of the literature on the correlates of correctional staff job satisfaction. *Criminal Justice and Behavior, 29,* 115–43.

Lambert, E.G., Hogan, N.L., & Barton, S.M. (2004). The nature of work-family conflict among correctional staff: An exploratory examination. *Criminal Justice Review, 29,* 145–72.

Lambert, E.G., Hogan, N.L., & Tucker, K.A. (2009). Problems at work: Exploring the correlates of role stress among correctional staff. *The Prison Journal, 89,* 460–81.

Lambert, E.G., & Paoline, E.A. (2010). Take this job and shove it: An exploratory study of turnover intent among jail staff. *Journal of Criminal Justice, 38,* 139–48.

Lanthier, R. (2003). *Towards a policy for Canada's penitentiaries. The evolution of Canada's prison system and the transformation of the correctional officer's role (1950–2002).* Retrieved from www.ucco-sacc.csn.qc.ca/Documents/UCCO-SACC/National/documents/Research/Towards%20a%20policy%20for%20Canada_s%20Penitentiaries.pdf

Lariviere, M.A. (2002). The importance of attitudes in predicting job stress, job satisfaction, and organizational commitment: Results from a national staff survey. *Forum on Corrections Research, 14,* 1.

Lariviere, M.A., & Robinson, D. (1996). *Attitudes of federal correctional officers towards offenders.* Ottawa: Correctional Service Canada.

Lash, S. (2001). Technological forms of life. *Theory, Culture & Society, 18*(1), 105–20.

Lash, S. (2003). Reflexivity as non-linearity. *Theory, Culture and Society, 22*(2), 49–57.

Lavoie, J.A., Connolly, D.A., & Roesch, R. (2006). Correctional officers' perceptions of inmates with mental illness: The role of training and burnout syndrome. *International Journal of Forensic Mental Health, 5*(2), 151–66.

LeBel, T.P. (2012). Invisible stripes? Formerly incarcerated persons' perceptions of stigma. *Deviant Behavior, 33*(2), 89–107.

Lester, D. (1983). Why do people become police officers: A study of reasons and their predictions of success. *Journal of Police Science and Administration, 11*(2), 170–4.

Liebling, A. (2000). *Prisons, criminology and the power to punish: Or a brief account of the "state of the art" in prison research.* Paper presented at the British Criminology Conference, Leicester.

Liebling, A. (2004). *Prisons and their moral performance.* Oxford: Oxford University Press.

Liebling, A. (2008). Why prison staff culture matters. In J.M. Byre, D. Hummer, & F.S. Taxman (Eds.), *The culture of prison violence.* Boston: Pearson.

Liebling, A., Crewe, B., & Hulley, S. (2011). Conceptualising and measuring the quality of prison life. In D. Gadd, S. Karstedt, & S.F. Messner (Eds.), *The Sage handbook of criminological research methods.* London: Sage Publishing.

Link, B.G., Cullen, F.T., Frank, J., & Wozniak, J.F. (1987). The social rejection of former mental patients: Understanding why labels matter. *American Journal of Sociology, 92*(6), 1461–1500.

Link, B.G., & Phelan, J.C. (2001). Conceptualizing stigma. *Annual Review of Sociology, 27,* 363–85. doi:10.1146/annurev.soc.27.1.363

Link, B.G., Struening, E.L., Rahav, M., Phelan, J.C., & Nuttbrock, L. (1997). On stigma and its consequences: Evidence from a longitudinal study of men with dual diagnoses of mental illness and substance abuse. *Journal of Health and Social Behavior, 38*(2), 177–90. doi:10.2307/2955424

Lois, J. (2005). Gender and emotion management in the stages of edgework. In S. Lyng (Ed.), *Edgework: The sociology of risk taking* (pp. 117–52). London: Routledge.

Lovrich, N.P., & Stohr, M.K. (1993). Gender and jail work: Correctional policy implications of perceptual diversity in the work force. *Review of Policy Research, 12*(1–2), 66–84.

Lyng, S. (1990). Edgework: A social psychologist analysis of voluntary risk taking. *American Journal of Sociology, 95,* 851–86.

Lyng, S. (2005). Edgework and the risk-taking experience. In S. Lyng (Ed.), *Edgework: The sociology of risk-taking* (pp. 3–16). Abingdon, UK: Routledge.

Lyng, S., & Matthews, R. (2007). Risk, edgework, and masculinities. In K. Hannah-Moffat (Ed.), *Gendered risks* (pp. 75–98). Abingdon, UK: Routledge-Cavendish Glass House.

MacKenzie, D.L. (1989). Prison classification: The management and psychological perspectives. In L. Goodstein & D.L. Goodstein (Eds.), *The American prison: Issues in research and policy* (pp. 163–89). New York: Plenum.

MacKenzie, D.L., Posey, C., & Rapaport, K. (1988). A theoretical revolution in corrections: Varied purposes for classification. *Criminal Justice and Behavior, 15*(1), 125–36.

Madriz, E. (1997). *Nothing bad happens to good girls.* Berkeley: University of California Press.

Maguire, M. (2004). *The environment of the correctional institution: An exploratory study of staff attitude and institutional characteristics* (PhD). Portland State University, Portland, OR.

Maier, K. & Ricciardelli, R. (2019). The "Prisoners' dilemma": How male prisoners experience and respond to penal threat while incarcerated. *Punishment & Society, 21*(2), 231–50. doi: 10.1177/1462474518757091

Management and Training Corporation Institute. (2011). *Correctional officers: Strategies to improve retention.* Centerville, UT: Management and Training Corporation.

Manitoba Government and General Employees' Union. (2012, 9 February). MGEU president Wales' presentation underscores the overcrowding crisis in Manitoba jails. Retrieved from http://nupge.ca/content/4806/mgeu-president-wales-presentation-underscores-overcrowding-crisis-manitoba-jails

Manitoba Justice. (2015). *Criminal legal process: Corrections.* Retrieved from www.gov.mb.ca/cgi-bin/print_hit_bold.pl/justice/criminal/corrections/index.html

Maruna, S. (2012). A signaling perspective on employment-based re-entry: Elements of successful desistance signaling. *Criminology & Public Policy, 11*(1), 73–86. doi:10.1111/i/1745-9133.2012.00789

McCormack, N. (2017). Manslaughter charges and the opioid crisis in Canada. *Australian Law Library, 25,* 27.

McMahon, M.W. (1999). *Women on guard: Discrimination and harassment in corrections.* Toronto: University of Toronto Press.

McMahon, T., Friscolanti, M., & Patriquin, M. (2014, 15 June). The untold story of Justin Bourque." *Maclean's.*

McShane, M.D., Williams, F.P., Schichor, D., & McClain, K. (1991). Early exits: Examining employee turnover. *Corrections Today, 53,* 220–25.

Merecz-Kot, D., & Cębrzyńska, J. (2008). Aggression and mobbing among correctional officers. *Medycyna Pracy, 59,* 443–51.

Messerschmidt, J W. (1997). *Crime as structured action: Gender, race and class and crime in the making.* London: Sage.

Messerschmidt, J.W. (1999). *Nine lives: Adolescent masculinities, the body and violence.* New York: Westview Press.

Messerschmidt, J.W. (2012). Engendering gendered knowledge: Assessing the academic appropriation of hegemonic masculinity. *Men and Masculinities, 1*(15), 56–76. doi:10.1177/1097184X11428384

Micucci, A., & Monster, M. (2004). It's about time to hear their stories: Impediments to rehabilitation at a Canadian provincial correctional facility for women. *Journal of Criminal Justice. 32*(6), 515–30. doi:10.1016/j.jcrimjus.2004.08.008

Miller, E. (1991). Assessing the risk of inattention to class, race/ethnicity and gender: Comment on Lyng. *American Journal of Sociology, 96,* 1530–4.

Ministère de la Sécurité publique. (2013, 29 October). Operation of correctional services in Quebec. *Services Correctionnels.* Retrieved from www.securitepublique.gouv.qc.ca/services-correctionnels/publications-et-statistiques/population-carcerale-prospective/sommaire.html

Ministère de la Sécurité publique. (2014). Établissements de détention. *Services Correctionnels.* Retrieved from www.securitepublique.gouv.qc.ca/services-correctionnels/milieu-carceral/etablissements-detention.html

Ministry of Justice. (2012). *Custody, supervision and rehabilitation services.* Retrieved from www.justice.gov.sk.ca/cp-cr

Ministry of Justice. (2013a). *Adult custody division.* Retrieved from www.pssg.gov.bc.ca/corrections/about-us/people/adult-custody-div.htm

Ministry of Justice. (2013b). *BC corrections workforce facts.* Retrieved from www.pssg.gov.bc.ca/corrections/about-us/people/workforce.htm

Ministry of Justice. (2014). *Our facilities.* Retrieved from www.pssg.gov.bc.ca/corrections/about-us/facilities.htm

Moran, D. (2012). Prisoner reintegration and the stigma of prison time inscribed on the body. *Punishment & Society, 14*(5), 564–83. http://dx.doi.org.ezproxy.library.yorku.ca/10.1177/1462474512464008

Mottaz, C. (1987). An analysis of the relationship between work satisfaction and organizational commitment. *Sociological Quarterly, 28*(4), 541–58.

Nacci, P., & Kane, T. (1984). Sex and sexual aggression in federal prisons. *Federal Probation, 48*(1), 46–53.

Newton, C. (1994). Gender theory and prison sociology: Using theories of masculinities to interpret the sociology of prisons for men. *The Howard Journal, 33*(3), 193–202.

Northeast Nova Scotia Correctional Facility; Priestville, Pictou County. (2013). *Correctional services.* Retrieved from http://novascotia.ca/just/Corrections/NENS.asp

Northwest Territories Justice. (2015). *Corrections and probation.* Retrieved from
www.justice.gov.nt.ca/en/browse/corrections-and-probation/

Office of Justice Programs. (1999). *Conference Proceedings.* Paper presented at the
National Symposium on Women Offenders, Washington, DC.

Office of the Auditor General. (2014). *Managing the province's adult offenders.*
Winnipeg, MB: Government of Manitoba. Retrieved from www.oag.mb.ca/
wp-content/uploads/2014/03/Chapter-6-Managing-the-Provinces-Adult-
Offenders-Web.pdf

Office on Women's Health. (2014). *Premenstrual syndrome (PMS) fact sheet.*
Retrieved from www.womenshealth.gov/publications/our-publications/fact-
sheet/premenstrual-syndrome.html

O'Kane, J. (2014, 13 June). "I had a job to do," says lawyer who represented
Bourque. *Globe and Mail.* Retrieved from www.theglobeandmail.com/news/
national/duty-to-defend-representing-justin-bourque/article19151262/

Onojeharho, J.E., & Bloom, L. (1986). Inmate subculture in a Nigerian prison.
Journal of Psychology: Interdisciplinary and Applied, 120(5), 421–32.

Ontario Ministry of the Attorney General. (2013). *Criminal law.* Retrieved
from www.attorneygeneral.jus.gov.on.ca/english/justice-ont/criminal_law.
asp#aboutOntario Ministry of Community Safety and Correctional Services.
(2013). *About correctional services.* Retrieved from www.mcscs.jus.gov.on.ca/
english/contact_us/contact_us.asp

Ontario Ministry of Community Safety and Corrections. (2010). *Correctional
services.* Retrieved from www.mcscs.jus.gov.on.ca/english/corr_serv/adult_
off/earned_rem/earned_rem.html

Parlee, M.B. (1982). Changes in moods and activation levels during the
menstrual cycle in experimentally naive subjects. *Psychology of Women
Quarterly, 7,* 119–33. doi:10.1111/j.1471-6402.1983.tb00824.x

Parole Board of Canada. (2012). The Safe Streets and Communities Act (Bill
C-10): Changes for the Parole Board of Canada. *Fact Sheets.* Retrieved from
www.pbc-clcc.gc.ca/infocntr/factsh/sscagenchng-eng.shtml

Pearlman, L.A., & MacIan, P.S. (1995). Vicarious traumatization: An empirical
study of the effects of trauma work on trauma therapists. *Professional
Psychology: Research and Practice, 26*(6), 558–65.

Pearlman, L.A., & Saakvitne, K.W. (1995). *Trauma and the therapist.* New York:
W.W. Norton & Company.

Phelan, M.P., & Hunt, S.A. (1998). Prison gang members' tattoos as identity
work: The visual communication of moral careers. *Symbolic Interaction, 21*(3),
277–98. doi:10.1525/si.1998.21.3.277

Philips, C. (2012). *The multicultural prison: Ethnicity, masculinity, and social
relations.* Oxford: Oxford University Press.

Phillips, J. (2001). Cultural construction of manhood in prison. *Psychology of
Men & Masculinity, 2*(1), 13–23. doi:10.1037//1524-9220.2.1.13

Plecas, D., & Maxim, P. (1991). *Correctional officer career development study: A six-year longitudinal study of 527 correctional officer recruits hired by the correctional service of Canada in 1984 and 1985.* Ottawa: Correctional Service Canada.

Poirier, S., Brown, G.R., & Carlson, T.M. (2008). *Decades of darkness moving towards the light: A review of the prison system in Newfoundland and Labrador.* St. John's, NL: Department of Justice and Public Safety.

Pollack, S. (2009). "You can't have it both ways": Punishment and treatment of imprisoned women. *Journal of Progressive Human Services, 20,* 112–28.

Pollock, J. (1984). Women will be women: Correctional officers' perceptions of the emotionality of women inmates. *The Prison Journal, 64,* 84–91.

Pollock, J. (1986). *Sex and supervision: Guarding male and female inmates.* Westport, CT: Greenwood Publishing Group.

Pollock, J. (2002). *Women, crime and prison.* Belmont, CA: Wadsworth.

Poole, E., & Regoli, R. (1980). Role stress, custody orientation, and disciplinary actions: A study of prison guards. *Criminology, 18,* 215–26.

Pope, H., Phillips, K., & Olivardia, R. (2000). *The Adonis complex: How to identify, treat and prevent body obsession in men and boys.* New York: Simon and Schuster.

Pratt, J. (2007). *Penal populism.* New York: Taylor & Francis.

Pratt, J. (2008a). Scandinavian exceptionalism in an era of penal excess: Part I: The nature and roots of Scandinavian exceptionalism. *British Journal of Criminology, 48*(2), 275–92.

Pratt, J. (2008b). Scandinavian exceptionalism in an era of penal excess: Part II: Does Scandinavian exceptionalism have a future? *British Journal of Criminology, 48*(3), 275–92.

Pratt, J. (2013a). Punishment and the civilizing process. In J. Simon & R. Sparks (Eds.), *The SAGE handbook of punishment and society.* London: Sage Publications.

Pratt, J. (2013b). *A punitive society: Falling crime and rising imprisonment in New Zealand.* Wellington, NZ: Bridget Williams Books.

Rennie, S. (2014, 25 August). Nunavut jail unchanged after watchdog report. *Canadian Press.* Retrieved from http://globalnews.ca/news/1525374/nunavut-jail-unchanged-after-watchdog-report/

Rennie, S. (2015, 9 March). Nunavut jail poses "significant constitutional and legal risks": Memo. *Canadian Press.* Retrieved from www.cbc.ca/news/canada/north/nunavut-jail-poses-significant-constitutional-and-legal-risks-memo-1.2987692

Ricciardelli, R., (2011) Masculinity, consumerism, and appearance and Consumerism: A look at men's hair. *Canadian Review of Sociology, 48*(2), 181–201.

Ricciardelli, R. (2013). Masculinity in Canadian prisons: Parolee experiences. *Journal of Gender Studies.* doi:10.1080/09589236.2013.812513

Ricciardelli, R. (2014a). An examination of the inmate code in Canadian penitentiaries. *Journal of Crime and Justice, 37*(2), 234–55. doi:10.1080/0735648X.2012.746012

Ricciardelli, R. (2014b). *Surviving incarceration: Inside Canadian prisons.* Brantford, ON: Wilfrid Laurier University Press.

Ricciarelli, R. (2016a). Canadian prisoners' perceptions of correctional officer orientations to their occupational responsibilities. *Journal of Crime and Justice, 39*(2), 324–43. doi:10.1080/0735648X.2014.972430

Ricciarelli, R. (2016b). Canadian provincial correctional officers: Gendered strategies of achieving and affirming masculinities. *Journal of Men's Studies, 25*(1), 3–24. doi:10.1177/1060826515624389

Ricciardelli, R., Carleton, R.N., Groll, D., & Cramm, H. (2018). Qualitatively unpacking Canadian public safety personnel experiences of trauma and their well-being. *Canadian Journal of Criminology and Criminal Justice,* 1–12.

Ricciardelli, R., Carleton, R. N., Mooney, T., & Cramm, H. (2019). "Playing the system": Structural factors potentiating mental health stigma, challenging awareness, and creating barriers to care for Canadian public safety personnel. *Health.* doi:10.1177/1363459318800167

Ricciardelli, R., & Clow, K.A. (2009). Men, appearance, and cosmetic surgery: The role of confidence, self-esteem and comfort with the body. *Canadian Journal of Sociology, 34*(1), 105–34.

Ricciardelli, R., Clow, K.A, & White, P. (2010). Investigating hegemonic masculinity: Portrayals of masculinity in men's lifestyle magazines. *Sex Roles: A Journal of Research, 63*(1/2), 64–78.

Ricciardelli, R., & Gazso, A. (2013). Investigating risk perception among Canadian corrections officers with experience handling inmates in Canadian provincial jails. *Qualitative Sociological Review, 4*(3), 96–120.

Ricciardelli, R., Maier, K. & Hannah-Moffat, K. (2015). Strategic masculinities: Vulnerabilities, risk, and the production of prison masculinities. *Theoretical Criminology, 19*(4), 491–513. doi: 10.1177/1362480614561456849

Ricciardelli, R. & Martin, K. (2017). Why corrections? Motivations for becoming a Canadian provincial or territorial correctional officer. *Journal of Criminological Research, Policy and Practice, 3*(4), 274–86, https://doi.org/10.1108/JCRPP-01-2017-0001

Ricciardelli, R., & Moir, M. (2013). Stigmatized among the stigmatized: Sex offenders in Canadian penitentiaries. *Canadian Journal of Criminology and Criminal Justice, 5*(3), 353–86. doi: 10.3138/cjccj.2012.E22

Ricciardelli, R. & Perry, K.H. (2016). Responsivity in practice: Prison officer to prisoner communication in Canadian provincial prisons. *Journal of Contemporary Criminal Justice, 29*(3), 179–98. doi: 10.1177/1043986216660004.

Ricciardelli, R., Perry, K.H. & Carleton, R.N. (2016). Prison officer orientations and the implications for responsivity with incarcerated youth. In J. Ireland, C. Ireland, M. Fisher, & N. Gredecki (Eds.), *International Handbook on Forensic Psychology in Prison and Secure Settings.* Abingdon, UK: Routledge.

Ricciardelli, R., & Power, N. (in press). How "conditions of confinement" impact "conditions of employment": The work-related wellbeing of provincial correctional officers in Atlantic Canada. *Victims and Violence.*

Ricciardelli, R., Power, N., & Simas-Mederios, D.M. (2018). Correctional Officers in Canada: Interpreting workplace violence. *Criminal Justice Review,* *43*(4), 458–76. doi: 10.1177/0734016817752433

Ricciardelli, R., & Spencer, D.C. (2014). Exposing "sex" offenders: Precarity, abjection and violence in the Canadian federal prison system. *British Journal of Criminology, 54*(3), 428–48. doi: 10.1093/bjc/azu012

Ricciardelli, R., & Spencer, D.C. (2017). *Violence, sex offenders, and corrections.* Abingdon, UK: Taylor & Francis.

Ricciardelli, R., & White, P. (2011). Modifying the body: Canadian men's perspectives on appearance and cosmetic surgery. *The Qualitative Report, 16*(4), 949–70.

Roberts, J.V., Stalans, L.J., Indermaur, D., & Hough, M. (2002). *Penal populism and public opinion: Lessons from five countries.* Oxford: Oxford University Press.

Robinson, D., Porporino, F., & Simourd, L. (1993). The influence of career orientation on support for rehabilitation of correctional staff. *The Prison Journal, 73*(2), 162–77.

Roy, P. (2010). *Jobs in community and correctional services.* Charlottetown, PEI: Government of Prince Edward Island.

Rutherford, A. (1994). *Criminal justice and the pursuit of decency.* Winchester, UK: Waterside Press.

Saakvitne, K.W., & Pearlman, L.A. (1996). *Transforming the pain: A workbook on vicarious traumatization for helping professionals who work with traumatized clients.* New York: W.W. Norton & Company.

Samak, Q. (2003). *Correctional officers of Correctional Service Canada and their working conditions: A questionnaire-based study.* Montreal: CSN Labour Relations Department. Retrieved from: https://ucco-sacc-csn.ca/wp-content/uploads/2015/05/Correctional-Officers-and-their-working-conditions1.pdf

Sapers, H. (2013). *Report of the Office of the Correctional Investigator (Canada) on the Baffin Correctional Centre and the legal and policy framework of Nunavut corrections.* Iqaluit, NU: Nunavut Corrections.

Sargent, J.P. (1984). The evolution of a stereotype: Paternalism and the female inmate. *The Prison Journal, 64*, 37–44.

Savicki, V., Cooley, E., & Gjesvold, J. (2003). Harassment as a predictor of job burnout in correctional officers. *Criminal Justice and Behavior, 30*(5), 602–19.

Saylor, W. (1989, Fall). Quality control for prison managers: The key indicators/strategic support system. *Federal Prisons Journal,* 39–42.

Saylor, W. (1991). *The key indicators/strategic support system: A tool for efficiently managing rapid population growth.* Washington, DC: Office of Research and Evaluation; US Federal Bureau of Prisons.

Saylor, W., & Wright, K.N. (1992). A comparative study of the relationship of status and longevity in determining perceptions of the work environment among federal prison employees. *Journal of Offender Rehabilitation, 17*(3/4), 133–60.

Schlosser, L.Z., Safran, D.A., & Sbaratta, C.A. (2010). Reasons for choosing a correction officer career. *Psychological Services, 7*(1), 34–43.

Schmalleger, F., & Smykla, J. (2005). *Corrections in the 21st century* (2nd ed.). New York: McGraw Hill.

Schram, P.J. (1997). *The link between stereotype attitudes and behavioral intentions among female inmates, correctional officers, and program staff* (PhD). Michigan State University, East Lansing, MI.

Schram, P.J., Koons-Witt, B.A., & Morash, M. (2004). Management strategies when working with female prisoners. *Women & Criminal Justice, 15*(2), 25–50. doi:10.1300/J012v15n02_02

Schroeder, K. (2004). Hypermasculinity. In M. Kimmel & A. Aronson (Eds.), *Masculinities: A social, cultural and historical encyclopedia,* vol. 1 (pp. 417–19). Santa Barbara, CA: ABC-CLIO.

Scrivens, R. & Ricciardelli, R. (2019). "Scum of the earth": Animus and violence against sex offenders in Canadian penitentiaries. In N. Blagden (Ed.), *Sexual Crime and the Experience of Imprisonment.* London: Palgrave Macmillan.

Seidman, B.T., & Williams, S.M. (1999). The impact of violent acts on prison staff. *Forum on Corrections Research, 11*(1), 30–4.

Shaffer, J. (1999). Life on the installment plan: Careers in corrections. *Corrections, 61*(7), 84–174.

Shearing, C.D., & Ericson, R.V. (1991). Culture as figurative action. *British Journal of Sociology, 42*(4), 481–506.

Simon, J. (2002). Taking risks: Extreme sports and the embrace of risk in advanced liberal societies. In T. Baker & J. Simon (eds.), *Embracing risk: The changing culture of insurance and responsibility* (pp. 177–208). Chicago: University of Chicago Press.

Simon, J. (2005). Edgework and insurance in risk societies: Some notes on Victorian lawyers and mountaineers. In S. Lyng (Ed.), *Edgework: The sociology of risk-taking* (pp. 203–26). Abingdon, UK: Routledge.

Simourd, L. (1997). *Staff attitudes toward inmates and correctional work* (PhD). Carleton University, Ottawa, ON.

Skolnick, J. (1966). *Justice without trial: Law enforcement in democratic society.* New York: John Wiley & Sons.

Slate, R., & Vogel, R. (1997). Participative management and correctional personnel: A study of perceived atmosphere for participation in correctional decision-making and its impact on employee stress and thoughts about quitting. *Journal of Criminal Justice, 25,* 397–408.

Sorensen, J., Cunningham, M., Vigen, M.P., & Woods, S.O. (2011). Serious assaults on prison staff: A descriptive analysis. *Journal of Criminal Justice, 39*(2), 143–50.

Sparks, R., Bottoms, A., & Hay, W. (1996). *Prisons and the problem of order.* Oxford: Clarendon.

Spencer, D.C. & Ricciardelli, R. (2017). "They're a very sick group of individuals": Correctional officers, emotions, and sex offenders. *Theoretical Criminology, 21*(3), 380–94. doi: 1362480616647590

Stamm, H.B. (1995). *Secondary traumatic stress: Self-care issues for clinicians, researchers, & educators.* Lutherville, MD: The Sidran Press.

Stanko, E. (1997). Safety talk: Conceptualising women's risk assessment as a technology of the soul. *Theoretical Criminology, 1*(4), 479–99.

Statistics Canada. (2014a). *Adult correctional services, average counts of offenders, by province, territory, and federal programs* (CANSIM Table 251-0005). Ottawa: Statistics Canada. Retrieved from www.statcan.gc.ca/tables-tableaux/sum-som/l01/cst01/legal31c-eng.htm

Statistics Canada. (2014b). *Adult correctional services, average counts of offenders, by province, territory, and federal programs (Provinces and territories)* (CANSIM Table 251-0005). Ottawa: Statistics Canada. Retrieved from www.statcan.gc.ca/tables-tableaux/sum-som/l01/cst01/legal31b-eng.htm

Stein, J., Leslie, M., & Nyamathi, A. (2002). Relative contributions of parent substance use and childhood maltreatment to chronic homelessness, depression, and substance abuse problems among homeless women: Mediating roles of self-esteem and abuse in adulthood. *Child Abuse & Neglect, 26*(10), 1011–27.

Stohr, M., Self, R., & Lovrich, N. (1992). Staff turnover in new generation jails: An investigation of its causes and preventions. *Journal of Criminal Justice, 20,* 455–78.

Strauss, A.L., & Corbin, J. (1990). *Basics of qualitative research: Techniques and procedures for developing grounded theory.* Newbury Park, CA: Sage Publishing.

Sykes, G.M. (1958). *The society of captives.* Princeton, NJ: Princeton University Press.

Sykes, G.M., & Messinger, S.L. (1960). The inmate social system. In R.A. Cloward, D.R. Cressey, G.H. Glosser, R. McCleery, L.E. Ohlin, G.M. Sykes, & S.L. Messinger (Eds.), *Theoretical studies in social organization of the prison* (pp. 5–19). New York: Social Science Research Council.

Thomas, A. (1990). The significance of gender politics in men's accounts of their "gender identity." In J. Hearn & D. Morgan (Eds.), *Men, masculinities, and social theory* (pp. 143–59). London: Unwin Hyman.

Toch, H. (1978). Is a "correction officer," by any other name, a "screw"? *Criminal Justice Review, 3,* 19–36.

Toch, H. (1998). Hypermasculinity and prison violence. In L. Bowker (Ed.), *Masculinities and violence* (pp. 168–78). London: Sage Publications.

Toch, H. (1992). *Living in prison* (Rev. ed.). Washington, DC: American Psychological Association (APA Books).

Toch, H. (1981). A revisionist view of prison reform. *Federal Probation, 45*, 3–9.

Toch, H., & Klofas, J. (1982). Alienation and desire for job enrichment among correctional officers. *Federal Probation, 46*, 35–44.

Trammell, R. (2009). Values, rules and keeping the peace: How men describe order and the inmate code in California prisons. *Deviant Behavior, 30*(8), 746–71. doi:10.1080/01639620902854662

Trammell, R. (2012). *Enforcing the convict code: Violence and prison culture.* Boulder, CO: Lynne Rienner Publishers.

Trevethan, S. (2000). *An examination of female inmates in Canada: Characteristics and treatment.* Paper presented at the Women in Corrections: Staff and Clients Conference convened by the Australian Institute of Criminology in conjunction with the Department for Correctional Services, Adelaide, AU. www.aic.gov.au/media_library/conferences/womencorrections/trevetha.pdf

Turcotte, M. (2013). *Women and education.* Ottawa: Statistics Canada. Retrieved from www.statcan.gc.ca/pub/89-503-x/2010001/article/11542-eng.htm.

Valverde, M. (2003). *Pragmatist and non-pragmatist knowledge practices in American law.* Paper presented at the Cornell conference on pragmatism, Cornell University, Ithaca, NY.

Vandello, J., Bosson, J.K., Cohen, D., Burnaford, R.M., & Weaver, J.R. (2008). Precarious manhood. *Journal of Personality and Social Psychology, 95*, 1325–39.

Van Voorhis, P. (1993). Psychological determinants of the prison experience. *Prison Journal, 73*(1), 72–102.

Van Voorhis, P., Cullen, F.T., Link, B.G., & Wolfe, N.T. (1991). The impact of race and gender on correctional officers' orientation to the integrated environment. *Journal of Research in Crime and Delinquency, 28*(4), 472–500.

Vincent, D. (2014, 24 July). Disciplinary measures against Canadian prison guards skyrockets. *Toronto Star.* Retrieved from www.thestar.com/news/canada/2014/07/24/disciplinary_measures_against_canadian_prison_guards_skyrockets.html

Vygotsky, L. (1987). *The collected works of L.S. Vygotsky: Problems of general psychology* (Vol. 1). New York: Plenum Press.

Watterson, K. (1996). *Women in prison: Inside the concrete womb.* Boston: Northeastern University Press.

Weekes, J.R., Pelletier, G., & Beaudette, D. (1995). Correctional officers: How do they perceive sex offenders? *International Journal of Offender Therapy and Comparative Criminology, 39*, 55–61.

Weinrath, M. (2009). Inmate perspectives on the remand crisis in Canada. *Canadian Journal of Criminology and Criminal Justice, 51*(3), 355–79.

Weinrath, M. (2016). *Behind the walls: Inmates and correctional officers on the state of Canadian prisons.* Vancouver: UBC Press.

Weinrath, M., & Coles, R. (2003). Third generation prison classification: The Manitoba case. *Criminal Justice Studies, 16*(4), 305–16.

Westley, W.A. (1970). *Violence and the police: A sociological study of law, custom and morality.* Cambridge, MA: MIT Press.

Whitehead, J.T., & Lindquist, C.A. (1989). Determinants of correctional officers' professional orientation. *Justice Quarterly, 6*(1), 69–87.

Willer, R., Rogalin, C.L., Conlon, B., & Wojnowicz, M.T. (2012). Overdoing gender: A test of the masculine overcompensation thesis. *American Journal of Sociology, 118*(4), 980–1022.

Williams, J. (1998). Domestic violence and poverty: The narratives of homeless women. *Frontiers: A Journal of Women's Studies, 19*(2), 143–65.

Winnick, T.A., & Bodkin, M. (2008a). Anticipated stigma and stigma management among those to be labeled "ex-con". *Deviant Behavior, 29*(4), 295–333. doi:10.1080/01639620701588081

Winnick, T.A., & Bodkin, M. (2008b). Stigma, secrecy and race: An empirical examination of Black and White incarcerated men. *American Journal of Criminal Justice, 34*(1–2), 131–50. doi:10.1007/s12103-008-9050-2

Wolf, N. (1991). *The beauty myth.* London: Chatto and Windus.

Wood, S.E., Wood, E.R., Wood, E., & Desmarais, S. (2002). *The world of psychology* (3rd Canadian ed.). Toronto: Pearson Education.

Wright, K.N., & Saylor, W.G. (1991). Male and female employees' perceptions of prison work: Is there a difference? *Justice Quarterly, 8*(4), 505–24.

Wright, K.N., & Saylor, W.G. (1992). A comparison of perceptions of the work environment between minority and non-minority employees of the federal prison system. *Journal of Criminal Justice, 20,* 63–71.

Yeater, E., Austin, J., Green, M., & Smith, J. (2010). Coping mediates the relationship between posttraumatic stress disorder (PTSD) symptoms and alcohol use in homeless, ethnically diverse women: A preliminary study. *Psychological Trauma: Theory, Research, Practice, and Policy, 2*(4), 307–10.

Young, J., & Antonio, M. (2009). Correctional staff attitudes after one year of employment: Perceptions of leniency and support for inmate rehabilitation. *Corrections Compendium, 34*(3), 9–15.

Zarate, G. (2010, 3 May). Nunavut prison is hell for inmates and staff alike. *Nunatsiaq Online.* Retrieved from www.nunatsiaqonline.ca/stories/article/987679_nunavut_prison_is_hell_for_inmates_and_staff_alike/

Zimmer, L. (1986). *Women guarding men.* Chicago: University of Chicago Press.

Zimmer, L. (1987). How women reshape the prison guard role. *Gender & Society, 1*(4), 415–31.

Zulehner, P.M., & Volz, R. (1998). *Manner im Aufbruch: Wie Deutschlands Manner sich selbst und wie Frauen sie sehen [Men awakening: How Germany's men see themselves and how women see them].* Ostfindern, DE: Schwabenverlag.

Zupan, L. (1986). Gender-related differences in correctional officers' perceptions and attitudes. *Journal of Criminal Justice, 14*(4), 349–61.

Index

occupational risk, 113–31; class
dimension of, 177n1; context:
about, 115; context: co-workers,
114, 115, 120–2, 124; context:
government policies, 126–9;
context: institution, 115, 122–6,
134; context: prisoners, 116–20,
124, 125, 128; differences between
federal and provincial systems,
119–20; hyper-vigilance, 99, 115,
116, 128, 131; lack of resources,
61–2; officers' vulnerabilities, 119;
outside the workplace, 129–31,
176n5; prison environment,
113–15; public perception, 119–20;
storytelling, power of, 119, 135, 137,
140, 141; and victimization, 116–18.
See also edgework; edgeworkers,
officers as; risk; risk management
"offender," as label, 57
officers. *See* correctional officers
officers' code, 148–9
"old boys club," 76
O'Malley, P., 19
open custody, 33, 148, 167
operators, as manager type, **27**
oral tradition, among officers, 119
organizational factors, effect of, 49, 50
"organizational logic," 74, 96
orientations: of officers, 24–6, 146–7,
154; and practice, 26–8; prisoner
interpretations of, **27–8**; punitive,
24, 26, 152; and stress levels, 153;
and vulnerability, 29
othering, of prisoners by officers, 19,
25, 95, 119
overcrowding, 15, 41, 45, 66, 85, 91,
114, 126–8, 131, 176n1 (ch. 5),
176n1 (ch. 6)

paranoia, redefined, 99
paternalism, toward women, 78–9
patriarchy, 55, 79

pay levels, 35, 41, 46. *See also* salaries,
of officers
peace officer, correctional officer as,
4–5
penal populism, 14, 15
penal system, failures of, 62, 64
perceptions, public, of officers, 30,
132, 134, 135, 136
police work *vs.* correctional work, 35,
38, 39, 43–4, 47, 134. *See also*
correctional officers; correctional
work
policy, and risk, 122–4, 125–6, 129, 134
politics, and prison policy, 14
Pollock, J., 85
populism, penal, 14, 15
positions, liberal/humanitarian, 24–6
power, and privilege, 12, 94, 112
Pratt, John, 14
predation, among prisoners, 65, 80, 81
pride, 40, 135, 137
Prison for Women (Kingston, Ontario), 97
"prison officer," as term, 4
Prison Social Climate Survey (Federal
Bureau of Prisons), 73
prison work. *See* correctional work
"prisoner code," 81–2, 86, 93, 96–7,
147, 148
prisoner need/officer stress dynamic, 85
prisoners: attitudes toward officers,
50–1, 147; classification, 158–9;
compliance, lack of, 66;
desegregation of, 129; experience
of "status insecurity," 95; with low
cognitive functioning, 84; male and
female, compared, 52, 82, 85, 86,
89–90, 96, 97; officers' influence
over, 50–1; officers' perspectives
and attitudes toward, 49–50, 146–9,
175n2; reintegration, 148; response
to female officers, 74; rights, 118;
transport, 68–9. *See also* prisoners,
female; prisoners, male